# AMERICAN
# SET
# DESIGN

# AMERICAN SET DESIGN

## ARNOLD ARONSON

FOREWORD BY HAROLD PRINCE

THEATRE COMMUNICATIONS GROUP    NEW YORK    1985

*For Kate Anne*

*American Set Design* is published by Theatre Communications
Group, Inc., the national organization for the nonprofit
professional theatre, 355 Lexington Ave., New York, NY 10017.

Design and typography by Joe Marc Freedman

Frontis: Rendering for *Porgy and Bess*, by Douglas Schmidt.
Back cover: Model for *Romeo and Juliet*, by John Conklin.
Front cover: Set for *The Entertainer*, by Ming Cho Lee; photo
by Joe Giannetti/The Guthrie Theater.

ISBN 930452-38-0 (cloth)
ISBN 930452-39-9 (paper)
LCCN 84-072626

Manufactured in the United States of America
Second Printing, April 1990

# CONTENTS

# FOREWORD

## by Harold Prince

When I began working in the theatre, a handful of designers held a monopoly on most of the work on Broadway. And Broadway was it. Today there are more talented, audacious designers experimenting in this country than in any previous period in our history. Arnold Aronson has done considerable justice to the careers of 11 of the most experienced and articulate of these.

Mr. Aronson himself shares the surname of one of the greatest designers the theatre has ever had. And, by coincidence, my career came into focus in the course of the many collaborations I enjoyed with Boris Aronson. It was Boris who first pointed out to me how limiting Broadway was for the artist. Pigeon-holing is an American phenomenon. You directed musicals OR dramas; sang and danced OR acted; designed extravaganzas OR plays.

He had spent his first 24 years studying and designing in Russia. And he worked consistently within the structure of a theatre company, part of an artistic collaboration. The designer as a member of a team did not exist when Boris arrived in this country, and when I arrived on Broadway 30 years later, the situation had little changed.

This past season I directed two plays: a serious one-set family tragedy called *Play Memory*, designed by Clarke Dunham; and a sophisticated black comedy with multiple settings entitled *The End of the World*, also designed by Clarke Dunham. William Ivey Long provided costume designs for both plays. Astonishingly, many people chose to comment on the double assignments: how could I *appropriately* cast the same designers for two such different plays?

Boris' angry words came thundering back at me. Why was a notion of a creative family anathema on Broadway? Why hadn't people realized how much more productive, *thrilling*, continuous collaboration could be? All the time spent getting to know the new members of the team could better be channeled into getting to know the nature of the material.

It's an easier matter to avoid the danger of repetition by altering the artistic components, but is it the brave course? Is it ennobling—respectful of the potentialities of the individual?

Well, Broadway hasn't changed much, but the theatre in our country *has*, and that's largely because of the proliferation of regional theatres. There were about 40 professional theatres in 1965. today there are over 200. Each of these not-for-profit professional companies has its directors, administrative staff, acting company and designers. No wonder the number of qualified theatre artists has multiplied, and nowhere is that more apparent than in design.

The theatre I entered in the mid-'50s was moribund. We were lazy, stage tricks ("astonish me!") were suspect. In the name of sophistication, we lacked a healthy respect for circuses, for vaudeville. We were isolated.

That isolation intensified. Television came along and appropriated our minds. We hibernated. Probably the speed and intensity with which that happened was a good thing. It couldn't last.

We woke up. We established theatres across the country. And those theatres, needful of material, seeking individual identity, artistic credos, battered down the isolation, acknowledged theatre as a world movement, running independent of borders and politics.

And the poisonous effect of competition from the tube, from pot-boiling films, forced us for our survival to redefine the uniqueness of theatre.

We explored the black box. We moved beyond Brecht (almost our sole frame of reference to the avant-garde) to Artaud and Meyerhold and Joan Littlewood, and Felsenstein and Grotowski and Lyubimov. The list keeps growing.

I think probably I was asked to write these words because my dependence on design is pretty well documented. It takes me an average of two years to direct a play or musical and the designer comes into the collaboration almost immediately. Occasionally, he or she is on the project before there's a play, on call as the play is being written.

I don't feel comfortable with the material until I have some notion of how it will work—its motor. Energy is a funny thing. There's a temptation, frequently with contemporary theatre, to be frantic— actors running around being energetic. But it doesn't fool anyone. Nothing has more energy than Noh theatre, which moves at minus a snail's pace. The problem is to locate within each project its authentic energy, its natural rhythm. And that can only result from the collaboration of director and designer.

In principle, the way Boris and I worked is the way I work now with Eugene Lee, with Dunham, with Timothy O'Brien. We talk. For months. More words than you can imagine—about places and things. We search pictures, photo magazines and newspapers of the period, editorials. We observe silhouettes, reflections in windows, the calligraphy of street signs. So many details which seemingly have nothing to do with a specific text.

We look at paintings, sculpture, architecture, furniture, the changing shape of household appliances. We look at faces. We study and stare at faces in the street, faces leaning out of windows; we dissect expressions or the absence of them.

And, of course, we talk about the project. The quality of the writing. Boris made a strong distinction, for *his* purposes, between good writing and good theatre.

However, an opinion of how a play should move carries with it a well-defined vision of the shape of the space—whether to operate on a turntable or a unit. Is it elevated or flat or undulating? Whatever. All of these I share with the designer and sometimes he creates a collage, an abstraction of everything we talked about over these many months.

Then he goes away.

When he comes back, he has designed a set, preferably a quarter-inch model (I hate blueprints!). Sometimes he has disregarded my turntable, or my elevation, or my undulating structure, but always he has provided me with the arena, a capability of serving the motor of the play as I perceived it.

In every successful instance, the designer provides a bonus. It can be the texture from which the set is made. Or, in Boris' case, it was the mirror in *Cabaret*, the elevator in *Company*. In Eugene Lee's, for *Candide*, a rain forest of green paper party tape triggering overhead and inundating actors and audience.

The point is: these are the designers and if they returned with what I expected, I would feel cheated. I expect more than I ask for. My job is to stimulate, not to dictate.

Boris was wary of what he called "the artist's handwriting." The designer must always be servant to the play. In the theatre he has an obligation not to overwhelm the production with his own chirography. Boris was a painter and a sculptor and he confined his individuality to those pursuits. He fought pigeon-holing by relinquishing that individuality. He knew that if he didn't, he would be designing the same play over and over again. He knew that when the designer dominated, the play failed. And he perceived himself part author, part director. In my mind, the qualified designer must share perception.

Reading the first-hand accounts of 11 very different artistic sensibilities, I'm struck by how similar their needs are to his. How lucky they are to have inherited an enlightened theatre away from Broadway. How much freedom to diversify they have been given away from the battering paranoia to which Boris and his peers were subjected.

What are these artists doing with all this freedom? How are they channeling the excitement it creates? They are absorbing and interpreting it. *Americanizing* it. There are writers experimenting in hybrid forms; actors training to handle any structures they come up with; unconventional spaces and growing audiences ready for anything.

I'm an optimist; still, there's no way I can reflect on this without acknowledging that the movement may be slowing down; that the theatres are in jeopardy; that the government position respecting arts endowments in recent years endangers them enormously.

Also, there are the problems borne within these new regional theatres as they face their second generation—problems of economically limiting repertoire, a filing down of aspirations, attrition born of the continuing relentless battle to do more. Compromises, alas, are a reality.

Still, the important thing is that these 11 designers, and many more, are making a life in the theatre—and that *is* progress.

Harold Prince
June 1984

# AUTHOR'S NOTE

In 335 B.C., Aristotle wrote, "The Spectacle has, indeed, an emotional attraction of its own, but, of all the parts [of drama] it is the least artistic, and connected least with the art of poetry."

Twenty-four hundred years later, many people still consider design a secondary form. Certainly, it rarely receives its due recognition. Nonetheless, there are an unprecedented number of designers at work in this country, and they are making significant contributions to the development of American theatre. This book was written to bring some greater degree of recognition to these designers and their art, and in the process, I hope, to help make critics, producers, photographers and audiences more aware of their contributions.

Choosing the specific designers was difficult. While few people would argue against the worthiness of the 11 included, there are at least twice as many who might claim an equal place. Together with Theatre Communications Group, I established several criteria. Each designer selected: 1) is currently active, primarily in the area of theatre design; 2) has a body of professional work spanning at least 10 years; 3) has worked extensively in resident professional theatre as well as on Broadway; and, 4) preferably, has experience in other genres such as dance, opera, film and television. These criteria still left some 30 to 40 possibilities and final choices were made with the usual mix of fairness and personal prejudice. The selection process also revealed an underlying inequity in the American theatre: Practically no women, blacks or other minorities met these criteria.

Tracking down illustrations for the text only reinforced my sense that design is undervalued by most people. Most designers keep poor records of their own work, and original drawings and photos are hard to come by. Production photos, whether of Broadway or regional theatre work tend to be publicity close-ups of actors, revealing little of the set and giving no sense of the context of the stage. Illustrations of some important productions are not included here, not out of choice, but because of the lack of availability of materials.

In preparing this book I talked to and interviewed too many people to thank individually. First of all, I must thank the 11 designers for their time, patience and cooperation. I wish to thank the designers' assistants who helped gather illustrations and data and talked to me about their work. I am grateful to the theatres' press departments and administrative personnel for their information and photo research, and their help in setting up interviews. I must single out Marion Simon at Trinity Square for her assistance. I interviewed many people whose quotes never made it into the text but whose information and insights were invaluable. I wish to thank Edward F. Kook, who first suggested that I write about American designers for *Theatre Design & Technology*; Christine Morris and Jeffrey West who helped transcribe tapes; Norma Adler who helped with research and proofreading. My research was made possible in part by a Sesquicentennial Fellowship from the University of Virginia. Finally, I wish to thank the Publications Department of Theatre Communications Group: Jim O'Quinn, Terence Nemeth and especially my editor, Laura Ross.

ARNOLD ARONSON

# AMERICAN SET DESIGN

# JOHN LEE BEATTY

"I grew up near Disneyland and I've been there over 30 times. I'll go to any amusement park and love it. At Yale, Ming Cho Lee used to say, 'I think, John, you perhaps have gone to Disneyland once too often.'" This is John Lee Beatty explaining his love for theatricality and even a quality of phoniness, crudity and trickery in design. Yet this is the same John Lee Beatty who is viewed by many as the master of lyric or poetic realism, and who, by the age of 32, had established himself as a major Broadway designer with such plays as Jules Feiffer's *Knock Knock* (1976), Lanford Wilson's *5th of July* (1978) and *Talley's Folly* (1980) and *Crimes of the Heart* (1981) by Beth Henley. (All of these shows originated in the intimate surroundings of Circle Repertory Company and the Manhattan Theatre Club—theatres which have fostered the resurgence of poetic realism, and theatres at which Beatty continues to work.)

Beatty's love of amusement-park theatricality is not readily evident in the evocative, moody renderings for these plays. Even for the less lyrical plays, the renderings are suffused with soft, warm light and seem bathed in a romantic glow. Nor is this theatricality always apparent in the sets themselves, where Beatty's most persistent scenic element to date has been the board planking that he uses again and again to represent a porch, a provincial stage, a dock, a platform or a floor. "I like wood," says Beatty, "because it doesn't have to pretend to be anything else. In the temporary world of scenery, it seems to me to be the most honest material." While the boards are sometimes smooth and symmetrical, they are more often rough and uneven, radiating out toward the audience at a variety of angles. This basic scenic approach is often used in conjunction with wooden posts, molding, gables, trellises and foliage. Beatty has done enough productions in this style that, in imitation of some critics, he facetiously dismisses his own work simply as "typical John Lee Beatty setting," which he describes as "romantic, slightly primitive interiors, with great warmth." A study of his ground plans also reveals a seemingly romantic use of circles, ovals, curves and spirals.

So where is the Disneyland theatricality? First of all, despite his association with the lyrical plays of Lanford Wilson, David Mamet, Beth Henley and others, he has also designed several revivals of 1920s musicals like *Whoopee!* (Goodspeed Opera House, 1978; Broadway, 1979), as well as productions like *Livin' Dolls* (Manhattan Theatre Club, 1982). As a piece of sheer theatrical fun, *Livin' Dolls* ranks high on Beatty's list of favorite productions. The play by Scott Wittman and Marc Shaiman was a parody of old beach party and Gidget movies. Beatty's design was a combination of Barbie Doll motifs and *Gidget Goes Hawaiian*, which he screened before starting the design. ("A very important film in my childhood," he notes with a grin.) It consisted of a huge vinyl Barbie Doll carrying case that opened up to become the set all done in 1960s colors: aqua, orange, pink and hot pink. Props were stored in pockets in the sides of the case. To change scenes the case closed and then reopened to reveal a different locale.

While Beatty enjoys this sort of indulgent theatricality, more often he employs it in subtler ways. Explaining his approach to realistic plays he states,

*Facing page, rendering for Thomas Babe's* Rebel Women *(New York Shakespeare Festival, 1976). Typical of much of Beatty's rendering style is the use of light, a sense of warmth, soft but definite colors and the illusion of symmetricality.*

"I don't think of myself as a realistic designer. I think my strength is that I am *not* a realistic designer but I often do realistic scenery, so it always has a theatrical quality." This quality emerges in what might be called "gimmicks" that sometimes take the form of actual tricks or effects—such as Joan of Arc rising to heaven amidst the collapsing walls and elaborate clutter of *Knock Knock*—but more often, it expresses itself as a stylistic device or conceit, a way for Beatty as a designer to bring a play into focus artistically. This latter approach becomes clear as he talks about his admiration for the late Boris Aronson.

"I like Boris Aronson for the theatricality and inconsistency that makes for a certain rhythm in his work. His design for *Cabaret*, for instance, had very realistic scenery in one scene and painted effects in the next. It keeps things alive." Beatty offers *Talley's Folly* as his own equivalent. While the boathouse that makes up the bulk of the set is in forced perspective, the attached gazebo is not. For Istvan Orkeny's *The Tot Family* at the Arena Stage (1976), Beatty designed different roofs for the interior and exterior scenes although it was the same house.

Another example of the typical Beatty approach was the set for *Crimes of the Heart*. "I started working on the groundplan," he explains. "There's a bed in the kitchen—makes no sense. There's a door to the grandfather's bedroom off the kitchen—it doesn't make any sense. Then I finally realized, 'Oh, it doesn't make any sense,' and then it was clear to me. Once I understood that it was all crazy, I intentionally tried to make it seem thrown together even though it is a realistic box set. You don't want to have the same kind of box set for every play."

This is not to suggest that Beatty is frivolous. He approaches a design carefully, starting with the groundplan. "I spend a lot of time on the groundplan and I feel that if the groundplan of a set is beautiful, the set will be beautiful. I don't like to cheat in a groundplan." The asymmetries, juxtapositions and inconsistencies stem from a consistent view about the function of design in a production.

"If you make something too perfect," he explains, "it can intimidate the performance, it can intimidate the audience. It's hard to play against and it's boring to look at." He does not expect the audience to notice all the details—he simply wants to keep the set interesting "so your eye doesn't get too complacent."

An important aspect of Beatty's style is his sense of proportion and his ability to accommodate both the pictorial and sculptural aspects of stage design. Lynne Meadow, artistic director of the Manhattan Theatre Club, also feels that proportion is central to Beatty's design and comments that one reason she does not mind working from his renderings rather than models is that "I always trust what his sense of proportion is."

Despite this, Beatty feels he has been typecast and that producers only call him to do small-scale, realistic shows. Consequently, starting with the Broadway production of William Gibson's *Monday After the Miracle* (1982), he has worked to alter his style. "I feel that with *Talley's Folly*, *5th of July* and *Angels Fall* I did a good job with a certain kind of show and that's great, but you can't just keep doing that. It isn't even a choice really—you just have to grow as a designer." His attempts to change, however, have been subtle. All the usual elements were there in *Monday After the Miracle*—"the decks, molding and stuff," as he refers to it; "I just started pulling it away more and more." The real change was in the mood and feel. "I'd been doing a whole series of sets that tried to embrace or enfold the actors in a kind of cocoon, but I very consciously avoided that in *Monday*. Also, in the groundplans I usually do a little forced perspective—all of a sudden there wasn't any and everything was kind of on the square. It freaked me a bit."

Unfortunately, this experiment did not work very well for *Monday After the Miracle* and he blames it in part on the production—something he almost never does. "I didn't feel the production went the extra distance to make the change of direction successful," he states. The play went through three ver-

*Facing page top, rendering for Charles MacArthur's* Johnny On a Spot *(Brooklyn Academy of Music, 1980). Beatty reworked an earlier version of the design, breaking the symmetry through the addition of the chandelier stage right and the broken line of wall units and molding. Bottom, rendering for Lanford Wilson's* A Tale Told *(Circle Repertory Company, 1981). Although the sliding doors on either side of the fireplace opened to reveal the upstage space, the central wall unit, in critic John Simon's words, "teasingly interrupted our pursuit of upstage lateral movement [making] the impenetrable mystery at the core of this…house smartly objectified."*

sions and vestiges of each remained. The result, scenographically, was a scene change in the midst of the first act in which two bedrooms and a living room filled with furniture had to be struck in 30 noiseless seconds. The subsequent set remained for the next two and a half acts. Because the specific Broadway theatre was not known as the play went into rehearsal, Beatty could not depend on wing space for winch-driven stages. While he eventually designed a clever scheme (all the living room furniture was less than 3 feet high so it could slide under the bedroom platform on a slipstage), Beatty felt that the tone of the show demanded a basically bare stage but was loaded down with props and furniture because of the realistic demands. "You can't have a Shakespearean stage with winches," he notes wryly. Nonetheless, he continued to develop his new ideas in subsequent productions.

The set for *Baby* (1984) epitomized his changing approach. The set consisted of large scrim that moved in different configurations about the stage on overhead tracks. Other minimal scenic elements—including a large bed—glided on and off the stage as necessary. The scrim and the pastel colors gave the set a warm, romantic feel typical of Beatty's earlier sets, but in contrast, the stage was stark and very direct and frontal. The minimalism was, in large part, for flexibility, but in retrospect Beatty feels that the design needed more "values." It was, he says, "too pure."

While very different in tone, the simplicity of *Baby* was reminiscent of the deceptively simple *Ashes* by David Rudkin (Manhattan Theatre Club, 1976), Beatty's favorite production. It consisted of platforms and curtains, but designing such non-specific, flexible, yet suggestive scenery "is a very difficult kind of designing." Comparing the design for *Ashes* to *Talley's Folly*, Beatty says that the latter "is like falling off a log in some ways. When someone tells you to give them a ruined Victorian boathouse on the banks of the Mississippi with moonlight and stars, that's pretty easy—I mean you don't spend a long time worrying about the concept. But

when you have to have ambiguous platforming that somehow appears appropriate but does not describe any specific location, it's hard, real hard." Beatty describes the evolution of the *Ashes* set:

Lynne Meadow directed it, and she and I came up with something pretty simple. We thought it needed some sort of gimmick to make the many scenes progress—from beds, to chairs

and tables, off and on. I had designed an oval set (I like circles); it had something to do with the womb, which is what the play is very much about.

But when we took the idea to Joe Papp, who was co-producing the Manhattan Theatre Club at the time, he said he thought it should be more like the Noh theatre. In the bed scenes he suggested that the characters should be

*Rendering for David Rudkin's* Ashes *(Manhattan Theatre Club, 1976). This was Beatty's most spare and minimal setting, and one of his most difficult to achieve. Its simplicity was inspired by Joseph Papp's suggestion that the play be staged in the Noh style. It is one of Beatty's favorite designs.*

standing up against a flat that represented the bed. Well, I thought that was stupid, but at the same time I thought it was great. All of a sudden, when he said that, I understood completely what it should be like: Oriental in its simplicity. He didn't really mean they should stand in front of a flat, but he certainly gave the direction, and I gave up the egotism of the first design and came up with a set that was very simple and very highly structured.

I did, however, cant the hard wood floor slightly so that it would be a bit more interesting. When Lynne saw that she said, 'I think you should give that up, too.' It was the last little design conceit I was grabbing onto.

Beatty truly enjoys the collaborative process and seems content with a contributing role. "I love other people's ideas. It's always a wonderful feeling when you finally break through your own resistance and realize the other person's way works. It's exciting."

Beatty begins his work on a play by talking with the director or playwright. What he wants out of these meetings are ideas, not specifics. Beatty says that the conversations he has with the director or other designers "are fairly casual and not necessarily about the play. Just appreciating somebody's persona or point of view towards the world is the most helpful thing. Then I go home, take the groundplan of the stage, and start messing around."

Lynne Meadow has worked with Beatty so much over the years that this process is automatic and trusting. "When I work with John," she explains, "I never try to imagine what the play will look like beforehand. I try to bring out the most creative thing in him by not hampering his imagination. He says that he is a 'psychiatrist for directors.' This is only partially true because, God knows, he is not passive. He has very strong feelings about things and he will put in his two cents worth. But he has a funny way of eliciting information from you. He is interested in what I feel about a play—not how I visualize it, but how I feel about the material itself."

The evolution of *Baby*, directed by Richard Maltby, Jr., was one of Beatty's more interesting experiences in the theatre. The concept was developed over a three-year period, and, even as the show went into previews, scenes were being added and deleted. Furthermore, the play was written in a style Beatty calls "television realism," and contained more than 30 settings. There was no way to accommodate this with realistic scenery. Beatty had to find a scheme that would allow for frequent shifts of locale, as well as for ongoing development of a production that was constantly in flux right through opening night. During production meetings—at which Maltby and the designers sometimes lay on couches while discussing possible ideas—Maltby suggested the possibility of elevators coming out of the stage floor, but he kept describing the production with a circular or spinning motion of his hands. Beatty picked up on this gesture and translated it into curtains moving on spiral or concentric circular tracks.

There was another reason for the use of curtains. Beatty states, "I'm not keen on modern, contemporary musicals with kitchen sets and bedroom sets. They're not visually interesting and they can detract. When I identify with a character, I don't want to see what his or her taste in living room furniture is—it may alienate me or it may be different from what I expected."

The scrims in *Baby* were also part of Beatty's attempt to move away from his earlier work. Prior to the 1981 production of *Crimes of the Heart* he had never used scrim. He decided to use it in that production simply because it was something new for him, but he did not want to use it in a conventional way. He was not interested in scrim for special effects or tricks but for its texture. "In my mind," he explains, "a scrim had always been used for a wall that you looked through and saw someone in another room. I still don't believe in that junk. I don't like that sort of wishy-washy, now-you-see-it-now-you-don't quality. An actor is either there or he isn't. I like presence in the theatre. But scrim on its own is perfectly nice." Beatty subsequently used scrim in the Circle Rep's production of *The Sea Gull* (1983), and in *Baby* he employed four different types of scrim.

After developing the groundplan, Beatty does a rendering. He is almost unique among contemporary designers in that he rarely works with models. His renderings are often works of art in themselves and he paints remarkably quickly. As an assistant for Douglas Schmidt, Beatty worked on sketches and renderings. "When Douglas found out how fast I could render," he relates, "he would do roughs and have me do 13 renderings for a show. I became like a rendering machine." But Beatty claims to have great difficulty building models and does not like doing it. "When I change my mind I'd rather change it in ink than some other form. I envision things in three dimensions, but when I see a model I just get confused in terms of scale. I know that sounds silly, but you are looking at a model as an object. I just can't get the head-on view to scale the people right." When Beatty does build models, it is usually after he has worked out the scale through renderings, and they are used for directors to work with or to work out specific problems. For *Baby* he built a 1-inch scale model—unusually large for a model—so that the creative staff could work out the movement of the curtains.

Another unusual aspect of Beatty's work is that he does his own drafting—a job most designers assign to assistants. He claims that "this is the only way I learn the show—to see where all the pieces end up and fit together. They make an enormous number of technical decisions in the shop, and how could I go there and say, 'No, this is what I meant,' unless I had drafted the show and knew it?" This desire to be in total control of his work and to be intimately involved in the whole process leads Beatty to employ few assistants. "I've avoided some larger shows because of that," he says. "I'd rather do it myself. I like to think there's something unique to what I do that nobody else does. Where the molding goes on the wall, for instance—maybe I would have made it six-and-a-half inches lower and a

draftsman would have made it seven inches. Maybe that's no big difference, but it is to me. I feel that the instincts in my hands must be important for something." Off Broadway, where he is not hampered by union rules, Beatty does his own scene painting.

When specifics are necessary, Beatty does research, but it is not an integral part of his process. He turns to picture books for mood or an occasional detail and he often draws on memories from extensive travel and museum going. Lanford Wilson's *Angels Fall*, for example, is set in a northern New Mexico mission so he studied pictures of small missions while drawing on personal memories of the area and its architecture.

The most important elements for Beatty, however, are composition and scale. Referring to his experience with musicals he explains:

> You don't design the same type of background for a musical as for a drama because people move so much. Oftentimes, I've used a sort of grid background—either very strong horizontals or verticals—for a musical so that the performers' movements are more obvious to the audience. In *Ain't Misbehavin'* [Broadway, 1978], for example, I used some very strong horizontal lines. For a musical you try to focus on the whole body.
>
> In a conversation play like *Talley's Folly* I try to focus the composition on the actor's face and upper torso. For that play I designed a bull's eye—a circular design that kept circling. I drew a figure of an actor and drew concentric circles around him, and then filled in the scenery to match—arches, curving vines, curving portals.

Compositional focus can also be achieved through color. In *Knock Knock*, everything was a "sort of nut brown" so that the actors would stand out from the scenery.

A major aspect of the design process, according to Beatty, is finding the "gimmick" within the de-

*The Cincinnati Playhouse in the Park production of Lorca's* The House of Bernarda Alba *(1978)—an unusually symmetrical setting from Beatty. The set was done in whites which were offset by Jennifer von Mayrhauser's black costumes.*

sign. Frequently, this manifests itself as nothing more than simple theatricality—pivoting tables pushed by actors and an upstage curtain that revealed the theatre in reverse in David Mamet's *A Life in the Theatre* (Off Broadway, 1977), for instance, or trees made of chenille bedspreads, pipe cleaners and raffia trivets in Neil Simon's *Fools* (Broadway, 1981). "The more simple a gimmick is, the more I like it," he says. "I like a gimmick that the audience can understand. The cleaner and more obvious, the better. I don't like complicated junk." Almost every Beatty show has some such device.

Yet Beatty's "gimmicks" can also be sophisticated and technically complex, while maintaining a simple charm. For *The Curse of an Aching Heart* he used two revolving stages and included a trolley that circled the entire set on an oval track. Critic John Simon noted his clever combination of theatricality and spatial composition in the 1981 Circle Rep production of Lanford Wilson's *A Tale Told:*

John Lee Beatty's set is of a noble simplicity compounded of ingenious stratagems, not least of which are shrewd apertures for the ghost to appear and vanish through, and a piece of central wall with a fireplace that blots out part of the wall beyond, even when sliding doors to the right and left of it are opened. Thus, our pursuit of upstage lateral movement is teasingly interrupted, and the impenetrable mystery at the core of this or any house smartly objectified.

Film and television would seem to be ideal media for a designer who likes tricks and gimmicks, but Beatty avoids them. He designed *Out of Our Father's House* for WNET's *Great Performances* (1978), and Eva LeGallienne's revival of *Alice in Wonderland* (1983) was adapted for television. These were enjoyable, but he calls it "cheating." "There can be a stagehand with a stick holding up some curtains for a three-second shot and the audience thinks

*Rendering for Lanford Wilson's 5th of July (Circle Repertory Company, 1978). The sense of light and texture, and the use of such elements as wood, posts and foliage were a trademark of sorts in Beatty's work into the early 1980s. The house was inspired by his childhood home in California.*

there's a room with a wall and a curtain. But there's nothing there," he explains. This is why he ultimately prefers theatre.

You can get away with murder in television but theatre is so hard. The TV camera looks at an old prop or flat and if it's dusty it doesn't register, if it's got a stain on it, it doesn't register. But you put something onstage with a crack or a stain and everything shows up immediately. I like the challenge of theatre—it's hard.

The differences between stage and television became painfully apparent with the *Alice* adaptation. Theatrical subtlety is lost, says Beatty. "I feel that television scenery tends to be shapes and colors rather than flat and graphic. You don't see a lot of detailed painting on television. But what we had [in *Alice*] was totally detailed painting and no dimension. Onstage we wanted a look as if it had been cut out of a picture book." The cross-hatching of the engravings, for instance, created a problem. Given the nature of the camera, if it was closer than nine feet the lines began vibrating. The stage production had been designed in subtle tints—"from a pale straw to a beige"—but the television camera does not pick up subtle colors. "Onstage," explains Beatty, "we had a blue-green scene followed by a blue scene, followed by a lavender scene. On television that became blue, blue, blue."

Ultimately, Beatty's unhappiness with television may stem from the lack of control of the frame that a designer or art director has in that medium. It is the camera that is controlling spectator focus, not the designer, and this can be disastrous for a designer whose strength is composition.

Beatty's fascination with theatricality began at the age of seven when he saw his first play, *Peter Pan.* "I was just fascinated by the wire—I thought it was just as wonderful to fly on the wire as it would be to fly without a wire. I've loved the phoniness of theatre ever since." This love was reinforced when at the age of eight or nine he spent a year in Europe

with his family and saw productions at the Old Vic, La Scala, the Paris Opera and Tivoli Gardens. But the most long-lasting impression was "a cheap extravaganza based on *The Loves of Don Juan*" that he saw in Madrid. "It was so deliciously phony. The raked stage was so obvious, and obviously covered with a ground cloth. Doves flew down from the balcony onto an umbrella during a harem scene. The blue lights came up and everyone went 'oooh!' The scenery shook. It was like a primer in crude theatre technique."

Beatty always wanted to be a designer. He remembers reconstructing the *Peter Pan* set out of construction paper and cardboard several times at home after seeing it. He and his sister staged productions on the sleeping porches of their clapboard, Victorian home in Claremont, California—the house that provided some of the inspiration for his design of *5th of July*. From the fourth grade through

*The Manhattan Theatre Club's production of* Livin' Dolls *by Scott Wittman and Marc Shaiman (1982) was a tribute to Barbie dolls and Gidget films. Beatty designed a set like a Barbie doll carrying case that opened to reveal different scenes painted in such 1960s colors as aqua and hot pink.*

high school, Beatty built miniature sets and even had his own puppet theatre. While he feels that puppets allowed him to work in theatre despite his shyness, he also liked them because of the visual control they allowed him in creating a complete picture.

He went to Brown University where he majored in English ("I don't believe in an undergraduate education in theatre") and began doing summer stock after his junior year. From 1970 to 1973 he attended Yale for his MFA and was in the first class fully trained under Ming Cho Lee. Aside from Lee, he was most influenced there by his scene painting class with Arnold Abramson. After graduation he passed the United Scenic Artists exam in both set design and scene painting.

Ming Cho Lee's influence is evident in his early work. "Being trained by Ming," says Beatty, "was somewhat like going into the studio of a Renaissance master. If you study with Botticelli you paint for awhile like Botticelli—when you get out you can become something else." Beatty readily acknowledges fairly classical influences: "I don't go long without looking through my Robert Edmond Jones, and I look at Jo Mielziner very often. I find Mielziner's sense of scale is brilliant, absolutely brilliant. I emulate Jones not so much for scale as for a sense of purity. As for painters, I'm fond of Vuillard, John Singer Sargent and Whistler . . . a little Botticelli here and there. I love secondary arts: architecture, furniture and great clothing."

His plan after Yale was to work in regional theatre for awhile and then go to New York, until he discovered that most resident professional companies were looking for "New York" designers. Beatty arrived in New York in September of 1973 and landed a job as Douglas Schmidt's assistant, working with him on seven shows including *Veronica's Room* and *Over Here*. Some of Beatty's interiors, like *A Tale Told*, seem to reflect Schmidt's influence. He also worked for awhile as a scenic artist at Nolan Studios and National Studios—scenery construction and painting studios.

Through a friend's invitation, he did sets and costumes for Kenneth Cavander's *Marouf* (1973) at the Manhattan Theatre Club and this led to several other shows. He designed a show for director Marshall W. Mason at the Queens Playhouse which led to an ongoing association with Mason at the Circle Repertory Company. Beatty designed the 1974–75 season for Circle Rep and won an Obie for that work. From that point on, he was constantly in demand. "I am nostalgic for my first year in New York," he sighs, "when I used to play solitaire. Now I can't imagine having the time."

Despite his success, Beatty maintains a commitment to Off and Off-Off Broadway and has turned down some Broadway offers in order to do shows elsewhere. This commitment, Beatty feels, has resulted in difficulty being accepted by the critics. "These 'paperback' productions have no money; I'm painting and propping myself and picking up a saw now and then. For *The Middle Ages* [Off Broadway, 1983] I got a used sofa for $100, because the one that would have been best for the romantic mood cost about $1,500. I drove the van to pick it up myself." (John Simon once referred to Beatty as the "designer who specializes in thinking small and cheap—albeit with taste and imagination.") Beatty is not saying this to pat himself on the back—he merely would like more acceptance from the critics under these circumstances. "The nature of our theatre is 'name brand,'" he says, and the critics notice his name and hold him to Broadway standards.

Beatty is a romantic with an unabashed love for the theatrical. His excitement at working with a legend like Eva LeGallienne on *Alice* is palpable; the thrill of the opening night of *Ain't Misbehavin'* on Broadway is still with him. At base is his love of the lunacy of it all. "I love the theatre," he explains with delight, "because there are so many intelligent people wasting so much effort on silly details."

*Facing page, rendering for Lanford Wilson's* Talley's Folly *(Circle Repertory Company, 1979 and Brooks Atkinson Theatre, 1980). Beatty calls plays of this genre "conversation plays" and tries to focus the spectator on the actor's face and upper body. Here he began the design with a bull's-eye, "a circular design that kept circling. I drew a figure of an actor and drew concentric circles around him, and then filled in the scenery to match— arches, curving vines, curving portals."*

# JOHN CONKLIN

Given the emphasis on new plays in the contemporary American theatre, it is rare that a designer, or any theatre artist for that matter, can carve out a career based upon the classics alone. John Conklin is one of the few that have. "I have a very strong emotional connection with the past," he says, and this statement sums up much of his approach to design. From his earliest work as an undergraduate at Yale in the late 1950s, through his long-time association with the Williamstown Theatre Festival and the Hartford Stage Company, and his increasing concentration since the 1970s on opera, Conklin has primarily designed historical and modern classics.

"If anyone asks me to do a Mozart opera or Shakespeare," he says, "I will always say yes because I learn so much from them. They are inexhaustible—so full, so mysterious. I think you have to keep doing them." Given a choice, he will usually reject most contemporary plays in favor of those that allow for large, operatic or conceptual settings. "It's not that I won't do new plays," he continues, "it's just that many of the ones I read I find somehow trivial. And since life doesn't go on forever, I want to fill it, if I can, with these other pieces. I've done five productions of *Cosi fan tutte*, *Marriage of Figaro* four times, and *Twelfth Night* six times. If somebody asked me to do *Twelfth Night* again I'd do it right away. But I don't think I could do six productions of *The Rose Tattoo* or *A Death in the Family*, for example."

Conklin is an eloquent, gentle person who looks a bit like a character out of a Russian novel. Almost everyone who has worked with him comments on his intellect—his eclectic knowledge of art, architecture, music and literature from which he draws inspiration for his designs. And those who have worked most closely with him inevitably talk about his profound influence. Mark Lamos, artistic director of the Hartford Stage Company comments, "John is somebody whose whole involvement in my life has changed it considerably . . . . Having that sensibility to work with has just been the most extraordinary experience of my work in the theatre." Designer Santo Loquasto, who assisted Conklin at the Williamstown Theatre Festival, talks about "a kind of reverberation in his work that really inspires me."

Because of his predilections, Conklin has designed very little on Broadway and those shows he has done have been box-office failures. Perhaps more important than the type of play that Broadway offers is Conklin's philosophy of theatre, a philosophy more easily accommodated by the conditions of resident and repertory theatres. "It is nice to be given a lot of money to do a lot of scenery," he explains, "but in a way it's just showing off. And I don't think it really has anything to do with theatre. Real theatre exists only when it can illuminate or move an audience, or make all of us understand something better. Bruno Bettelheim writes about how children need and use fairy tales to help them cope with terrible feelings and problems that they have—well, theatre is like that. If somebody asked me to do a Las Vegas show, I might do it just for fun. There is pleasure in technique, it hones your skills. But I wouldn't spend my life doing that."

Much of Conklin's work is informed by a Roman-

*Facing page, model for Bertolt Brecht's* The Resistible Rise of Arturo Ui *(Williamstown Theatre Festival, 1979). The cemetery scene was created in silhouette in front of bleachers meant to suggest a Nazi stadium. Scenic pieces that had been white flowers in the previous scene pivoted to become black tombstones; other black pieces were flown in and performers entered with black umbrellas. Conklin also designed the costumes.*

tic sensibility that clearly fits with his liking of "operatic" scale. Even when he uses pipe scaffolding it seems to have a period flavor, created, perhaps, through touches of realistic detail. When dealing with interiors he often creates whole worlds complete with offstage spaces, nooks and crannies, shadowy corners, and great detail. But he is just as capable of creating a minimalist setting—even for a play that would seem to demand detail, such as Chekhov's *Three Sisters* (Hartford Stage Company, 1984), which employed two columns, a gray wall, some curtains and windows. And despite his fondness for what might be perceived as old-fashioned values, Conklin enjoys shocking the audience on occasion.

Opera audiences in the U.S. are so complacent in the worst sense, mindlessly complacent. So sometimes you have to make them mad, upset them, make them think. We did a *Don Giovanni* in St. Louis [directed by Mark Lamos] that was black, spare and empty. There was not a lot of scenery and the audience had to pay attention to the piece. It drove them crazy. They were indignant because it wasn't "Mozart"—in other words, pretty, harmless and meaningless. They were face-to-face with the piece and most of them hated it. (In some ways it was not successful from our point of view either, so that confuses the issue.) That image of opera as gaudy and big is just as bad as the image of opera consisting of fat ladies waving their arms around onstage.

Conklin believes that the recent practice of broadcasting opera on television will shatter old attitudes. Television shows faces—hence, emotions—and minimizes the scenery and costumes. This tendency to shock was noted by director Andre Gregory for whom Conklin designed Rochelle Owens' *Beclch* at the Theatre of the Living Arts in Philadelphia (1967). This was probably the first modern environmental production in America, predating Richard Schechner's landmark environmental pro-

duction, *Dionysus in 69*. The basic concept—a sort of hallucinatory version of Africa—was Gregory's, but the sensibility was Conklin's. As Gregory remembers, "I wanted to turn the whole theatre into a jungle, and I knew that I wanted a lot of the action to take place in a real mud pit. John's fantastic contribution was this absolutely diabolical sensibility he had then. There were skulls everywhere. He gave it a bizarre, surreal aesthetic." Around 1968 or 1969, Gregory was asked to direct a contemporary production of Richard Strauss' *Salome* at the Santa Fe Opera—"very much 'of today.'" He asked Conklin to design. The resulting proposal included nudity, a hallucinating, drugged Salome, performers floating in bubbles over the stage, five pink Cadillacs, and a Las Vegas revue version of the "Dance of the Seven Veils." It was rejected by Santa Fe. "I think John enjoys taking something to the point of almost being vulgar, but actually being quite beautiful," concludes Gregory. "Then, at any rate, he walked a fine line between terror and kitsch, never falling into the kitsch."

Conklin's work is eclectic. If there is a unifying stylistic element it is his architectural approach and his settings tend to have strong physical structures. Many of his designs are also marked by a strong frontality—sets squarely facing the audience, filled with lines parallel or at right angles to the front of the stage. But two ideas strongly inform the conception of his designs: he believes in the theatre as a psychological space, and almost all his designs emanate from explorations of culture—the art, architecture and social milieu of a play.

As a result, many observers have commented on the intangible sensibility or reverberations in his work—a musical quality. Rhoda Levine, who has directed several Conklin-designed operas in Santa Fe and Amsterdam, tells an anecdote about *Cosi fan tutte*. She and Conklin had just begun working on the project and he had built a rough model that was sitting in his studio. Mark Lamos stopped by—he knew nothing of the *Cosi* project—and while waiting to talk to Conklin idly glanced at the model. He

*San Francisco Opera's production of Wagner's Ring of the Nibelung (1982-85) has been Conklin's biggest project to date. Far right top, ½" elevation for the terrace of Valhalla in* Das Rheingold *(1983). The upper section is a copy of the Dresden Opera House, the midsection is based on Leo von Klenze's neo-classical version of the Propylaea—the Konigstor—in Munich. This rests upon a recreation of a vast idealistic 18th-century project by the architect Boulee, and the base is modeled after an 18th-century women's prison. Far right bottom, working sketch for burned Valhalla in* Götterdammerung *(to be staged in 1985). Because the upper part of Valhalla is based on the Dresden Opera, this is meant to suggest the fire-bombed Dresden of World War II as well. Right, photo of* Die Walküre, *Act III (1983). At the end, the island slowly moved upstage and became enveloped in smoke, seeming to vanish and leave Wotan alone looking into space.*

then absent-mindedly began to hum fragments of the opera. Perhaps something concrete triggered the association in Lamos' mind, but Levine feels it was the sense of the music in the setting.

As Conklin talks about design, the word that seems to come up most often is "connection"—the way in which historical work connects with the present, the way in which scenic elements connect with one another, the way in which the work on the stage connects with the audience. This helps explain his predilection for the classics. Conklin feels that they deeply connect with audiences in a way that most contemporary plays do not. He strongly believes

that the past is "alive and fascinating." But, it is important to note, he is adamantly opposed to theatre and opera as museum pieces; at the same time he vehemently dislikes gimmicky productions that try to make the classics "relevant" or palatable to modern audiences. Neither approach connects with the work itself, he feels, nor does it connect the work to a contemporary audience.

Conklin's approach is to seek out that aspect of the play or opera that resonates in the 20th century. "I often get fed up with museums, but I love to travel—to see cultures and images [past and present] that are just living together in a very unself-

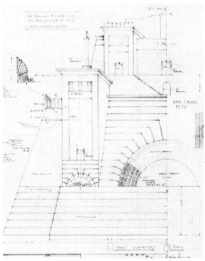

BURNED
VALHALLA

conscious way. Those Roman Baroque churches still have people praying in them; they are very alive. If you hear a great performance of a Mozart opera, it can only be 'modern,' but it affects a modern mind through our perceptions of the sensibilities of the 18th century. I'm very interested in exploring that sort of psychological impetus behind a piece, behind a work of art."

The fascination for Conklin is that any work that survives through time brings with it into the present an accumulated history. All plays and operas accrue cultural and historical references that have nothing necessarily to do with the author's original intent. "We really can't do Mozart the way Mozart wanted it to be—whatever that means. When you do *Don Giovanni* today there are nearly 200 years of people experiencing it, so there are all those varying perceptions and changes floating about. I can't look at Wagner without seeing it in terms of Naziism—there is no way to erase images of Bayreuth and Hitler. It has just been added to Wagner—he didn't mean it, he didn't want it, we may not want it to have happened, but it has." What remains the same, however, according to Conklin are the "psychological core instincts which are the bases of everything—love, hate, power, ambition, death. That's what all those people were writing about." These elements are as understandable today as they were when they were written, and it is out of this that Conklin finds the impetus for his sets and costumes.

Conklin possesses a knowledge of art and architecture—especially Renaissance through 19th century—that is perhaps unsurpassed among American designers and he brings this to his work. The names of artists like Goyá, Canaletto, Guardi, Longhi, Tiepolo, and Schinkel permeate Conklin's discussions of his work. "When I work with a director," he explains, "I work a lot with paintings, pictures and architecture—the artifacts of the social world of the piece." He uses art not simply for a proper historical flavor or for superficial references to the past, but for a deeper psychological insight into the world of the play that allows him to connect the

work to the present. "You're connecting lives and feelings," he exclaims, "not just using it as decor." He quotes British director Jonathan Miller, with whom he did a *Cosi fan tutte* for the Opera Theatre of St. Louis, to the effect that you should *use* the past, not just ransack it. Rhoda Levine has commented on the way in which Conklin can absorb a work of art into his personal sensibility. "John doesn't use paintings," she says, "he *owns* them."

An example is *The Marriage of Figaro* at the Santa Fe Opera (1982). Conklin points out with some amusement that the opera is based on a play set in Spain and written by an Austrian—and he created a setting based on Dutch interiors. He and director Levine saw the setting in terms of the triumph of bourgeois values ("in the best sense," Conklin emphasizes) and he explains that "Dutch painting, to me, has always had that feeling of the best of a kind of domestic harmony—small spaces filled with light and just enough decoration. But it's sort of honest and clean and clear." Throughout the course of the evening, the rooms became increasingly elaborate as the characters became more embroiled in the complex plotting.

The best example, however, of Conklin's use of "quotations" from the past and from visual arts is in the largest project he has ever undertaken—Wagner's *Ring* cycle for the San Francisco Opera (*Die Walküre*, 1983, *Das Rheingold*, 1983, *Siegfried*, 1984, *Götterdämmerung*, 1985). For a designer of operas, to design the *Ring* is the achievement of a major goal, and the San Francisco Opera has supported some of the most innovative design projects in this country in recent years. The *Ring*, therefore, serves as a prime example of Conklin's style and technique.

"The Ring is almost entirely quotations from the 19th century," says Conklin.

Some people will recognize them and some won't. They are often quite literal; sometimes they are collaged together. There is a reason for it and I don't care if nobody knows exactly what

the quotation is. It is not so much that the audience recognize it, it's important to *me* that it is a quotation. The quotations bring power to those pieces—even if people don't know what they are—because of the way they look, because of the way they're assembled. There is a connection that I find fascinating and very energizing.

The facade of Valhalla in *Das Rheingold* is an amalgam of at least four very specific architectural sources including Gottfried Semper's Dresden Opera House and a 19th-century women's prison. It creates a Valhalla that reflects a 19th-century German sensibility—the architecture that surrounded Wagner as he wrote—and it relates back to Conklin's idea of connection. "How," he asks, "does the

psychological core of the piece work itself out through the outward manifestations in terms of architecture, costume, and decoration? If you can understand that, then the connections are just made."

Conklin, of course, did not randomly choose these artistic quotations. The approach was arrived at in conjunction with the director, Nicholas Lenhoff. More important are the connections in Conklin's mind between the elements selected and the opera. Semper, for instance, was responsible for preserving Wagner's career after the 1848 revolution. Architecturally, the arrangement of elements in the Valhalla set results in an opera house sitting above a fort. "The gods," explains Conklin with great delight, "live over a fort in an 'opera house' because they are 'opera singers.' Valhalla symboli-

*Model for* Miss Havisham's Fire *(New York City Opera, 1979). This was a unit set with three doors. Most scenes occurred in the protagonist's house; there were some garden scenes. The back wall was a collage applique on muslin that allowed light to shine through. Thus, sunlight could suffuse the room through the wall and at times the wall just glowed.*

cally is a set!" The worlds of the myth, the opera and the stage all intersect in Conklin's settings for the *Ring*.

In the *Ring*, and in some half-dozen other productions since the mid–1970s, Conklin's architectural style has taken on a quite literal application through the construction of miniature cities or buildings as background. In *Das Rheingold*, for example, Valhalla was not a painted facade; it was a detailed dimensional model presented in two versions—first as a small structure in the distance, and then at the end of the opera as a 30-foot by 48-inch set piece, but still a "model." The change from small to large model gave the impression of the fortress mysteriously moving towards the audience. He attributes the use of this device in part to an "obsession with models as a way of working." But most

designers work with models and few incorporate them into their settings. More importantly, this seems to reflect Conklin's emblematic thinking. To place a model on the stage is to acknowledge the reality of the stage while creating an illusion. It is, as he says, "both real and fake at the same time." It is an emblem of the theatre itself.

Occasionally, Conklin plays games with perception—primarily as a means of correlating an audience's contemporary eye with an historical work. "My favorite thing is to build something with a lot of detail and then paint it as though it were a flat, painted surface. Then it looks painted but lights as though it were real." He used this technique in his setting for Verdi's *Ballo in Maschera* (San Francisco, 1977). The three-dimensional scenery in the *Ring* (Wagner had basically used two-dimensional sce-

*Left, rehearsal photo of the Netherlands' Opera production of Massenet's* Don Quichotte *(1981). The general imagery for this design was based on the paintings of Goya. The back wall was made of plaster built up to a cyclorama. The horse's head had movable ears and mouth and was strikingly real, although the horse's body was obviously two performers in a costume. Facing page, Hartford Stage Company's production of* Skinflint Out West *(1967), based on Molière's* The Miser, *was an early example of Conklin's use of elements of "movie realism."*

nery), created much the same effect. "We discovered that one of the ways to do an 'avant-garde'-looking production of Wagner was to do a stage full of real scenery derived from a 19th-century sensibility," says Conklin. "It is shocking when you view that because you so rarely see it." For Conklin, replacing the 19th-century painted scenery with dimensional decor creates a "modern" look that is in keeping with current sensibilities. "The audience's perceptions have to be taken into account," he continues. "Not by making the production 'relevant,' but by taking into account those perceptions and using them."

The fascination with illusion and reality has led to some highly naturalistic productions—what Conklin calls "movie realism." This might seem the antithesis of opera, but it is the scale that attracts Conklin to both. Some of the best examples of this naturalistic style are Jean Anouilh's *Ardèle* (1980) and *Rain* (1977), the adaptation of Somerset Maugham's novel—both done at the Hartford Stage Company—and R.C. Sheriff's *Journey's End* (1979) at the Long Wharf.

*Ardèle* is described by Conklin as "a good example of my work at its most florid." The play is set in the great hall of a French country house around 1910. In Conklin's version, a balcony with several doors opening onto it ran along the upstage wall. There were stairs with ornate balustrades, a skylight and seemingly infinite detail. The walls and ceiling were painted to suggest inlaid tiles—there were at least 30 different patterns! It was a full, rich setting, filled with period furniture and accessories. "It was busy," notes Conklin, "but I don't think it became maniacally unwatchable." In order to create that sense of movie realism, Conklin decorated the "rooms" behind the doors—he calls this the "offstage syndrome." During the technical rehearsals he went down to the prop room and pulled furniture and dressing to furnish these rooms, thereby creating a whole world offstage. "It's a recreation of a world. It's like you're making a 1910 French reality, not just a set." He feels that this is possible at a place

like Hartford, but would be unlikely on Broadway because of the time and expense.

Conklin takes great delight in this detail. Describing the set for *Rain* that the audience saw as they entered the theatre he said, "It was as if you were in Tahiti. It was like the best 3-D movie you've ever seen."

In an interview in *Theatre Crafts* (May/June 1980) Conklin described the offstage syndrome in *Journey's End*, a production that, for instance, used real mud:

There was a passage off the main dugout set that had bunk beds and some period pinups from 1915 London theatrical magazines cov-

ered with dirt and mud. Now I don't think anybody could really see what those scraps of paper were—and I wasn't really doing it for the actors—but it was a kind of homage to the idea of a set—that you can somehow recreate a piece of historical truth through research and detail and poetic feeling, and it will have an energy that an audience will respond to. I don't really have any interest in doing movies—it's that feeling that can exist only in live theatre that intrigues me.

While Conklin thrives on this kind of setting, and on the large scale of opera, he does not like to do abstract settings. "My mind simply won't work that way," he states. The one time his designs tended toward the abstract was, interestingly, for *Die Walküre* and *Das Rheingold*. In a misguided attempt to make the productions more modern, "and not just a stage full of old-fashioned scenery," he and the director decided upon a shiny black floor and platforms and sculptural objects. They later realized that this was wrong and opted instead for the three-dimensional painted scenery. Because operas tend to return periodically as part of a company's repertoire, Conklin has had the opportunity to alter the set and for the 1985 completion of the full cycle, the shiny black platforms will be gone.

Conklin is one of the few designers who designs costumes as well as sets, and one of the only Americans to design both together on a regular basis. He is aware that, at least in the United States, if designers combine two disciplines it is generally sets and lights, but in Conklin's mind sets and costumes function together and he has difficulty separating them.

For one thing, the sets and costumes can each fulfill a different aspect of the overall design, thereby creating more freedom. In the St. Louis production of *Don Giovanni*, for instance, the costumes were based on paintings by the 18th-century Venetian artist Longhi and were very realistic and detailed. "That suddenly allowed the scenery to

drift off into an abstraction," he explains. "In my mind you don't do the set and then put the costumes into it. They are always there together. In *Don Giovanni* I knew the set could be a certain color because the costumes were a certain color."

Conklin sees both sets and costumes as composed of the same elements—color and texture. "They exist in an unbreakable embrace," he exclaimed in the *Theatre Crafts* article. In large-cast operas especially, the sheer number of people on the stage becomes a type of scenery and he feels it is essential to be in control of the total visual aspect. In *Ballo in Maschera* there are 120 performers onstage in the final scene. "I must do the clothes, for they are as crucial an element in the overall design picture as any amount of scenery."

Conklin's costume-designing has led to work with masks including a grotesque towering puppet for Brecht's *Galileo* (Hartford 1979), animals suggested through a clever use of wicker baskets in the American premiere of Hans Werner Henze's *Pollicino* (Cabrillo Festival, 1983), and a horse's head for *Don Quichotte* (Amsterdam 1981) so real that the proverbial "suspension of disbelief" was created in the audience despite the fact that the legs of the two men embodying the horse were undisguised. *Don Quichotte* also included grotesque human masks influenced by Goya's drawings.

Conklin arrives at his designs by a seemingly circuitous route. Directors who have worked with him describe the early conceptual meetings as rambling conversations about apparently unrelated subjects or tangential points. Rhoda Levine recalls her first meeting with Conklin to discuss Massenet's *Don Quichotte*. She arrived at his apartment/studio and he said, "Would you like to look at doors?" Although, as Levine remarks, conversations often range from spaghetti to novels, the most frequent theme is art. When Conklin talks about a painting, however, he is not suggesting copying a particular work, or even borrowing specific elements—although that sometimes happens—he is using the work of art for its sensibility.

Because Conklin brings his great wealth of knowledge to these discussions, they inevitably have a profound effect on the production that goes beyond the design itself. Mark Lamos describes the process of working with him:

I had a feeling that I wanted to set *Hamlet* [1980] in a kind of Hapsburg Empire setting. That was all based on a book I'd been reading about the Mayerling tragedy. So we just started talking about things Germanic in relation to the play—from concentration camps to palaces, to certain architects like Otto Wagner whom I hadn't known about until he showed

me. And as the whole thing evolved, we ended up with a setting that had the immensity and order of an Otto Wagner foyer with a giant staircase, huge pillars, funereal wall sconces and a grate in the ceiling through which light occasionally came. It was an amazing construction all based on Otto Wagner. Because of its color—a sort of gray marble—there was a feeling of outdoors, of snow and ice. The Hapsburg idea became slightly more Russian, for reasons which I no longer remember. The basis of the overall production became a kind of attention to detail that came completely out of our work on the designs. It all came from the

*Rendering for Act III, Scene 1 of* Werther *(Houston Opera, 1979). Although Conklin rarely does finished renderings, he is capable of beautifully evocative ones. This is really a collage: the floor and window unit are made of poster board glued onto the backing and painted over; the trees are a color photocopy glued onto the rendering and painted.*

text—a sense of rottenness that John was able to foster with every piece of brocade, with every egret feather and every marble pillar. It was an astounding thing.

Then sometimes I'll just say to John, 'I'm doing this play and I want to hear all your ideas about it,' Which is how *Kean* [1981] evolved. I said, 'I really don't know quite why I like this play, and I don't know how it should be done.' He had 1,000 ideas, all of which actually formulated the production and made it what it was—ideas about the acting, ideas about the staging, all of which just came out in one meeting and I suddenly knew how the production should work and why I had wanted to do it. I put the script together in a completely different way and that's how it began.

Because of the degree of Conklin's participation, Rhoda Levine proposed that the billing for her productions with him read simply: "Production by Rhoda Levine and John Conklin" rather than a separate listing for director and designer.

The design process for Conklin is a period of evolution. "Ideally, no production should be designed until it has been in rehearsal for at least a month," he proclaims. Ideas are constantly tossed about, developed, changed and abandoned. Because of this, his working models are rarely finished. "John

*The Hartford Stage Company production of Jean Anouilh's* Ardèle *(1980). One of Conklin's most detailed settings, the floor and ceiling were painted to suggest more than 30 patterns of inlaid tile. The offstage rooms were filled with furniture and props to create "a 1910 French reality, not just a set."*

knows the value of a paper model," notes his long-time assistant Leigh Rand. "It's just a means to an end." When working out an idea, Conklin can very quickly throw together a model out of paper and tape just to get a sense of the setting. "I work very quickly," he says. "I might do a rough sketch or a rough groundplan and then I do very rough models—*very* rough. I have absolutely no patience because I am desperate to see what it might look like. I don't have the patience to be very exact or even careful. I just try to get an effect. Then I can work with the director." He prefers working with these "sketch" models, as he calls them, so that the design does not get "too tight too quickly."

Conklin employs two assistants to work on sets—one who primarily drafts, and one for model-building. Most designers' assistants come and go, but Conklin has worked with Leigh Rand, who does most of his drafting, since the early 1970s and Josie Caruso, who builds models, since 1980. Rand and her husband, designer David Jenkins, live across the hall from Conklin and the doors to the two apartments are usually open, creating an amorphous mixture of studios and apartments, work and family life.

Over the long collaboration between Rand and Conklin a sort of shorthand has developed. "John gives me a very rough drafting," she says. "If he gives me three lines I know that's a particular kind of molding he wants me to work out." Although he is specific when he needs to be, Conklin gives his assistants a great deal of freedom in drafting and building from his rough sketches or models. Conklin uses other assistants for his costume work and except for occasional research, these people come into the process late.

Conklin's apartment appears vastly disorganized. He seems not to care, or not to have the time to furnish or decorate it except for the necessities and an occasional decorative touch. There is a baby grand piano in what should be the living room, but it is generally covered with drafting and model pieces. Books are piled everywhere—he has an enormous collection of art and reference books, magazines and file drawers filled with pictures for research. He is contemplating buying a computer in order to catalog his collection. There are also collections of fabric swatches.

He tends to work within a fairly limited palette for each production. *The Turk in Italy* (New York City Opera, 1979), for example, had sets and costumes designed all in pale, neutral colors except for the heroine's brilliant red dress and one red theatre scene in the second act. Rand notes that he frequently uses rust and gold in his sketches, and that his costume sketches are generally done in terra cotta colors with colored pencil and occasional touches of paint.

Like most designers, Conklin is generally working on several projects at a time. The opera work complicates schedules because the preliminary work begins as much as three years in advance. But he thrives on this. "I would go crazy if I wasn't doing a lot," he says. "When I began to work on the *Ring* I thought, 'This is the biggest thing I'll ever do in my life. I shouldn't work on anything else, just concentrate on this.' Well, that lasted for about two months. I just needed other things. I *need* to have three things going on at once. If you have a strong enough image for each one, they don't meld together because they are so totally different. And it helps your mind get going. You get excited and you can't sleep. It's not very relaxing and it's probably not good for you, but it is great fun."

When working, Conklin is often up at 4:00 a.m. The early morning hours allow him undisturbed time to work and it is when he accomplishes the most. He takes short naps in order to get through a work day that lasts well into the evening.

Conklin grew up outside of Hartford, Connecticut. He saw little theatre, although his grandmother took him to see opera in Boston. As a child he began to present performances in his backyard and from the beginning evinced an interest in sets and costumes. He used to do what he jokingly calls "ideal theatre" in which the curtain would open to reveal a set and and actors in costume and then close—no script, no direction.

He went to Yale as an undergraduate where he began to design sets for the Yale Dramatic Association—an undergraduate producing organization. Since there was no design training for undergraduates, Conklin essentially taught himself. It was at this time that he began to design costumes as well. He says that there was an excellent student lighting designer there—Peter Hunt—so that his sets looked wonderful under lights but the costumes were bad. He began to design his own costumes "as a sort of self protection." To this day he still does not design lights. He explains this not only in terms of training but because of his desire to have one other "visual person" collaborating. At Hartford and elsewhere, this has most frequently been lighting designer Pat Collins. "Working with Pat and Mark," notes Conklin, "you almost cannot tell who did the lighting, who did the sets, and who did the direction. We all sit together and talk about the show. And Pat and Mark have a facility for doing something that I think is important and rare—the productions don't exist at all until they're on the stage—then the real work of all three begins."

While at Yale, Conklin began to work at the Williamstown Theatre Festival because of Nikos Psacharopoulos, who taught directing at Yale and was artistic director of Williamstown. As a senior, Conklin was allowed to enroll in Donald Oenslager's graduate design course. After graduation he enrolled in the Yale School of Drama for a year before coming to New York as Will Armstrong's assistant, where his career developed through what he calls "the infamous Yale mafia." It was these contacts that led to his association with the Hartford Stage Company and also his career in opera.

One of the strongest influences on his development was Oenslager. "Here was this man who had been designing forever, teaching forever, and he was still as excited about things as a 15-year-old. You waited for his lecture on Robert Edmond Jones. It was an incredible sense of connection. Also, looking

at his designs, he had no 'style' and, paradoxically, I think that is very important for a designer. You look at Mr. Oenslager's work and everything was totally different. His mind seemed to be fresh each time he went into a design."

Beyond his formal training, the greatest influences on Conklin have been certain European designers and directors. Although Conklin is architecturally oriented—or perhaps because of it—he admires Lila de Nobili's "amazing painterly style." In Luchino Visconti and Walter Felsenstein he sees "the psychological relevance of detail." Conklin also studied briefly with German designer and director Wieland Wagner at Bayreuth. "His work was seemingly the total antithesis [of Visconti's and de Nobili's]: it was pure space—pure psychological space. The stage was a huge 'empty' void filled with light. Everyone thought that Wieland was abstract, but he created visual abstractions and then worked with the performers as if he were doing Chekhov. There was a startling contrast between this intense acting and a very liberating abstraction that allowed the singers to fill the space. You didn't need or want a lot of scenery. The scenic space should free the energies of the singers or the actors and the piece."

In 1980 Conklin began teaching design at New York University's Tisch School of the Arts. Following Oenslager's example, he actively encourages students to find their own styles and means of expression—he does not impose "correct" solutions to problems. As one observer noted, he trusts his students. Conklin also says that teaching is a good way to "get out of your own self. As a designer you're always in your own mind visualizing a design, revising it, moving things around, talking and thinking—caught in your own ideas. But when you're working with students it's their problems, their minds."

Conklin is one of the few designers who seems able to articulate the attraction of the profession. Design, as a profession, does not have the immediate, overt rewards of other aspects of theatre—there is rarely the applause that actors receive or the crit-

ical acclaim and credit given to directors. Certainly there is little monetary reward. But, as Conklin explains,

It is a peculiarly powerful profession. At a place like the San Francisco Opera, for instance, there are all these people—the shop is full of highly skilled technicians, craftsmen and painters—who are all literally creating your fantasies. In an appropriately crazy way, it's like being Ludwig II of Bavaria. Up on the stage it's *your* world—the fantasy is suddenly real. Because you are producing environments that are bounded by the small dimensions of the stage, you almost begin to live in a totally controlled world. It is a little like being a god. In the 'real' world that often seems totally without order or control, it is a way of focusing everything—focusing on something very specific and complete. Ideally, it is shared with the director, but basically it is *yours*. This sounds ridiculously egotistical—and it is—but it is a fact, and I think most designers have to deal with it for good or ill.

So how do you keep from going mad, as Ludwig of Bavaria did? One way is to get away from the world of the theatre, which Conklin claims he does by traveling. Another way is to work, as Conklin does, with and through art. "When you are dealing with Vermeer or Friedrich [the German Romantic painter who was Conklin's inspiration for much of the *Ring*] you are dealing with very powerful forces and they are much bigger than you are; they are bigger than the theatre. You are constantly learning because you are faced with people like Goya or Verdi whom you have to work very hard to understand. And you are ultimately absorbed into the never-ending energizing mysteries of artists like Shakespeare or Mozart."

*Model for John Colton and Clemence Randolph's* Rain *(Hartford Stage, 1978). Conklin describes the set as "like the best 3-D movie you ever saw."*

# KARL EIGSTI

Karl Eigsti loves to talk about design. Perhaps it is the teacher in him—he has taught at New York University since 1967—but he is more articulate about the theory, process and history of design than most of his fellow artists. One of his favorite topics is the impact of stage design on audience perceptions—and the failure of American critics to realize this. He passionately denounces those who see theatre as little more than a branch of literature. Typical of his theoretical approach, however, is his analysis of the problem in terms of the differing impacts of Catholic vs. Protestant heritages on European and American cultures. Pointing out that by and large it is the southern European or Catholic societies that have the more visual theatres, he notes the long tradition of pictorial imagery in the Catholic Church, and the Protestant rejection of this tradition. While the theory may not be totally valid, it is indicative of the way Eigsti approaches his work. He is primarily interested, he says, in "the elusive nature of what people see."

What people see when they see an Eigsti set is apparently many different things. Reading reviews of a single production often gives the impression that the critics have seen different plays. For instance, referring to *Murder at the Howard Johnson's* (1979), an ill-fated Broadway production set in a Howard Johnson's motel room, one critic called it "frighteningly accurate," while another described it as a "shrewd and wild caricature." This sort of response is typical for most of Eigsti's realistically based settings and it emphasizes one of his great strengths as a designer: his ability to select and abstract elements in order to create an illusion of reality.

There are essentially three ways to deal with a real location in a play. It can be recreated as accurately as the conventions of the theatre will allow; it can be presented as a totally abstract space whose reality exists solely in the imagination of the spectator; or, it can be suggested through fragmentary and stylized elements. The last approach has certainly been the most common in the 20th century, but what Eigsti does that is unusual is to present these fragments so that the casual observer is generally unaware of their theatricality. The viewer is presented with just the right clues so that the mind reads the setting as "real."

While Eigsti is fascinated by this perceptual illusion, and consciously tries to create it through what he and critics call "evocative" settings, he has no formula or specific approach that enables him to do so. He can talk about the effect, but not exactly how he achieves it. "The essence of what is onstage physically is evocative of something much larger," he explains. "It evokes a reality that is more real than what is being seen." But how this is created—by eliminating every third flat, or using only certain colors, for instance—is not easy to pin down; it arises from an essentially intuitive response to the material.

Eigsti does talk about how the stage setting must overcome its physical limitations if it is to suggest that reality. Noting that the real world extends beyond the realm of one's view, he points out that on the stage "the *reality* of what you're seeing stops

*Facing page, rendering for Arthur Miller's* Death of a Salesman *at Arena Stage (1974). Overcoming Jo Mielziner's famous 1949 design is difficult enough—mounting the play in the round presents even more difficulties. "What I had to do," says Eigsti, "was figure out how to penetrate the space and still make it evocative of Miller's play." The vertical poles were suggested by director Zelda Fichandler. Eigsti suspended emblems of Willy Loman's life above the stage. Ming Cho Lee says that this production influenced his own arena designs.*

and beyond that is the back wall of the theatre, which is something entirely different—*unless* it is all made part of how the audience experiences it. The backdrop has to suggest limitations that have been exploded."

The result is a sort of scenographic gestalt. While most designers talk about how to deal with space or images, Eigsti talks about the spectators' physical and emotional responses. "Humans have this great ability to imagine and to convince themselves that they *see* what they imagine," he says.

This approach came together most successfully on *Knockout* (Broadway, 1979), Eigsti's favorite set, which earned him a Tony nomination and one of his two Joseph Maharam Foundation Awards. The locale was a gym in Hoboken, and Eigsti's setting created not so much a specific gym as an archetypal gym whose mood rang true to anyone who had ever seen a classic boxing film or had ever frequented old neighborhood gymnasiums. For research Eigsti visited a gym on 31st Street in Manhattan—not to copy it or photograph details but to absorb a mood. Part of the mood was a glare created by the frosted storefront window. The resulting set did not look anything like the one he visited, but it was dominated by a large frosted-glass window and a boxing ring. The window in the upstage wall permitted subtle changes in mood through lighting. The ring had to be realistic enough to accommodate a boxing match, yet it could not be so large as to usurp the entire stage since many scenes occurred outside the ring. Eigsti solved the problem by making the ring smaller than regulation size and angling it along the stage's center line so that one corner pointed downstage, almost at the curtain line. The result was not a real gym at all—the space was distorted, the arrangement of elements was unrealistic—yet it was perceived as a meticulous recreation of a run-down gymnasium.

*Cold Storage* (Broadway, 1977), set in a hospital, was similar. Though not a photographic reproduction of any hospital, nor even a detailed amalgam of hospital elements, the set was seen as an "accurate" recreation of a hospital by critics.

Michael Murray, former artistic director of the Cincinnati Playhouse in the Park, attributes this effect to Eigsti's sense of texture—his feeling for the textures of materials and for the texture or feel of a particular place. "There is a kind of honesty in Karl," explains Murray, "that is not all pretty. He doesn't go for the pretty but for a very direct experience." While this directness is obvious in contemporary realistic plays, Murray feels that it is most striking in classical plays, giving the sets a "uniquely American" quality. "Even when Karl designs Shakespeare," Murray explains, "it has an Edward Hopper sort of American poetry and bluntness, as opposed to the elegance and refinement one finds in other designers. Not that he's not elegant, but even when he goes for elegance it's always with his feet on the ground." He cites a production of Molière's *The Imaginary Invalid* (1977) which evoked both the elegance of 17th-century style and the street roughness of a commedia troupe.

Perhaps it is the actual elements Eigsti selects that evoke such strong images. Even if he cannot formulate a system for doing so, he is very sure of his choices. *The Woolgatherer*, for instance, is set in a one-room tenement but for Circle Repertory Company's 1980 production Eigsti added a long dark hallway. That addition was not necessary to the action, but it added a bleakness to the setting—and to the play—which brought out a mood that might have otherwise remained hidden. While audiences react to such images, they are usually unaware of the cause. Eigsti marvels that art critics can write pages on a single painting while theatre critics can barely write one sentence on multiple settings that crucially affect the success of a production.

The confidence of his choice-making could be seen during the technical rehearsals of *Amen Corner* (Broadway, 1983). The background colors were neutral shades of beige, so that any "constant in front of it will pop." One item that did "pop" was a marvelous 1960's wire-leg couch with blue, beige and red plaid cushions. The director and producers

*Facing page top, sketch for Preston Jones'* The Last Meeting of the Knights of the White Magnolia (*Arena Stage, 1975*). *Facing page bottom, photo of the same production.*

were unhappy with it and wanted it changed. In a soothing, phlegmatic tone Eigsti assured them that the couch could be changed but it would alter the "balance," not to mention that the overstuffed couch the producers were suggesting would block audience sightlines when three performers sat on it. But mostly it is the balance that Eigsti wants—the relationship of a particular piece of furniture to the rest of the setting. "You have to know where your ideas came from," he notes.

Eigsti is aware that his approach works well for television and he is very proud of the four movies he has designed for PBS. His approach, he explains, is to take "certain elements out of a variegated landscape for the camera to see." Because the camera functions as the spectator's eyes, the selection process becomes much more controlled.

It is the aforementioned *Murder at the Howard Johnson's*, however, in which selective details and fragmented images seemed to coalesce best into an illusionistic whole. As originally conceived, each of the play's three acts was to take place in a room of a different Howard Johnson's motel. The set was composed of floating scenic pieces—three window units, two doors and a backdrop and furnishings provided by Howard Johnson's. For each act the elements were to be rearranged "like a Chinese puzzle." There was a change of directors midway through rehearsals and it was decided to keep the action in one room. The scenery became stationary against a black backdrop; but it was still composed of unconnected flats. The backdrop could be seen between the segments of wall. Yet this was perceived as a realistic, solid room. "Audiences get into a frame of mind where they create a vision of something that is much more real than you could ever possibly do," he concludes.

But there is another side to Karl Eigsti that New York audiences rarely see—the symbolist and theatricalist. At the Guthrie Theater, Cincinnati Playhouse in the Park and several other resident professional theatres, and most especially at Arena Stage where he has done more than 40 productions,

Eigsti often creates abstract, symbol-laden sets. While this is not a surprising approach to the classical repertoire, he finds ways of making it work even for more realistic plays. One of his most surprising applications of this style was in the Arena Stage production of *Death of a Salesman* (1974), which had to be designed in the round. Eigsti notes that for the first 10 years of his career he hardly ever worked on a proscenium. Arena staging forces a sculptural approach to design. In an interview in *Theatre Crafts* (Nov/Dec 1980) he states:

The penetration of space is much more important than in a proscenium theatre. In a proscenium theatre you don't really penetrate the space. You're dealing with a series of planes that the audience looks through. In the arena format you're dealing with three-dimensional, sculptural space which has to be penetrated with forms. That's the basic difference. What I had to do in designing *Death of a Salesman* was figure out how to penetrate the space and still make it evocative of Miller's play.

The result was an essentially bare space with several wooden porch posts placed about the stage rising up to a grid about 20 feet above the floor. The key elements of Willy Loman's life were turned into emblems floating above the stage—a slightly smaller-than-real car, a larger-than-real softball

*Dario Fo's* Accidental Death of An Anarchist *(Arena Stage, 1984). The set had an almost cartoon-like quality and the vista of Milan was painted on a diorama-type drop that rolled up when the action moved to a higher floor of the police station. The set also used one of Eigsti's favorite devices—chaser lights.*

trophy, a scale model of the house, and a vastly over-sized coin. Much of this approach, of course, came from the ideas of director Zelda Fichandler. "I get my first intuitions about a play visually," she explains. "I began to see *Death of a Salesman* in a cube of space with verticals, with the angles of viewing changing for each section of the audience as the performers moved around these verticals. The verticals represented alternately partitions, doorways, trees in the yard, barriers. They were psychological barriers, the linchpins of psychological movement—Willy's search around these poles to find out that memory that he was trying not to find out."

Another Arena Stage production in a similar vein was *Duck Hunting* (1977). The setting consisted of about a dozen aircraft cables strung at angles from the grid through the gray carpet on the floor to suggest rain or room dividers, among other things. The actors moved through the maze of cables without taking notice. Suspended above the stage were plaster sculpted ducks in flight. Suspended just above the floor were wooden decoy ducks. The image was striking, although some critics found it too overtly symbolic. But Eigsti defends his use of emblems. "I think emblematic devices are extremely important. A play doesn't need realistic images—it can be done with an emblematic feature. They present themselves more in some plays than in others. I always like to try to find the emblem."

One of Eigsti's favorite examples of emblematic scenery was a wheel, 12 feet in diameter, that dominated the set of John Arden's *Serjeant Musgrave's Dance* (Guthrie, 1968). The setting—a mine head—was inspired by the paintings of Lowry, a Midlands' painter. These and other paintings of mines inspired the wheel which became a symbol of the industrial revolution, and an abstract suggestion of momentum. Creating the *Musgrave* set required dismantling the permanent structures that English designer Tanya Moiseiwitsch had designed for the Guthrie stage. There was some resistance to this on the part of the producers, but later, when Moiseiwitsch saw photos of the production, she said

that Eigsti had proven that scenery was possible on an open stage.

Regardless of whether it is abstract or real, the important thing, says Eigsti, is to "be drawn into another world that you can become a part of. That is a really great moment."

When the play permits, Eigsti easily abandons the "moody, gray interiors" for the highly playful. For a production of Dario Fo's *Accidental Death of an Anarchist* (1984) at Arena, a backdrop was painted in a cartoon-like manner to represent a view of Milan through an office window. Scene One occurred on the second floor of the police station, Scene Two on the fourth floor. As Scene Two began, a character noticed that the vista out the window had not changed from the first scene—he ran off

*Rendering for Alexander Vampilov's* Duck Hunting *(Arena Stage, 1978). The vertical space was penetrated by diagonally hung aircraft cables. This production incorporated Eigsti's most blatant use of symbolic scenery.*

stage and cranked the drop down so that the audience saw the vista from a higher viewpoint.

But Eigsti had the most fun with the New York production of Andrew Lloyd Webber and Tim Rice's *Joseph and the Amazing Technicolor Dreamcoat* (Off Broadway, 1981; Broadway, 1982). The curtain opened to reveal a 40-foot pyramid and two lesser pyramids textured with a plethora of materials including kitty litter (although this was not apparent to the audience). Later scenes included a mobile camel and an Egyptian sun icon that suddenly lit up with chaser lights. The pyramids revolved to reveal other scenes.

Despite the gimmickry and cleverness of *Joseph*, Eigsti sees it as the epitome of his emblematic style.

The director, Tony Tanner, had told him, "I want to do Egypt, not rock 'n' roll." Eigsti researched the historical period and Egyptian iconography and based his design on that, but he actually suggested Egypt through emblematic shapes. The pyramids were nothing but two-dimensional triangles leaning against the back wall—"There was nothing on the stage that said Egypt," he explained, "except three triangles painted gold. The magic of the moving pyramids was just the shifting of abstract shapes." The limited, suggestive use of imagery created a whole world.

In other productions Eigsti has used multiple projection screens, chaser lights and, in another musical, *Eubie!* (1979), he created a light and glitzy

*A scene from Rice and Webber's* Joseph and the Amazing Technicolor Dreamcoat *(Entermedia Theatre, 1981 and Royale Theatre, 1982). Eigsti considers this the epitome of his emblematic style—Egypt was suggested by "pyramids" created by the simple device of three triangles painted gold, leaning against the upstage wall. The pyramids were textured with net and kitty litter. The central pyramid turned to become Potiphar's condominium.*

setting that included illuminated, plexiglass stairs and light borders on set pieces. He enjoys these productions and would like to do more musicals, but producers tend to see him as an evocative realist.

Regardless of the style, Eigsti is most happy when the "magic" occurs that transports an audience—when the limitations are broken:

Every theatre is finite. Every stage has a border, a limitation. Yet it is a premise of most plays that they exist in a universe with infinite borders. Every play seems to suggest a much larger world of which it is a part. When a character walks out the door we believe he is going to another room, another country, the moon. But in actual fact he is going to a backstage area which is finite, closed. I think the great moments happen when the audience suspends its awareness of the limitations of the theatre and just emotionally and intellectually participates in this world. That is not always done by *masking* the limitations of the stage. It's done in many elusive, different ways. You don't just put up a drop and say "this is the sky." Often you do the opposite and take it down and expose the back wall of the theatre and the audience sees sky in some magical way. It deals with this great ability humans have to imagine and to convince themselves that they see it. For me, the great moments are when I experience that.

Eigsti's basic design process is not unusual. He starts with a rough sketch, then a white model, then a more detailed model and finally a full-color model, although he admits that on occasion the final model is completed after the show opens. It is, after all, the final production that counts. "The drawings, the models, the sketches, everything you do," he explains, "is merely an indication of something. You're not going to really know what it is until it gets up."

He generally employs one or two assistants who work in his cramped, two-room studio overlooking Union Square. The assistants, working from Eigsti's sketches, draw up the groundplans and build the models, as well as shopping for materials and doing research and routine work on a production. For *Julius Caesar* at Cincinnati Playhouse in the Park (1984), his assistant James Fenhagen sought out photographs of South American revolutions and the Perons from the picture collection of the New York Public Library. During the rough sketch period these photos were scattered about the studio, almost as decorative elements. They were being used for a sense of mood and for broad images rather than any specific details.

Eigsti likes to find a specific idea from which his designs can grow; to find a way in which to turn "words and ideas into visual images." Boris Aronson was his ideal because of his ability to find an image for each play. If possible, Eigsti will talk about the play in general before discussing the specifics of design in order to find the metaphors, the images, and to discover how the play works. He has developed his closest rapport with Michael Murray and this process is most successful in his productions in Cincinnati.

Murray describes their collaboration:

I throw a whole bunch of images at him and in a short time Karl brings me a model. I feel free to reach my hands into the model and rip things away. And Karl has the same relationship with me. The model will take some aspect of the ideas we've talked about and explore it. Nine times out of ten we get rid of [the first model] except for one element—the one thing that seems exactly right. I hope that our goal is always to get rid of as much as possible.

An example of this process was seen in the Cincinnati production of *Macbeth* (1982). Murray and Eigsti were trying to incorporate some medieval battle engines which Eigsti had designed as a scaffold-like structure. At one point in the evolution of the production these structures moved about the stage and included trap doors and other moving

*Rendering for Athol Fugard's* Boesman and Lena *(Circle in the Square, 1970). The set suggested a desolate Garden of Eden.*

elements. They were eventually simplified into a stationary tower that appeared to be some sort of wall buttress. As Murray explains, "It didn't make logical architectural sense but it became an abstraction of all the complicated and cumbersome things we had gone through."

Murray suggests that an element of Eigsti's style is the inclusion of architectural elements and that buildings—either realistic or abstracted—frequently enter his settings. *Julius Caesar* was set in a locale of contemporary strife like Beirut or El Salvador—the idea being that Caesar was a revolutionary leader who had just overthrown some previous repressive regime. Murray found an image in a newspaper of a bulldozed heap of a building at a military checkpoint and it became part of the stage setting—a dirt heap covered with rubble. Eigsti balanced this image against a Roman arcade on the other side of the stage. The arcade was covered with contemporary posters and images but was unmis-takably Roman and could logically have been there. Thus, he was able to secure a contemporary interpretation of the play to its historical roots and take a director's image and incorporate it into a balanced and original setting.

The collaborative process, and Eigsti's ability to "understand the heart of the play," as Murray says, allow him to contribute not only to the shape of a production but, in the case of new scripts, to the very writing itself. *Buddy System* (Cincinnati, 1979) originally jumped from locale to locale in a way that caused many scenographic difficulties. In attempting to solve the scenic problems, Eigsti suggested a way in which the play could gain a greater coherence.

Sometimes Eigsti's scenic clarity can help a playwright's vision of his work. Eigsti is fond of an incident in which he took a playwright's description of a house and transformed it into something completely different. When the playwright saw the de-

*Left, rendering for* Murder at the Howard Johnson's *(John Golden Theatre, 1979). Eigsti created an uncanny illusion of a Howard Johnson's motel through fragmented wall units and actual motel furniture. In the final production, the backdrop was replaced by black velour at the insistence of the producers. Many critics saw the set as a detailed recreation of the locale. Facing page,* Julius Caesar *at Cincinnati Playhouse in the Park (1984). Eigsti and director Michael Murray combined images of ancient Rome, current-day Beirut and El Salvador, and a South American revolution.*

sign he exclaimed, "That's exactly what I meant."

*Twelfth Night* at Cincinnati (1979) provides a good example of both the collaborative process and the evolution of an image. The play was to be performed by an interracial cast and the setting needed to accommodate that approach. After considering several possibilities, director Michael Murray suggested that Eigsti read Gabriel Garcia Marquez' *One Hundred Years of Solitude*. That ultimately suggested a solution. Macando, the locale of the book, inspired the design of the play—which they set in South America around 1820—and the result was a lush, verdant setting featuring several hundred plants and many bird cages (complete with stuffed birds). It was, said Eigsti, "like a tropical oasis."

For *Amen Corner* the director originally wanted a revolve to make the change between the two basic locales, but Eigsti, upon hearing the music, felt that the rhythm of the play was more a back-and-forth movement. The result was two wagons that moved on diagonal tracks from the upstage corners of the stage to a down center position. They were both visible at all times.

Sometimes, what in retrospect are truly irrelevant factors determine the look and very groundplan of a set. John Guare's *The House of Blue Leaves* (1971) at the Off Broadway Truck and Warehouse Theatre was the first successful New York production with which Eigsti was associated. The setting, a Queens apartment, was in Eigsti's words, "fragmented realism." The edges were vague and suggestive of the outside world. It was, Eigsti explains, an attempt to make the play more relevant in the context of an era heavily influenced by theatrical innovators like Jerzy Grotowski. Some of the directorial and design choices were inappropriate for the style of the play—although it was successful at the time. Several years later, Eigsti designed a revival of *The House of Blue Leaves* at the Westport Country Playhouse that was straight, situation-comedy realism. He claims it worked much better and prefers the second version.

Although he has a special rapport with Michael Murray, Eigsti's longest design relationship is with Zelda Fichandler and the Arena Stage. "I get in there and something happens—it's just kind of magical," he says. Fichandler describes the collaboration:

We argue a lot, we talk a lot. We start off by talking about the play. In *After the Fall* [1980], for instance, we were working on two sets—one for the Arena and one for the Hong Kong Arts Festival, a proscenium. So we just talked and talked and talked about what the central image of that play was—man's capacity for destruction, its furthest extension being the concentration camp. 'After the Fall,' all of us are possessed of evil. It's a simple idea, but it took us months to find out how to embody it physically. In the early phases we work very much as

co-directors, and in some ways as co-designers. Neither has possession of the whole truth. There is a circle that we draw around ourselves that is permission to argue within the search. When I'm teaching, I let Karl take my class if I can't make it because we really have the same basic viewpoint. I visualize a play psychologically—the psychological movement of a scene. The designer thinks visually. I like it if the designer thinks both visually and psychologically.

We did an obscure Hungarian play called *Screenplay* [1983]. It was very difficult—since it's a play about the lie within truth, and the evanescence of truth under any dogmatic system. We couldn't decide whether the place was as it was described to be—whether it was really the Great Circus of Budapest—or whether it was some shabby little provincial town that was pretending to be the Great Circus. Now there's a conversation for you! It began in June over the telephone and we went into rehearsal in December. That's what I like about working with Karl—we'll have what seem to be aimless conversations about the text. When we did *Duck Hunting* we arrived at an extraordinarily simple set that took us months to evolve. It was really simplicity achieved through complexity.

After we talk about images it goes to sketching—lots of sketching. We throw out books of them. The ideas change and the elements change. In *After the Fall* there was a slab in the middle of the arena which was, in our mind, a monument to the dead of Auschwitz. And there were brick walls that had been knocked down. For me, those were the things that were going on in Quentin's head although they might make you think of the brick walls of a ruined city. And there were various levels of platforming and steps in the corners. This evolved over months. After idea-sketch, idea-sketch, idea-sketch we hesitatingly move toward a model, always with the injunction, one to the other, that this is nothing concrete—its just the best sketch. It lets you walk around inside of it psychologically. You might find that one of the corners is true and something else washes away. Eventually out of that comes a more finished model. I work slowly because if the design isn't right, I know that I'm never going to make the play happen.

Karl Eigsti has one of the most eclectic backgrounds of any designer currently working. Unlike many who knew early on that they wanted to be designers, Eigsti came to it through trial and error, and in a certain sense is still not sure that it is what he wants.

His parents were Mennonites, a religion that frowns upon theatre and painted images, although Eigsti's family was very liberal in that respect. They played music and he studied piano as a child. Studying in Europe for a year when his parents were there he discovered art, developed an interest in it and thought he would go to art school. In high school he began to do some acting and when he went to Indiana University it was as a playwright.

*Facing page,* Twelfth Night *(Cincinnati Playhouse in the Park, 1979). The imagery was derived from Gabriel Garcia Marquez' novel* One Hundred Years of Solitude. *Eigsti describes the set as a "tropical oasis." Below, rendering for John Guare's* The House of Blue Leaves *(Truck and Warehouse Theatre, 1970). Despite the situation-comedy realism of the play, the production was vaguely influenced by experimental trends of the time and Eigsti made the edges of the set shadowy so as to blend into the surrounding world outside the apartment.*

He acted a lot at Indiana and took no art classes. In the summer of 1959 he acted at the White Cloud Playhouse in Michigan, but when the designer quit, he took over and designed his first two productions: *Speaking of Murder* and William Inge's *Picnic*. The following year he went into the Army and was based in Washington as a script writer and announcer for the Army Chorus. At the same time, he took courses at American University where he was given credit for designing sets since he could not attend classes regularly.

In 1962 he applied for a Fulbright Scholarship to study in England and also auditioned for the CBS News. He was offered both and decided to take the Fulbright, figuring he could resume broadcasting when he returned. He spent two years in England at the Bristol Old Vic and wrote a Master's thesis at the University of Bristol. During that time he saw hundreds of plays—one almost every day. Although he had seen some professional theatre before—a Broadway production of *Peter Pan* in 1949 and *Guys and Dolls* in London in 1953—this was his first real adult introduction to the theatre and it was a total immersion in the exploding world of British theatre of the early 1960s.

When he returned to the U.S. in 1964 he was of-

*Arena Stage production of Sam Shepard's* Curse of the Starving Class *(1979). The interior sat like an island in the midst of the surrounding terrain.*

fered a job at the Arena Stage as a supervisor of Robin Wagner's sets (Wagner's career was beginning to blossom in New York and he could not devote himself full-time to Arena). Eigsti wound up designing three shows at Arena that season, launching his career as a designer. He began to work at other regional theatres and assisted Ming Cho Lee at the New York Shakespeare Festival. But he was unhappy with the working conditions. As Eigsti explains, in those days designers did everything—props, building, painting—and he did not enjoy the all-nighters. "It wasn't designing, it was torture." After two years he quit and in 1966 came to New York University as a directing student in the first class of the School of the Arts. It was then that he began to do some teaching of undergraduate classes. He also did some directing at La Mama E.T.C. in New York, the Actors Theatre of Louisville, and in Traverse City, Michigan, occasionally designed a set. In 1968 he was asked to design a show at the Guthrie and it was a whole new experience. There was a staff of about 40 people and Eigsti felt that this was how it had been in England. He also spent six months as head of the New Plays Program for Jules Irving at Lincoln Center while continuing to mix designing and directing. But there was an 18-month stretch in the late 1960s in which he did no designing. During that time he attended the School of Visual Arts to "learn how to express my ideas with a pencil." With the productions of *Boesman and Lena* (1970) and *The House*

*of Blue Leaves*, however, he was finally established as a designer. But, he claims, it was not until 1978 or 1979 that he felt fully "in control." Now, he says, there isn't any play that he cannot "get his hands on."

Eigsti's varied background has also engendered an ambivalent attitude toward collaboration. Almost all designers claim to thrive on the interplay of ideas that can result from successful collaboration, and Eigsti does too. But he also craves the total control of the solo artist. "When critics refer to 'Karl Eigsti's scenery,'" he laments, "it isn't my scenery. It is my designs for scenery that was built by somebody else and put on the stage by somebody else!"

In Eigsti's studio are box sculptures, somewhat like those of artist Joseph Cornell, that Eigsti creates as an outlet for his artistic energies. "One of the things about set design," he explains, "about design in the theatre, is that it is such a collaborative art that sometimes it is hard to feel your own artistic fulfillment. You have to channel those energies somewhere. These sculptures are a way to achieve something which is autonomous, something in which you have the final say—beginning, middle and end. There's always a need to satisfy that aspect of your artistic personality."

Discussing the eclectic and seemingly unfocused directions that design and theatre in general have taken in the past decade, Eigsti asks a question that may reveal a personal quest as much as an artistic one: "What should we be doing?"

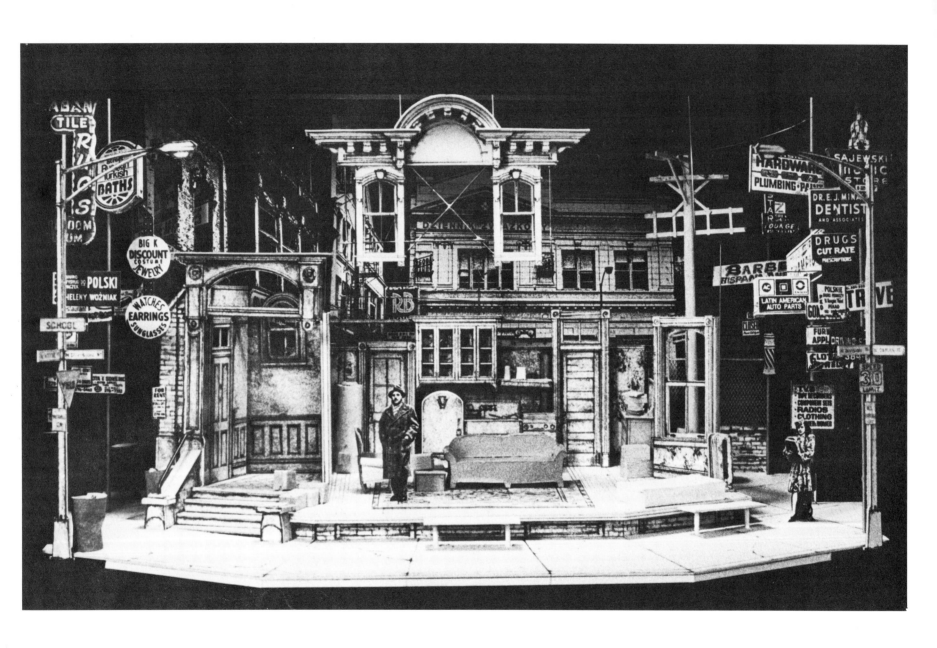

# RALPH FUNICELLO

In a world where stage designers are not well known, Ralph Funicello is less well known than most, at least in the East—although this may change with the 1984 New York City Opera production of Puccini's *La Rondine*. He was born in Mamaroneck in 1947, and started his career in New York City, but he has been a "West Coast designer" since 1972. But among theatre people, Funicello has an outstanding reputation as a designer of sophisticated and elegant sets. "Ralph is really good," says his former teacher, Ming Cho Lee. "He seems to be so quiet and unassuming, yet every time he comes out with something it is always startling. You never expected that this play could have been done this way, but it is always right. He is superb." Kenneth Brecher, associate artistic director of the Mark Taper Forum in Los Angeles, refers to him as "poetic, elegant and sensitive." With little recourse to the trademarks of the last few decades such as scaffolds, erosion cloth or raw-wood plank stages, and without obvious stylistic conceits, Funicello has created a personal style and infused his settings with an understated elegance whether creating an Elizabethan study, a Chekhovian house or a Chicago tenement.

Funicello is also highly regarded as one of the few American designers skilled in the art of repertory design. When considering a difficult season that included Shakespeare's *Richard III* and Turgenev's *A Month in the Country* (1983), the Mark Taper's artistic director Gordon Davidson was primarily concerned that Funicello would be available to design the shows, for then he would not have to worry about the physical demands on the space.

A resident designer at San Francisco's American Conservatory Theatre (ACT), Funicello designs steadily at a network of theatres that include the Mark Taper Forum, Seattle Repertory Theatre, Berkeley Repertory Theatre, South Coast Repertory, Denver Center Theatre Company and the Guthrie Theater. After his first season with ACT he realized that the steady work and variety of projects he was enjoying there would be difficult to find in New York. And in New York, of course, there would rarely be the possibility to design for repertory, which Funicello loves. Consequently, he chose to stay out West—a decision he has not regretted—and make only occasional working trips to New York. (He designed the 1981 Broadway production of Steve Tesich's *Division Street*.)

Funicello's poetic approach to design becomes apparent in an interview published in a 1983 Mark Taper Forum program: "I imagine a set—for any play—as being like two cupped hands, or some nurturing structure that holds the characters together in a specific relationship." Because of his long association with ACT, which, under general director William Ball, is first and foremost an actors' theatre, Funicello has become acutely aware of actors' needs, and the relationship of a play's characters to its setting. When starting a design, he explains, "I always begin by asking myself what environment or space the characters might exist in."

But what does a "nurturing structure" look like? How does "elegance" translate into specific scenery? At first glance it is hard to pin down Funicello's style. Many of his sets feature strong horizontals in relation to vertical lines. Diagonal lines are rare

*Facing page, model for the Broadway production of Steve Tesich's* Division Street *(1981). Although Funicello researched Chicago neighborhoods for a sense of the signs, streetlamps and the like, the final design, in keeping with the farcical nature of the play, was more a pop-art collage than gritty realism.*

in a Funicello design, although several of his sets are placed on a diagonal within the stage. "I think some plays seem comfortable set in a corner," he explains. Another element, as he describes it, is "planes intersecting other planes. I find that for the creation of mood, the more perforation—the more ways of getting light into and involved in the scenery—the better off I am and the more successful the design." While he has done his own lighting on occasion, he simply feels he is not as good at it as he is at set design. And he notes the invaluable input he has received from excellent lighting designers like Duane Schuler.

The perforation, the intersection of planes and the strong horizontals become apparent upon studying almost any of his designs, but Ibsen's *Pillars of the Community* (ACT, 1974), with its back wall of windows and doors, a skylight in a raked ceiling and open wall sections, provides a striking example. Even in a spare set, such as the one he created for the Mark Taper's 1984 production of Arthur Miller's *American Clock*, Funicello created a grid-like structure of intersecting planes to frame and unify the design. The set essentially consisted of two platforms and a floating wall that also served as a projection screen, but, as described by Gordon

Davidson, "He created a system of vertical poles connected by horizontals in the air. It tied the set together. It was not functional, it was not architectural—it was literally a way of unifying the space."

This stylistic motif is not, in Funicello's mind, a purely aesthetic choice. He sees it as a manifestation of character needs. He wants a setting to which the characters can respond emotionally, and he feels that the "perforated space" designs allow that, and as a result ring true to the audience.

Given the repertoire of the theatre for which he works, Funicello has designed a lot of classic plays, from Shakespeare and Molière to Chekhov, Ibsen, Strindberg and O'Neill. And regardless of when the play was written, he has found that many directors place plays in the pre-World War I milieu, necessitating what he calls "realistic motivation" in scenery.

That doesn't necessarily mean that you need a box set. But it does mean that the actors and director will be looking for a certain kind of reality onstage. When the actor crosses from stage right to stage left there is going to be a reason and the reason will not be because the director has told him or her to do it. The character will be crossing to pick something up, to go look at something, to get the knitting off the table. The set and props will have to provide a justification and motivation for those actions.

In order to create "realistically motivated" sets without slavish adherence to naturalism, Funicello relies on carefully selected detail. He refers to the result as "non-box-set-realism." Ken Brecher says that "detail—acute attention to detail, without fussiness" is the key to Funicello's style. Director Tom Moore describes him as a designer "willing to keep working until every last detail fits into the concept, even though most of the audience will never know."

Examples of this attention to detail abound. For *Number Our Days* (Mark Taper Forum, 1982) by Suzanne Grossmann, Funicello studied and photographed the actual location of the play—a building on the boardwalk in Venice, California. The set was the exterior of a Jewish community center, but through the addition of a few careful details—fluorescent light fixtures, broken down folding chairs and an "ironic Biblical quote" on an overhead sign—the set became the interior of the center as well. Funicello even painted the trash cans to recreate the chipped look of layers of paint.

For David Mamet's *American Buffalo* (Berkeley Repertory Theatre, 1983), set in a junk shop, Funicello carefully divided the junk into categories and areas within the setting, with some objects, like a television and the pornographic magazines placed so that they obviously belonged to Donny, the shop owner. As a result, the audience could sense Donny's presence even before he came onstage.

What is most important to him is the impression on the audience. The details do not necessarily add up to an historically or physically accurate recreation. Rather, they achieve a look that conveys the mood of the play. In talking about his use of research, for example, Funicello states, "I will be blatantly inaccurate if I feel it serves the emotional value of the play." According to Tom Moore, "Ralph's brilliance is his ability to use a few very special elements that added together create one very bold visual idea."

For *A Month in the Country* Funicello created, in Brecher's words, "a celebration in wicker." He got a local craftsman to create wicker furniture in the period style. It was not a literal recreation but it captured the spirit of the play and thus it rang true to the spectators. Moore had originally envisioned a simple background of curtains that changed and shifted. "Ralph took my simplistic idea and turned it into a magical set. He took those restrictions and made them his own." The curtain motif remained, but various scenes were created by actors tying the curtains in different configurations. Although Funicello could have left this as a problem for the actors and director, he worked out three or four methods of dealing with the curtains. Moore cites this as an

*Facing page, Athol Fugard's* Master Harold...and the boys *(Seattle Repertory Company, 1984).*

example of Funicello's concern for detail, for the actor and for the overall production.

Perhaps no playwright creates greater challenges for a designer than Chekhov, with his combination of symbol and reality. For *Uncle Vanya* (ACT 1983), director Michael Langham wanted to suggest a feeling of people lost in the space of a vast house, but without specifying doors, windows and the like. Funicello used a rear projection screen backdrop and suggested the house through very detailed but highly selective set pieces. It was an oppressive

house, but not a "real" one. Funicello says it is a question of selective reality. "If someone is sitting in a drawing room, how much do they have to have around them for the audience to see it as a drawing room?"

While almost any production can serve as a model of style and process, three Funicello productions stand out both for the difficulties they presented (and the way he solved them) and for the look of the finished product: *The Taming of the Shrew* (ACT, 1975), Marlowe's *Doctor Faustus*

*Left, Mark Taper Forum production of Division Street (1980). The play is a farce in which doors are an essential element. Taking advantage of the thrust stage, Funicello was able to design a set in which all the doors were not simply aligned along the upstage wall. Facing page top, Peer Gynt at the Pacific Conservatory of the Performing Arts (1974). The central platform both tilted and revolved, creating a great variety of configurations on an otherwise simple and spare set. Facing page bottom, the Seattle Repertory Theatre production of Christopher Hampton's Savages (1982). As in Peer Gynt, Funicello was able to define space with the simple use of vertical and horizontal pieces.*

(Guthrie Theater, 1976) and *Division Street* (Mark Taper Forum, 1980; Broadway, 1981).

The look of *The Taming of the Shrew* was determined largely by director William Ball. Ball generally exercises firm control over the designer's color palette in order to completely control the focus. He does not want any jarring scenic elements or colors that would in any way distract from even the smallest gestures by the actors. According to Funicello, for *Shrew* Ball wanted to create the sense of a troupe of commedia performers emerging out of darkness into the space and performing for no one—or for God. The result, in Funicello's words, was "a slightly surreal or ethereal design": a wooden plank stage in raw-wood colors with touches of "tomato soup red" as an accent.

The production was very physical, employing TV wrestling techniques and commedia pratfalls, so the stage had to be padded. Funicello used a springy wood like spruce or cedar, and each plank was then covered with dense, black foam rubber, encased in duck cloth and painted.

Individual scenes were framed by a chorus-like grouping of actors; but for a later television version, two tower-like structures were added to serve as a background for the cameras to shoot against, or an environment to shoot through. They provided a more tangible visual frame. Interestingly, Funicello had wanted these structures in the original production but Ball insisted on the more open space.

Of all the productions Funicello has designed, *Doctor Faustus* was perhaps the most difficult. Director Ken Ruta had provided him with some specifics in terms of a groundplan, such as the need to place a character above the stage floor and where the devils should appear, and there was some discussion of themes and images such as transformation and Faustus' "rotted-out existence." But both the groundplan and the look of the show eluded Funicello for a long time. Finally he sent Ruta a sketch and Ruta responded, "Fine! Just take the entire thing and turn it upside down."

Funicello had designed a "recessive" set, one that

pointed inward and upstage. By essentially turning the plan around the set thrusted forward like the Guthrie stage itself. Funicello has remarked wistfully that the Guthrie stage, before Liviu Ciulei's renovation, was his favorite. The original was an asymmetrical five-sided thrust with steps on all sides leading into a pit area. Now it is a raised, rectangular platform. "If you didn't compete with the theatre," Funicello explains, "and just allowed the excitement of the space to carry you, then you didn't have to try to pump excitement into the set. It was there and if you followed it and worked with it, the set would be fine." He likes the stage of the Berkeley Rep for the same reason.

The final design for *Faustus* was a skeletal construction that looked like a charred, burned-out frame of an Elizabethan study. Funicello felt that a "see-through" set embodied well the idea of transformation, and the charred look reinforced the image of a "rotted-out hell." The imagery also came from Albrecht Dürer etchings Ruta suggested he look at. There was a catwalk cantilevered off the skeletal structure creating a partial ceiling for use by devils and apparitions.

*Doctor Faustus* was also one of the few sets in which Funicello has employed special effects. There was a crucifix—again, skeletal and rotted—hanging over a vomitorium and Ruta felt that it should

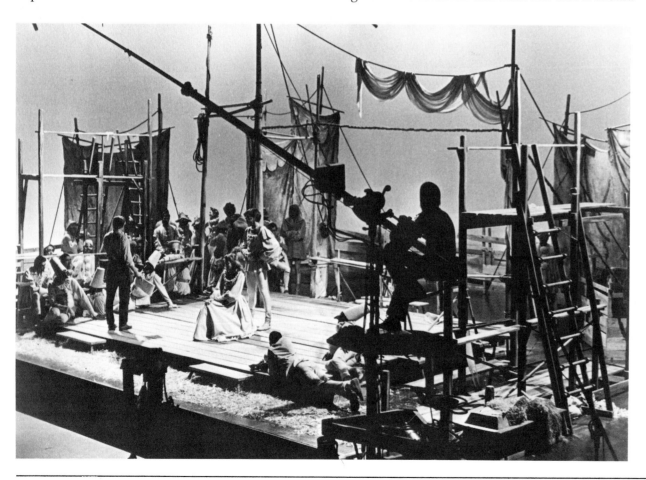

*The television production of American Conservatory Theatre's* The Taming of the Shrew *(1976). The scaffolds on either side of the stage were an addition for the television production. Although Funicello would have liked such structures for the ACT stage production, director William Ball wanted a more open space.*

not be there at the end of the play. Funicello decided to make it disappear in style. An airplane cable dipped in glue and gunpowder and attached to a starter was threaded through the cross. As Faustus made his final appeal to God the cross suddenly erupted in flame and smoke. The unexpected and violent reaction practically over the heads of the audience provided a stunning conclusion to the production.

As Gordon Davidson suggests, *Division Street* presented two problems: How do you do farce on an open stage, and then how do you make that set work on a proscenium when the show moves to Broadway?

The Taper production used a backdrop of photo blowups that Funicello describes as "a Warholesque, 1960s pop-art representation of Chicago in rather garish greens, violets and magentas." He had carefully studied street signs and lampposts in the appropriate sections of Chicago. Where the backdrop met the back wall of the set it slowly blended and evolved into wallpaper. Gordon Davidson still marvels at how Funicello "twisted and turned that space so the doors were part of the whole environment." When the show moved to New York, director Tom Moore felt that the entire production needed a tighter focus. There were rewrites and he asked for changes in the set, making it more realistic in order to let the farcical elements of the script emerge. The arrangement of images in the latter production, says Funicello, "made more sense. It still couldn't be read as real, but it wasn't as *unreal*."

Allowing for the necessary changes in moving from thrust to proscenium, the groundplan remained essentially the same. Funicello notes that because *Division Street* is a farce and the relationship of doors and windows is crucial, the groundplan was the first aspect of the set he worked on. When the show moved, he had to figure out how to arrange the set to maintain the timing of the stage actions that were developed in Los Angeles.

Funicello has a fairly consistent working process. "My personality leads me to do a lot of work in my

head," says Funicello. "I'm not the sort of person who can lay out 15 different approaches to something. In my head I sort through those 15 approaches and reject 14 before I put anything down on paper." This does not mean that Funicello has never abandoned an approach to a particular play, of course, but he does begin with a strong, definite choice to which a director can respond.

Funicello is a strong believer in the need to completely subjugate the design to the needs of the script and the desires of the director. His ability to listen and respond has made him more successful than most in working with "difficult" directors—several directors have commented on this quality. Funicello says that many of the directors with whom he works, such as Allen Fletcher at ACT, are "reactive," meaning that they can react to ideas presented to them, but are not especially good at presenting concrete ideas themselves.

*Dear Antoine (Loeb Drama Center, 1973). Funicello considers this early design one of his first truly successful creations. The play—which is a play-within-a-play-within-a-play—is about the staging of a piece about the protagonist's life. The set was an image of a Baroque chateau, but was composed of pieces of scenery under construction—suggesting both a chateau under repair and a set being built. The audience could see the bracing holding up the set.*

After the listening period come rough sketches. "They're sort of guideposts to where I want to go and are almost unrecognizable to anyone but myself." This is often followed by a groundplan which, he notes, is especially important in realistically motivated plays where entrances, exits, furniture arrangement and the shape of the space are crucial. "Once I have a groundplan that will work," he explains, "I can tell whether the show will work and whether it will be an exciting or a more mundane design."

The next step is a rough model, usually in quarter-inch scale, and usually constructed from sepia-tone architectural presentation paper which is a bit sturdier than blueprint paper. In evolving a design he finds it very helpful to have three-dimensional scenery present to play with. Funicello claims to think far better spatially than pictorially. Consequently he hardly ever does renderings. ("I don't like to draw very much," he states.) Because the pre-production discussions with the director are often carried on over long-distance (one of the few drawbacks to working all over the western half of the country), Funicello photographs the rough model and sends the photos to the director. This is his solution to the problem of not working with renderings. "I can draft the models and get a photo off to someone in almost no time," he claims. Since he has developed long-term working relationships with directors such as Fletcher and Moore, Funicello finds that detailed, complete models and sketches are usually not necessary in the early stages. He says that a "shorthand" or "trust" develops that allows that sort of communication.

The rough model is generally followed by a more detailed one. Funicello often cannibalizes old models to construct new ones—taping bits and pieces together. He compares it to the German practice of building a full-scale mock-up of a set for rehearsals out of old scenery. He is aware, however, of the potential dangers of such a habit to his designs. "It's bad enough that certain personal stylistic elements constantly show up in your work without designing the same door over and over," he says with a smile.

Bearing this spatial approach in mind, a study of his sets reveals how deceptive they are. Because so many of the productions include highly realistic elements, and because many of the sets give the illusion of being box sets, it is easy to forget or overlook the fact that Funicello is basically a sculptural designer. The sculptural approach becomes strikingly clear in productions such as *Doctor Faustus* and Ibsen's *Peer Gynt* (Pacific Conservatory of the Performing Arts, 1974). He much prefers an open stage to a proscenium for this reason. *Peer Gynt* included a revolve in the center of a raked, wood-plank stage. As the revolve turned it could also tilt, creating a variety of shapes and spaces on a seemingly simple stage that was bare except for some dozen thin tree trunks piercing the vertical space.

When it comes to the execution of his designs, Funicello seems to do more for himself than many designers. Although ACT has an associate designer on staff and interns whom he uses to help draft and build models—"I sometimes hire them on weekends. It is a way to pay them more money to do for me what they do for ACT for a little bit of money"— he seems a bit uncomfortable with assistants and rarely uses more than one. He generally paints his own models and has been known to sneak onto sets to help paint scenery. He has an excellent rapport with crews. Funicello has high praise for the technical crews at most of the theatres but singles out Bob Scales at the Seattle Rep for his open and unique approaches to problems.

True repertory—where plays can change every day—places certain limitations and demands upon his work. "What it means," he explains "is knowing where to make compromises. I think that as a result, my designs are more minimal or more refined. I take things down to fairly essential elements." In purely practical terms, this means creating sets that can be changed over easily by a small crew in as little as one-and-a-half hours. Furthermore, storage problems must be taken into consideration. At ACT this is not as crucial—it has enormous fly space that

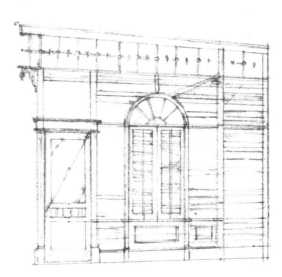

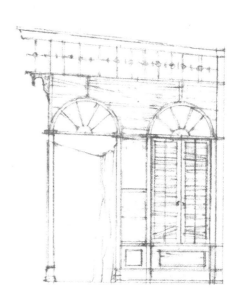

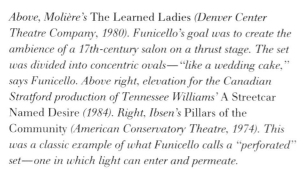

Above, Molière's The Learned Ladies *(Denver Center Theatre Company, 1980). Funicello's goal was to create the ambience of a 17th-century salon on a thrust stage. The set was divided into concentric ovals—"like a wedding cake," says Funicello. Above right, elevation for the Canadian Stratford production of Tennessee Williams' A Streetcar Named Desire (1984). Right, Ibsen's Pillars of the Community (American Conservatory Theatre, 1974). This was a classic example of what Funicello calls a "perforated" set—one in which light can enter and permeate.*

allows as many as four shows to be hung at once. But the Mark Taper Forum was originally designed as a concert hall—there is no fly space and the minimal wings have eight-foot ceilings. There are few, if any, designers more capable of dealing with both the logistics and aesthetics of such a situation and Funicello's ability to handle such complexities are a key element in the Taper's planning.

The evolution of a specific design approach varies from show to show and director to director. For *A Month in the Country*, Tom Moore came in with some very specific ideas that Funicello says he would not have thought of himself. With Allen Fletcher he usually meets two or three times before committing anything to paper. Whatever the specifics, however, it is the collaboration and the input of many minds that Funicello finds exciting. Furthermore, he has been able to work out a schedule—

usually no more than eight or nine shows a year—that allows him to be involved continuously in the process of bringing a production to opening night. Especially with the more realistic, prop- and furniture-laden shows like *American Buffalo* or *The Front Page* (Seattle Rep, 1982), he notes, "It's fun to think through the placement of every object onstage—what it would be and why it would be there—character studies in set dressing." He discusses objects with the actors to explain his choices and to get their input. "At its best," he says, "you really feel like part of the rehearsal process, as opposed to someone who is funneling actors in directions they might not want to go."

One of his most successful collaborations in this respect was for the Pacific Conservatory of the Performing Arts' production of Duerrenmatt's *The Visit* (1975), directed by James Moll. The scene

*Model for Lillian Hellman's* Another Part of the Forest *(American Conservatory Theatre, 1981).*

changes were executed by the actors, and Funicello had a strong vision of how scenes should begin and end. Moll allowed his constant input to help shape the production.

Because his father was a carpenter, Funicello developed an early interest in crafts and making things but had no special interest in theatre. In high school he became involved in theatre primarily for social reasons—"the community nature of the work." To this day he finds that aspect of theatre the most appealing and enjoys the sense of interdependence. The process of creating a production is often more rewarding than the final product. Because of his craft skills he was immediately involved in the design and technical side of theatre and never had an interest in acting or directing.

Funicello notes with amusement that the first professional production he saw—a school matinee at the American Shakespeare Festival when he was in high school—was directed by Allen Fletcher, for whom he has since designed more than 25 plays.

He spent two years at Boston University but found it unfulfilling and transferred to the just-founded New York University School of the Arts where he received a BFA in 1970. Designers Wolfgang Roth and Ming Cho Lee taught there at the time and were profound influences. "Ming was the foundation of my professional career," he claims. Among the things he learned from Lee was that there were no set rules. Roth took him to Germany as an assistant on a production and introduced him to European production methods and styles—a reason, perhaps, for Funicello's fondness for repertory. The European experience also taught him that "a simple, well thought out representation of a wall can suffice for an entire room." He also notes the influence of another teacher at NYU, Robert Rabinowitz, who "opened the door to the idea that I had an influence in shaping a production."

A later influence came from designer Desmond Heeley whom he met at the Guthrie. As Funicello describes it, his training to that point had been "for want of a better word, Brechtian or Expressionistic—presentational; materials speaking for themselves; no transformations. Desmond's work stood in opposition to that." From him, Funicello says, he learned the importance of "the weight of everything placed on the stage," and how all the "mundane materials could come together to create something magical, something that could transport you."

After NYU he passed the exams mandatory for entrance into the design union, then traveled around Europe for a year. Upon his return he got a job through his former teacher, lighting designer Jules Fisher, as Robin Wagner's assistant and worked on several shows with Wagner, including *Jesus Christ Superstar*. Fisher subsequently recommended him to ACT where he was eventually interviewed by Ball in the spring of 1972. ACT originally offered him one show but then asked him to come for six months and design three shows. The staffing and organization of ACT reminded him of the European theatres and the relatively steady work was appealing. He decided to stay.

Living in what he describes a bit facetiously as "idyllic, bucolic Marin County" and away from the hectic pace of New York can have its advantages. Funicello has the closest thing to secure, steady employment that most designers are likely to get in the theatre. And he can pace his schedule so that he is rarely designing three productions at once. But he is constantly traveling, which is exhausting. His idea of rest and relaxation is to just sit at home and "try not to make decisions."

He is not without ambition but he is content with his situation. Given the opportunity, he would like to do more new plays, more opera and possibly ballet. But he seems genuinely uninterested in whether or not he ever designs on Broadway again. In an interview he once described the joys of repertory: "I can be working in the 15th century one moment, then turn around and find myself in the 19th century, among birch trees and wicker furniture. That's the fun of repertory!" And that is the reason Ralph Funicello is not anxious to return to Broadway.

# MARJORIE BRADLEY KELLOGG

Because of their shadowy depths, notes a professional photographer, Marjorie Bradley Kellogg's sets are difficult to shoot. But, he continues, "I would love to live in them." Kellogg is one of the leading realist designers in the American theatre today, creating remarkably atmospheric designs that evoke the deep feelings of a particular locale. She moves easily between the selective realism of "memory plays" like Hugh Leonard's *Da* (Broadway, 1978), and the photorealism of David Mamet's *American Buffalo* (Long Wharf, 1981 and Broadway, 1983) or Nell Dunn's *Steaming* (Broadway, 1982). When given the chance, however, she is equally at home with more abstract or non-realistic settings, as well as light and functional musical comedy design as demonstrated by her set for the long-running *The Best Little Whorehouse in Texas* (Broadway, 1978).

Her style, which is neither overtly naturalistic nor subsumed by stylistic idiosyncrasies, fills an important niche in American production since so many theatres produce plays in a realistic or poetic-realistic style. The brand of realism embodied in Kellogg's work is descended from the New Stagecraft and is perhaps closest in its use of elements to Lee Simonson, the principal designer for the Theatre Guild in the 1920s and '30s. The New Stagecraft, based on the theories and work of European designers Edward Gordon Craig and Adolphe Appia, rejected the slavish reproduction or illusion of reality that typified naturalism in favor of simplification and abstraction through the reduction of scenic elements to their essentials. Lee Simonson was famous for creating suggestive settings by stripping away almost everything that was not essential for defining the locale and mood. Kellogg's approach is a contemporary equivalent.

As this suggests, Kellogg's realism is not 19th-century illusionism. Comparing herself with other contemporary realistic designers such as David Mitchell and David Jenkins she notes, "We are not putting reality on the stage any more than a filmmaker puts reality on film. Everything is a very clear choice. We are interpreting reality." This is the key to Kellogg's art: the interpretive selection of elements from the real world used to create an emotional impact on the stage. "What I work to do," she explains, "is present the audience with details that make up a larger picture, with an emotional reality and focus that is more important than the sum of each of the details. There is a lot of choice based on making the material live not only in a physical way but in an emotional way."

Thus, Kellogg rarely reproduces a room or other locale in intricate detail. Rather, she selects out those elements that will convey the ambience of a given space. These elements are created with great care and often with real materials. Kellogg describes it as "realism that is not bound by realistic boundaries. It's real in its elements—the wood is real wood, if there's a door it's a real door—but it's not tied together in the usual way. It's real, but it's not *realistic*."

It is this sensibility that Edwin Sherin, artistic director of the Hartman Theatre, was referring to when he described her set for Ibsen's *Hedda Gabler* (Hartman Theatre, 1981): "It was one of the most extraordinary things I've seen in many years. It was

*Facing page, rendering for David Mamet's* American Buffalo *(Long Wharf Theatre, 1980 and Booth Theatre, 1983). The rendering is colored pencil on black poster board, creating a beautiful subtlety and romanticism in apparent contrast to the photorealism of the script. In the production, the outer edges of the set were sprayed with black paint to tone it down and focus attention on the performers.*

the interior of a room without being a room. It was just a series of planes of color."

While Kellogg, who is one of the most verbally articulate designers, can usually explain her choices quite logically and rationally, the initial process seems an intuitive one. She has no formula for selecting the key elements that will identify a place. "Any room or place can be boiled down to a major element, or major element and sub-elements," she says matter-of-factly. "I just look for what I consider to be the focus of that place and let everything else just coalesce around it."

This instinctual response is nowhere better demonstrated than in her setting for Lanny Flaherty's *Showdown at the Adobe Motel* (Hartman Theatre, 1980), a play about the confrontation of two old rodeo cowboys. The design was substantially different from the detailed and workable description provided in the script. She reduced the 25-foot deep Hartman stage to a mere eight feet and brought the 42-foot proscenium in to 35 feet. The result was an almost bas relief presentation of the two heroes in profile against the wall of the motel. Sherin recalls looking at her "wonderful, wonderful" drawings and, "I had nothing to say. She had solved it all!"

According to Kellogg, the solution essentially presented *itself*, almost as if there were no alternative. It was a play in which movement was minimal. "It wanted to be absolutely frontal," she states. "As confrontational as possible. It was the best way I could think of to get the necessary visual tension into the piece." She claps her hands together forcibly as she describes how the performers were "smack, right up against that wall. One of the things it did was give the feeling of watching the show in close-up. Sometimes, depth is *not* what you need; confinement is what you need."

Quite understandably, Kellogg does not like being pigeon-holed or typecast as a realistic designer. Such a designation limits her possibilities—she feels that producers and directors generally hire her when they are looking for a realistic design, and

turn to someone else for non-realism. As a result, she has not had the opportunity to design for opera, dance, or much of the classical repertoire—theatrical forms in which spectacle, non-realism, conceptual design and formalism thrive and areas she would like to explore. Even *Best Little Whorehouse* was not the sort of musical in which spectacular, kinetic scenery would have been appropriate. Yet her "realistic" designs constantly move beyond such narrow confines—her design for Harold Pinter's *Old Times* at the Roundabout Theatre (1984) is an excellent example.

The Roundabout stage has a 60-foot proscenium opening—one of the largest in New York—which makes it difficult to design intimate shows. The director saw the production as a series of movie closeups, whereas Kellogg had to deal with a vast space.

> Ultimately, I tried to give him realistic details in a space that was stretched into a bit of an abstraction. The confines of the room were not square like a real room. The space itself was extremely abstract. It was big, so that there was a sense of isolation. We "stretched" the furniture apart a little bit—placed the pieces farther apart than they would normally be. The furniture was "blocky" enough so that it could stand being stretched apart without feeling scattered. It had the weight to sit where it was and feel like it meant to be there. I think that a designer's first job is dealing with the weight and balance of the space.

The La Jolla Playhouse production of Barrie Keeffe's *A Mad World, My Masters* (1983), directed by Des McAnuff, on the other hand, placed few realistic restrictions on her and instead unleashed her creativity. The British play—an updated classical farce about the monarchy—had 17 or 18 scenes and needed to move quickly. "As I read it," recalled Kellogg, "I kept seeing the color green." McAnuff saw it taking place on a large lawn.

We evolved something that was carpet and velour painted in the shape of a huge Union Jack, but all green. There were big green portals and little, bizarre topiary trees to get that tight Edwardian feel. The trees weren't real, they were all paper and strange and out of scale. They looked a bit like the Looking-Glass chessmen.

What was fun was the opportunity to be really loose about it. Some of the elements were sort of realistic. When you have actors onstage, what's next to them has to be consistent with them somehow. You can distort the objects to the degree that the actors distort their performances. If you go beyond that, then you are indulging yourself in a way that can overwhelm the actors. That doesn't mean that the interstices have to be real. We had a lot of over-scaled objects in this, but the furniture was real.

One of Kellogg's longest-lasting collaborations has been with director Arvin Brown at the Long Wharf Theatre. While Brown classifies many of his Kellogg-designed productions as "heightened nat-

*Showdown at the Adobe Motel (Hartman Theatre Company, 1981). Kellogg created a very shallow acting space, forcing the production into a kind of bas relief.*

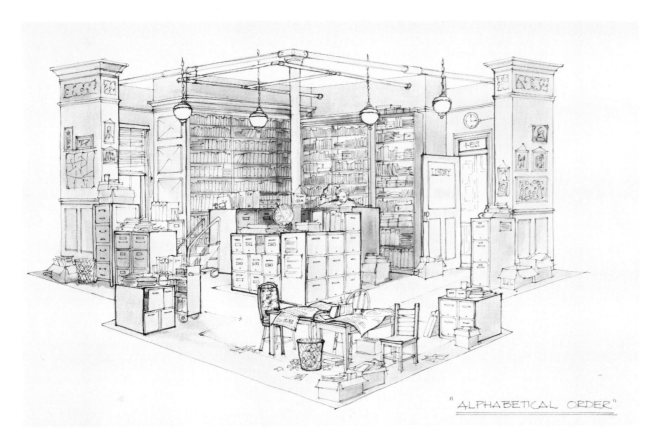

"ALPHABETICAL ORDER"

uralism," he is quick to point out that her selection of details results in "a kind of naturalism that is almost as much a product of the imagination as an abstract setting." He cites her setting for Rod Serling's *Requiem for a Heavyweight* (1984) as an example. Based on Brown's suggestions, Kellogg created a unit set suggestive of the "subterranean world of the fight game." Within that setting on a thrust stage, Brown explains, "were lots of different sets and playing areas created very efficiently that flowed remarkably well for three-quarter staging. It was not a totally realistic set by any means. It was a cinematic concept which she translated to the stage in almost musical terms. It flowed from place to place to place very quickly."

All designers, of course, say that the setting should serve the play. But some designers, through either intention or personal style, imprint themselves very strongly on a production. Kellogg is a bit more adamant than most about the need to "moderate" the design to the needs of the piece and even categorizes some of her designs as "recessive." She is well aware that the so-called recessive designs tend to be overlooked. *Whorehouse*—the most commercially successful show with which she has been associated—consisted of an unadorned, multi-level set in brass and burgundy, with two rolling stair units. She notes that, "The set did nothing but serve the show. It was a long collaborative process involving the director, choreographer and me, and occasionally the lighting and costume designers and the producer. We used to gather in Tommy Tune's

*Left, sketch for Michael Frayn's* Alphabetical Order; *right, photo of the production (Long Wharf Theatre, 1976). This set eloquently exemplifies Kellogg's eye for detail.*

apartment and sit on the floor and discuss what the show should look like. It was not a showy design in any way—it was an extremely recessive design. It didn't say. 'Look at me, I'm scenery.' So in the end it was considered a non-design." Such seemingly simple, minimal settings are among the most difficult for designers to achieve—it is always easier to provide a lot of scenery than to go through the long process of extracting the essential elements.

When the play allows or demands it, however— as with *Steaming* and *American Buffalo*—Kellogg can create settings that serve the play while having lives of their own. And they do what designs rarely do—make the critics take notice.

*Steaming*, a British play set in a bathhouse, had only a limited run on Broadway but virtually every critic commented on the remarkably atmospheric set that included a steaming pool of water downstage. Douglas Watt of the *Daily News* rhapsodized over the rusty pipes and discolored tiles so real that "you can practically smell the sweat and 'oil of wintergreen.'" Kellogg generously credits lighting designer Pat Collins for much of the effect, noting that it was the lighting that looked "wet."

The success of the set was due in part to Kellogg's research at the Portchester Baths in London. Typical of her research, she took dozens of photographs of such details as moldings, columns and furniture as well as the general architecture. The purpose was not to reproduce an existing Turkish bath but to get

an overall sense of that type of place—for "inspiration," Kellogg explains. Individual details from her London research ultimately found their way into the Broadway set but, she says, "it was not like any Turkish bath I know of."

Research is an indispensable aspect of Kellogg's design process. She feels that "it is the difference between a passing acquaintance and an in-depth friendship. When you know the atmosphere, the realities, the texture, the color, the spaces, the smells—when you know all those things about a space, then you can really put it onstage, even if you're not approaching it from a realistic point of view. The best designs that I've done were the ones in which I knew the place exactly—even if it was not a real place. Sometimes, if you're making it all up out of your own head, it gets a little blunted. You settle for cliches or weakly remembered details that are not special. Obviously, the thing that makes a great design is some kind of *specialness* either in concept, execution or in detail."

Although Kellogg wishes she had more time to devote to research, she notes that a designer's whole life is a process of looking; everything is research. It is undoubtedly this process of observation that informs the details and textures in her designs, giving them that realistic edge. One of the best examples is *American Buffalo*. The play takes place in a junk shop set slightly below street level. The sidewalk is visible through the shop windows and door that form the upstage wall. Although only part of the audience might ever see or notice, there are cracks in the sidewalk and chunks of concrete missing. It is the sort of detail that is crucial to the mood of the setting without drawing attention to itself in any way. For Kellogg, the idea of "just a plain sidewalk" is not conceivable. "If you can see it, it has to be right! That's supposed to be a rundown neighborhood, so it would be a rundown sidewalk. It makes it consistent with the reality of the play."

Kellogg sees details in terms of semiotics—what do the images, the "signs" convey to an audience? "We're taking an object and using it for its symbolic value—for what it tells you, what it conveys beyond its own reality. That's the art of it, after all," she explains. The designer's tools, such as color, line and texture, she sees as semiotic forces to be manipulated for subtle emotional effect. As a result, audiences often experience a reality that is not explicitly there. She provides signs and images that the spectators translate into personal experience.

Kellogg says that the purpose of scenery is to put the audience in the proper frame of mind and in the right place. Describing her work as a designer, in fact, she calls herself a "maker of places." She creates these "places" not only from research but from the rhythms she finds inherent in the script. Quoted in an article in *Ms.* (June 1984) she noted that "a good script has *movement* in it; you can *feel* the way people are going to move long before there is blocking. The words have a meter. You can feel that the people will move in groups or singularly, circuitously or at sharp angles. In *Steaming* there was a relaxed quality to the language that told me people were going to have to wander." The *Steaming* set included a large, central open space around the pool, and cubicles, corners and niches into which actors could recede.

One of the most troublesome spaces for which Kellogg has designed is the Circle in the Square. When the theatre—one of Off Broadway's oldest—moved to its current Broadway location in the 1970s, it recreated the notoriously difficult long, narrow thrust stage of its former downtown space. The problem it presents is connecting the long stage space with the decor against the back wall. When used as an arena, as it was for Noel Coward's *Present Laughter* (1982), there is the difficulty of creating discrete areas while maintaining a unified space. Kellogg has repeatedly demonstrated an ability to cope with what she calls "that horrible long tunnel." The "secret," she says, is to achieve a workable groundplan. "If you get the space working, if you can get it interesting and tie it together so that a move from upstage to downstage is comfortable, then you can put whatever else you want in it."

For *Present Laughter*, Kellogg created an Art Deco setting whose curves were echoed in the groundplan itself. Through the use of black carpet she visually eliminated parts of the stage to create a more dynamic and interesting space—the audience focused only on the illuminated, light areas of the stage. She calls this "negative shaping." The Art Deco curves, both in the patterns of the furniture and on the floor tiles as well as in the shape of the stage itself, created a smooth flowing line among several discrete stage spaces.

Kellogg often uses a frame or framing device to help take the design into a world of conceptual statement. Vaclav Havel's *A Private View* (New York Shakespeare Festival, 1983) is a series of three one-act plays about the effects of the Czechoslovakian regime on the day-to-day life of the characters. The plays themselves are not polemics and could almost be seen as domestic or social comedies, and the decor for each was essentially realistic—simplified by

a limited budget. But Kellogg completely framed the proscenium with a collage of Soviet-style agit-prop poster art. The stage thus resided in the midst of an agitprop billboard, clearly placing the action in its political context. It was a totally visual, not verbal, statement.

Color and texture become enormously important elements in selective realism. Kellogg tends to use neutral or earth-tone colors, an approach she learned from Ming Cho Lee. Shaw's *Heartbreak House* (Circle in the Square, 1983), for instance, which is supposed to "resemble the after part of an old-fashioned high pooped ship," was constructed and painted to appear like rich, wood planking. *Steaming* was done in the beige of discolored marble tiles with a slight greenish hue to the whole set. "Look at the world around you," she says. "Except for the ads, most of it is neutral or earth-toned."

More significant, however, than the basic palette from which she draws, is the way in which she limits

*Harold Pinter's* Old Times *(Roundabout Theatre, 1983). Kellogg used heavy furniture pieces to create a sense of unity and intimacy in a room that had to fill an unusually large stage.*

that palette within an individual production. Using a restricted range of color in any set, Kellogg has a remarkable ability to vary and offset the hues against one another. In *Heartbreak House*, for instance, there was a wide though subtle variety of shades from board to board, occasionally offset by bands of inlaid wood. "Subtly used," says Kellogg, "color and contrast are very important to keep the look clean, not mushy." She also uses color to abstract a setting from reality. In the 1982 Off Broadway production of William Mastrosimone's *Extremities*, for example, everything, including the props, was bleached and whitened. In *American Buffalo*, where the hundreds of props that filled the junk shop should have created a kaleidoscope of color, "everything was darkened with a patina of dust and age into a kind of bas relief of cast-off objects."

Although she feels that very bright colors in a background can compete with the performer, she admits that she is getting bored with neutral colors and has, since the early 1980s, begun to use color a bit more boldly. She cites *Requiem for a Heavyweight* as an example. "I found myself reaching for the red pencil. You know how in public buildings sometimes there is a painted wainscoting? I ended up with this dark red wainscoting—all across the back of the set and across the downstage portal. It was all dark red up to waist high. It made the whole thing much crisper and nastier." In the Hartman Theatre production of *Hedda Gabler* she used a palette of purple, gold and magenta and Sherin describes the set as having had "an incredible burning, autumnal color."

Kellogg notes that she has a strong emotional response to textures in the world around her. "I just love getting that texture onstage and playing with it like a sculptor." She continues:

Texture is the abstract way of thinking about realism for me. The interest that I have in realism has to do with texture and the different surfaces that one can play with. Desmond Heeley once said, "Scenery is what catches light." That's all it is for me. What catches light is texture or the lack of it. Because of light, you have to consider every material you put onstage in terms of its reflective quality. I think that texture gives depth—age, history, what it's made out of. Rich information.

Texture, of course, is one of the semiotic elements to which Kellogg refers, and textural effect, therefore, takes precedence over literalness. In *Da*, for instance, the house unit was constructed of wood, even though stone might have been more appropriate for an Irish cottage, because she felt that stone would create a heavier atmosphere and work against the humor in the script.

Like color, Kellogg's use of line is not so forceful that it constitutes a stylistic trademark, as it does for, say, Santo Loquasto or David Mitchell. But she is well aware of how she uses line and notes a tendency in the groundplans toward settings that are at right- and 40-degree angles to the proscenium. "It has something to do with the idea of a good relationship to the viewer—decent sightlines, yet oblique, she explains. "I also like the 'noncombative' quality of right angles. You accept a right angle; it's just there. When you force an angle, especially on a small scale, it can become contrived or pushed toward a stylistic statement of some sort."

At root, Kellogg sees herself as a sculptor—she is shaping and focusing space. Sculptural balance and volumetric composition are primary considerations in her designs.

When I was studying Michelangelo, I was taught that one of the great things about his sculptures was that they seemed to be made from the inside out, rather than the outside in. There is a form there and he was just taking away all the outside 'junk.' That's what positive and negative space is about—the statue is positive and the rest of the marble around it is the negative space. What we tend to think when we look at scenery is that the scenery itself is the positive, whereas what is really positive is the *space* contained within the scenery. It's positive because that's what the actors are going to be moving through. And that's what I feel I work with first—sculpting the space itself.

*American Buffalo* provides a sense of how she approaches volume and balance. The script called for a set that was really nothing more than an arrangement of props in a room—the items that fill a junk shop. "It's absolutely crucial to the design that the props have a certain mass coordination," insists Kellogg. "It looks uncontrolled but it's not. It is grouped to lead your eye from one place to another to form a frame around the central area." The props and scenery toward the outer edges of the set were sprayed black to tone them down, so that the viewer's eye was directed toward the center.

After Kellogg agrees to design a show, she spends "a lot of time staring at blank walls"—trying to remember, isolate and capture the first impression made by the script. "I used to just start sketching," she explains. "But now I think before I leap. I try to put boundaries around that first impression so that I can hold onto it longer. That impression is my natural response and therefore my most personal and probably most powerful image."

Kellogg's next step is to get the impression down on paper in some way. Most often it takes the form of a rough groundplan. "I see most shows in a three-dimensional way, as if they were all around me. I feel myself *in* them instantly," she says. The groundplan, then, is a means of delineating this three-dimensional space. There are some plays, however, that Kellogg claims to see "in a graphic way—as if from a distance." These are the ones that manifest themselves first as sketches. In searching for a pattern to explain which shows begin as groundplans and which as sketches, she ventures the idea that the less realistic ones appear as sketches—such as *A Private View*, in which the graphic portal "came before any sense of how the space was going to work."

After the first impression comes what Kellogg calls "the realities" like size, money and the input of others. The first conversation with the director is what she described in the *Ms.* article as "a dream conversation—you're trying to describe to each other something that does not yet exist. . . . You only get to talk, *really talk* with the director at the beginning, and that's where the process of inspiration happens, and it has to endure through the whole production." As important as the first impression is for Kellogg, she does not let it become so embedded as to interfere with input from the director. "If you form a design," she explains, "you become a little married to it. If it's not what the director wants, then you have to divorce yourself from it and start over again. It's less painful and probably more produc-

*Rod Serling's* Requiem for a Heavyweight *at the Long Wharf Theatre (1984). The set allowed for many different locales and playing areas. Director Arvin Brown described it as "a cinematic concept which [Kellogg] translated to the stage in almost musical terms. It flowed from place to place to place very quickly."*

tive to let the vague ideas float for awhile untethered until you have a clearer idea of where the director thinks the production should go. Hopefully, you're both going in the same direction."

Despite her practice of serving the playwright and director, she is not a quiescent designer. She is interested in a certain kind of control—the control of the audience's perceptual experience. This becomes clear when she discusses the drawbacks of designing for film or television. As she explained in *Ms.*, "You're not telling the audience where to look. That is what the camera does in the media. And that is what the *designer* does in the theatre."

Given this approach, one might expect that Kellogg would want control over all the design elements in a production, but she does not. She has no interest in designing costumes, in large part because they do not fit in with her sculptorly passion for "making places." She says that she could imag-

ine designing lights but "I love having other designers to work with. When it comes to design, three heads are better than one or two. Besides," she adds with a laugh, "if there weren't a lighting designer, who would you talk to during rehearsals?"

Although she has worked with many designers at many different theatres, her most frequent collaborators have been costume designer Jennifer von Mayrhauser and lighting designers Richard Nelson, Pat Collins and Arden Fingerhut. When working with these designers, Kellogg can move more rapidly because there is a mutual understanding of the working process. With the lighting designers, for instance, "even before there is scenery we can talk about what the quality of the light will be and how it will fill the space or change. We can talk about sources and color and I can work with that in mind. I have a full idea of what the set will look like." Often a shorthand develops that obviates the need

*Model of the basic set for Vaclav Havel's* A Private View *(New York Shakespeare Festival, 1983). Simple settings for each of the three one-act plays were created through the use of selective realistic elements. The frame was a collage of Soviet-style agitprop poster art.*

for full design conferences. Sometimes in working with Pat Collins, for instance, Kellogg simply discusses things over the phone. "There's a style there that I understand," she says, "and I can extrapolate from my knowledge of her. Doing a show with her is like feeling the pieces of a well-oiled machine fall into place."

Until the winter of 1984 Kellogg worked out of her apartment, but she now has a small studio on upper Broadway filled with supplies, old models and the noise from the street two stories below. It provides her with the space she needs and allows a certain separation of home and work. She employs one assistant full time, mostly for model-building, and occasionally hires others. Like most designers without a current hit musical or a lucrative film to her credit, her prodigious amount of work provides a modest living at best, and much of her income goes for design-related expenses.

Kellogg does not remember deciding to become a set designer. "I just sort of slid into it," she explains. She spent the first 11 years of her life near Boston, before moving with her family to New York City where she had her first introduction to theatre. With her high school friends she mounted productions of Shaw and Shakespeare in someone's living room, which they grandly named the 93rd Street Playhouse.

Kellogg went to Vassar College, and following her freshman year landed a summer job at the New York Shakespeare Festival. "It was like the sky opened. It was wonderful." She spent three summers there, first running and building props, then as prop mistress and finally as a painter for Ming Cho Lee, then the principal designer. After her graduation from Vassar, she took a job as an assistant to designer Elmon Webb—whose wife, Virginia Dancey, had taught design at Vassar—at the Lakewood Playhouse in Skowhegan, Maine. It was there that Kellogg got to design her first professional show, *Wait Until Dark*. "Everyone should do at least one summer of stock," she proclaims. "You don't learn a whole lot about design, but you learn a lot

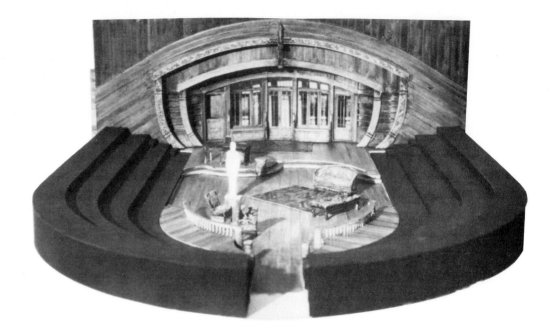

about the mechanics of the theatre. It prepares you for commercial attitudes in the city. Broadway is just summer stock grown up. The idea is not to let it cost too much, to get it up fast, and to make the audience like it."

She had done some acting in high school and college "but, quite frankly, I did not like what it did to me. There's something so self-centered about acting that you tend to forget about other people, particularly when you're a college student." As graduation approached, Lee suggested that she come and work in his studio, but Kellogg felt she was not ready: she wanted to try a completely different environment. So she applied to UCLA—somewhat to Lee's dismay, as he had gone there and dropped out. Kellogg, too, dropped out after less than a year, describing the situation tactfully as "not adequate." She returned to New York and began working in Lee's studio in the spring of 1968, staying until 1970 and passing the Union exam in the process.

Vassar had taught her about basics—and a lot about drama—but it was in Lee's studio that she

*Model for George Bernard Shaw's Heartbreak House (Circle in the Square, 1983). Kellogg has been notably successful in dealing with the long, narrow thrust stage of this theatre. She says that the key is to achieve a workable groundplan first. In this production, the large upstage unit helped to unify the space.*

feels she really learned design. "I learned the literary tools at Vassar," she explains, "and how to draw a decent line from Ming." She also acknowledges the help she received from Ming's chief assistant at the time, Leigh Rand. She began to get occasional design jobs—shows that Lee or Rand passed on to her—and she even co-designed a play called *Sambo* with Lee at the New York Shakespeare Festival. Webb and Dancey were responsible for getting her her first show at the Long Wharf Theatre in 1970 and since that time she has done at least one production a season there.

She was recommended for her first Broadway show, *The Poison Tree* (1976), by Martin Aronstein who had lit many of Lee's shows at the Shakespeare Festival. "The show didn't do too well," remembers Kellogg, "but it had Peter Masterson in it, who several years later called me up and asked me to do *The Best Little Whorehouse in Texas.*"

In the first few years after leaving Lee's studio she continued intermittently to assist other designers, including Robin Wagner, David Mitchell, Tony Walton and—very briefly—Boris Aronson. Of working for Wagner she notes, "It was the best thing that could have happened to me, going from one extreme [Ming Cho Lee] to the other; from ⅛-inch scale models to draftings on the backs of envelopes. It was very liberating. And Robin can really teach

Moose Murders *(Eugene O'Neill Theatre, 1983). Although the play was a classic Broadway failure, Kellogg's intricately detailed, somewhat tongue-in-cheek design was overwhelmingly successful.*

you about moving scenery, which is not Ming's forte. Tony Walton was also what she calls a "mitigating influence that pulled me away from being a Ming copy." But Lee remains the strongest influence on her development as a designer, an influence for which she is most grateful.

She also feels that two specific designs she saw early in her career had a profound effect on her. One was the 1967 Broadway production of Harold Pinter's *The Homecoming*, by British designer John Bury, and the other was David Jenkins' set for David Storey's *The Changing Room*, done first at Long Wharf and then on Broadway in the early 1970s. Bury's use of space and color, and the mixture of non-realism within a seemingly realistic environment—furniture sitting in the middle of space, away from the walls as she remembers it—opened up new possibilities for Kellogg. As for Jenkins' set, "I remember it almost detail-for-detail," she says. "It was like a revelation. When I first saw it at Long Wharf I thought it was the most wonderful thing I'd ever seen. It had all the detail and texture of Ming, with a kind of gritty realism that Ming is not interested in. I think David Jenkins is the real genius of realism in the theatre."

Despite her apparent success, it was not until sometime in 1982 with *American Buffalo* and *Present Laughter* that Kellogg felt fully in control of her work. "Before then, I had begun to fear that I would be nothing but a mediocre designer," she says. She still feels that the "big break" is yet to come, although she qualifies that by saying, "I don't know that I believe in such a thing. If the show is a hit, you get a break. Whether the scenery is good or not has very little to do with it." She is now quite confident in her abilities—and her future—though not in the future of the theatre in general. "I wonder," she told *Ms.*, "if soon it's all going to be *Nine* and *Cats*, Las Vegas in New York."

Most designers, when asked what they do in their spare time or what they do to relax, just laugh—the concept of spare time does not exist. It does not exist for Kellogg either, but she is one of the few designers who actively pursues other activities. She is the author of *A Rumor of Angels*, a highly praised science fiction novel, and she finds time to pursue this second career despite the demands of the theatre. Ming Cho Lee is enormously impressed with her intellectual as well as artistic abilities and proclaims, "She is probably smarter than all of us."

And she has devoted part of her time and energy to making the theatre community more aware of the discrimination against women in set design. "These days," she wrote in *American Theatre* magazine (May 1984), "the first (and sometimes the only) question I get asked is if it's harder being a woman scenic designer. Harder than what? Being a designer is hard. Let's talk about being a designer. But the questioners persist, and in their persistence is their answer. By setting women apart to press that question, they prove that the answer must inevitably be yes."

Kellogg encountered blatant sexism only once, working on a television production with David Susskind, but the real discrimination is more insidious. It is demonstrated in the fact that fewer than three percent of women set designers work on Broadway and that Kellogg is the first woman scenic designer since Aline Bernstein in the 1920s to work there so consistently. Yet, this translates into fewer than a dozen productions despite consistently good reviews.

Kellogg has no desire to be a crusader or to politicize the theatre. But because of her success as a designer, and probably because of her success as a gadfly, more and more women are moving into the ranks of set design, and it has been made a little bit easier by the hard work of Marjorie Kellogg.

# EUGENE LEE

"Designers shouldn't be so eclectic," proclaims Eugene Lee. "Artists have styles that you can recognize instantly, and I have always thought that that is what the stage designer should have. At base we're artists and craftsmen with a tradition. I have always thought there should be a point of view."

Lee's point of view, simply stated, is that the entire theatrical experience resides in the relationship between the performer and the spectator—all else is secondary. Consequently, he sees the stage and auditorium as a single, unified space. Most designers, of course, have a style; it is easy to spot their use of color, texture, sculptural forms or even idiosyncratic trademarks. Yet many of these same designers have submerged their points of view, espousing, instead, the necessity of serving the text and the director. Lee, too, believes in serving the text, but not through the creation of pretty pictures restrained by the proscenium arch. He approaches each play as if it were a puzzle or a problem to be solved. With no preconceived notions as to how the text is to be interpreted or how the theatre space is to be dealt with, he becomes an iconoclastic problem-solver in close and direct collaboration with the director.

The results have included such daring and innovative landmark productions as Amiri Baraka's *Slave Ship* (Chelsea Theater Center, 1969), the revival of Leonard Bernstein's *Candide* for which he won a Tony (Chelsea Theater and Broadway, 1974), Stephen Sondheim's *Sweeney Todd* (Broadway, 1979) for which he won another Tony, and dozens upon dozens of productions with Adrian Hall at the Trinity Square Repertory Company in Providence,

Rhode Island. These productions, in turn, led to designs for NBC television's *Saturday Night Live*, several movies, rock concerts, and collaborations with British director Peter Brook.

There are two stylistic elements that recur in Lee's work. First, his use of space is generally non-traditional—regardless of the usual configuration of the theatre in which he is working, Lee treats the entire theatre space as one room to be designed. Hence, his work is frequently environmental or at least audience-involving in some way. Second, he likes real materials and objects rather than the illusionistic imitations frequently employed in theatrical design. "I don't mean painting things to look real," he explains. "Once you start painting, it has a painted look. What please me are real textures used in the way nature left them. There's nothing like a real piece of rusted tin—really rusted—put up on the stage. I don't care how heavy it is, how dirty it is. Everyone says, 'We can paint it; we can make it.' You *know* they can't." For Andre Gregory's production of *Endgame* at the Theatre of the Living Arts in Philadelphia (1965) and Yale (1966) Lee constructed a wire-mesh cage to enclose the performance. He began constructing it outside, three months in advance of the production, in order to let it rust naturally. (He points out that he did his own construction—something he still likes to do, although union rules make this difficult.)

Because the terms "environmental" and "audience-involving" tend to have specific, perhaps negative connotations for some people, it should be emphasized that Lee's work is meticulous, technically sophisticated and highly conceptual—always

*Facing page,* Tom Jones *at the Dallas Theater Center's Arts District Theater (1984), for which Eugene Lee created a construction site environment using a real crane and other machinery donated by a construction company. The environment also included gravel, dirt and water. The theatre is a temporary structure, designed by Lee, with a tin roof and a dirt floor.*

evolving from ideas he and the director find implicit in the script or scenario. "I hate those theatres where people come up and talk to you," he says.

His interest in encompassing the audience within the scope of the design is an attempt to engage them on a psychological and emotional level. He becomes excited when discussing the atmosphere at Trinity Square, and the production of *Billy Budd* (1969) in particular: "We would roll big cannons out at the audience and they would climb out of their seats because they knew the cannons were going to fire. I love to shake them up, see them on their feet and moving—theatre that's outside and inside at the same time."

Lee has a reputation in some circles for being difficult or non-communicative. In fact, he is shy, and his speech falters in situations in which he is uncomfortable. Kevin Kelly of *The Boston Globe* describes the "hesitant, staccato, cyclical patterns of his speech . . . the exact opposite of the crafted, meticulous stage sets." If he is difficult—Harold Prince calls him stubborn—it comes from a passionate, uncompromising sense of theatrical values—values that sometimes fly in the face of commercial norms. As a result, his best work has emerged out of his collaborations with directors Andre Gregory, Adrian Hall, Harold Prince, Michael Lindsay-Hogg and Lorne Michaels. His unconventional approaches began to get him into difficulties in college—he attended several.

Trying to reconstruct Lee's past can be difficult. He is genuinely uninterested in past accomplishments and totally unable to recall dates. Of his patchwork college career, he states vaguely, "I don't think I have a degree from any place. Maybe I have a degree from Yale, I can't remember." (He told another interviewer that Carnegie "took pity on him" and granted him a BA.) He is not being facetious or affected; his memory is poor when it comes to his own accomplishments, and he is quite uncomfortable talking about himself. "I don't know what I do," he replies when asked to discuss his work. Sounding a bit like the Fortune Teller in *The Skin of Our*

*Teeth*, he continues, "I only have a sense of the future. I can't tell you about my past, only what I'm working on at the moment, or what I will be doing tomorrow."

Lee was born in Beloit, Wisconsin in 1939 and has a twin brother. As far as he remembers he always wanted to be a designer—not simply to go into theatre but specifically to design. His parents were active in community theatre—his father as an actor, his mother as a designer—and his high school theatre was unusually elaborate, Lee Simonson apparently having been the consultant when it was built. With this ambition, the only problem was to learn the craft. He did some summer stock and enrolled at the University of Wisconsin, which did not have a design program at the time. The summer after his first year at Madison he saw a television documentary about Carnegie Tech (now Carnegie Mellon University). According to Lee, he put his meager portfolio in his Volkswagen and drove to Pittsburgh where he stayed three years. "I don't think I enjoyed it too much at the time," he recalls. "I left in a traumatic state."

He went from there to Chicago where he enrolled in the Goodman School for another two years. While there he joined the union and did some work at the Chicago Lyric Opera. From Chicago he went to Yale. Fellow Yale student, costume designer Carrie Robbins, recalls that his sets there were stunning and innovative. But there, as elsewhere, Lee felt stifled by the faculty for his unconventionality. Although he admits that some teachers over the years were influential—Dan Snyder and Ted Hoffman at Carnegie, James Maronek at Goodman, and Donald Oenslager at Yale—he concludes that, "You learn nothing in school that you couldn't learn by traveling around the world for five years." He still has great respect for Oenslager and states that "there are no designers today who even remotely approach Oenslager's stature." The schools did, however, provide friendships that would help launch his career; lighting designer Roger Morgan whom he met at Carnegie, for example, brought

*Above, John Conklin's model for* Camino Real
*(Williamstown Theatre Festival, 1968). Right, another John
Conklin model, for the ballet* Romeo and Juliet *(Hartford
Ballet, 1980).*

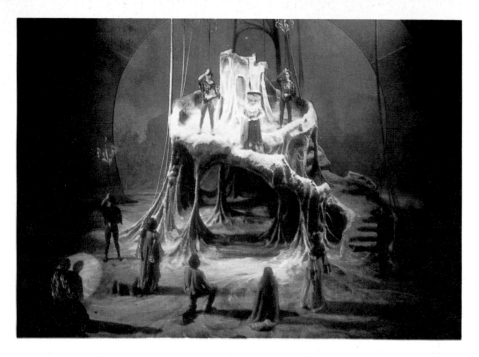

*Above, Ming Cho Lee's set for* The Tempest *(Mark Taper Forum, 1979). Near right, a rendering for* Hair *(New York Shakespeare Festival, 1967), also by Ming Cho Lee. Far right, Eugene Lee's Chinatown set for the 1982 film* Hammett. *Opposite page, Ralph Funicello's set for* The Front Page *(Seattle Repertory Theatre, 1982). Photo by Don Hamilton.*

*Two renderings by John Lee Beatty. Above, Neil Simon's* Fools *(Broadway, 1981). Right,* Look Homeward Angel *(Yale School of Drama, 1972).*

*Above, two examples of Santo Loquasto's work. Left, the set for* American Buffalo *(Broadway, 1977). Right, Touchstone's costume, worn by Roy Brocksmith in* As You Like It, *(Guthrie Theater, 1982). At right, a scene from* La Cage aux Folles, *designed by David Mitchell with costumes by Theoni Aldredge (Broadway, 1983). Photo by Martha Swope.*

*Left, Douglas Schmidt's set for the entrance to Isis' temple in Aida (San Francisco Opera, 1981). Photo by Ron Sherl. Above, another Schmidt design, for Saint-Saëns' Samson et Dalila (San Francisco Opera, 1980). Right, the paint elevation for a backdrop in the musical 42nd Street (Broadway, 1980), designed by Robin Wagner.*

*Above, Karl Eigsti's rendering for* Knockout *(Broadway, 1979). Right, Marjorie Bradley Kellogg's model for* Steaming *(Broadway, 1982). Photo by Martha Swope.*

him to the attention of Adrian Hall at Trinity.

It was Ted Hoffman, head of the theatre program at Carnegie, who recommended Lee to Andre Gregory in 1965. Like Lee, Gregory had a reputation for being difficult and unconventional and was having trouble finding a designer with whom he could work at the Theatre of the Living Arts.

Gregory had been strongly influenced by the unified theatrical approach of the Berliner Ensemble. He believes Lee was similarly influenced and in him he saw a kindred spirit. "The designers that I met prior to Eugene just didn't think that way," remembers Gregory. "Also, I couldn't find a designer who could really speak the language of theatre. It's like the language of marriage. The specificity of the word is important, but there's also a subtext which sometimes says something more precise. We're talking in the theatre about an unseen music, and poetry and rhythm that's not necessarily physical. The designers I met wanted to know how many walls I wanted—I didn't know how many walls I wanted. Eugene wasn't like that. When he showed up in Philadelphia he looked like a mad bomber. He was extremely shy, had very thick spectacles and a cap. He could hardly say a word. He just opened his portfolio and I was simply staggered by the beauty of his work and sort of fell in love with him, the way you do with certain colleagues—the way I feel about Wally Shawn or Twyla Tharp. It was never necessary to talk very much."

This early collaboration resulted in some startling work but, ironically, the set designer for Rochelle Owens' *Beclch* (1966), Gregory's first environmental production, was John Conklin. Lee designed the costumes. What was most beneficial about this early work with Gregory was the freedom he had to seek new solutions and to experiment with conceptual settings. It also marked the beginning of Lee's participation as a collaborator in the staging of productions—"I like to get involved in the script," says Lee. "If I can't, it's no fun for me. I get involved in how we do it—what the ideas are. I mean the real ideas, the directorial ideas." Gregory involved him

in this process. Lee is one of the few designers who truly enjoys sitting in on rehearsals.

This collaborative process has been most successful at Trinity Rep with Adrian Hall. "I would never have been able to fulfill myself as an artist without Eugene Lee," claims Hall. "It is a communal art that we deal with. The structured text is not what the theatre experience is. So any amount of wishing that you had a good text still does not mean that you would have good theatre. The designer is an integral part of structuring that experience."

Almost any Lee design could serve as an example of collaborative problem solving, but James Schevill's *Cathedral of Ice* (Trinity Square Repertory Company, 1975) stands out in Hall's mind as "the

For Son of Man and the Family *(Trinity Square Repertory Company, 1970), a play about the Charles Manson family, Lee created a prison environment based on his visit to a penitentiary. The metal grates helped create an aural as well as visual environment. The set also included working showers under which the family washed following the murders.*

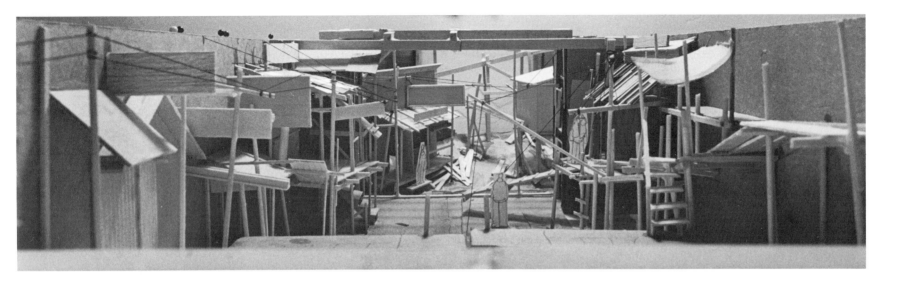

single most brilliant design effect I have ever seen, the most brilliant solving of a problem I have encountered." Lee created a carnival atmosphere for the play about Hitler's rise to power and American myths. The performance began in a tent outside the theatre that was set up to suggest a German beer garden, complete with long tables and free beer for the spectators. The play then progressed inside the theatre to a kind of carnival midway through which the audience was free to move. At the end of the second act—the moment Hall is referring to—the atmosphere had to change instantly from carnival frivolity to the gas chambers. Lee's solution, after much discussion, was for bodies to fall from trap doors in the ceiling. As Hall describes it, "The sky literally opened and hundreds of bodies plummeted out of the sky in one minute. It was the most horrifying moment you can imagine. It wasn't built on any kind of illusion. It was just there—bang! The audience looked up and just gasped."

When Lee arrived at Trinity they had just begun performing at the Rhode Island School of Design. His first designs there timidly poked out from the proscenium, but it was not until *Macbeth* (1969) that the iconoclastic style for which Hall and Lee

have become known emerged. There were two main impulses toward breaking through the proscenium plane. Trinity Square had a grant to perform theatre for students, and their first season of doing so had been disastrous in terms of student response. "We had to find a way of grabbing their attention and holding it," explains Hall. He began to realize that the physical barrier between the audience and the performers also acted, at least in the case of the students, as a psychological barrier.

Around the same time, Lee visited the Edinburgh Festival with the Trinity Company, where he saw Jerzy Grotowski's Polish Laboratory Theatre. Grotowski's company created total, audience-encompassing environments for each production. Grotowski also advocated "poor theatre" which, among other things, abolished the glossiness and illusionism of much contemporary theatre in favor of sets constructed out of found objects, illumination through simple white light, and simple costumes. (In explaining his use of an environmental approach, Lee also notes his fascination with medieval theatre and especially the 15th-century drawing of *The Castle of Perseverance*, a morality play performed in a series of "mansions" amidst the audi-

*Model for Michael Weller's* The Ballad of Soapy Smith *at the New York Shakespeare Festival (1984). This was Lee's first New York production in over two years, and his first environmental design in New York since the 1974* Candide. *An earlier, more-or-less proscenium version was done at the Seattle Repertory Theatre in 1983.*

ence in specially constructed earthen "rounds.")

For *Macbeth*, a pipe-scaffolding structure covered a wood-plank stage that extended into the auditorium with a runway. Characters entered and exited from all parts of the auditorium which was dimly illuminated by small fires in tin cans. The use of real fire recurred in a few of Lee's subsequent productions.

*Macbeth* was followed two months later by *Billy Budd*, based on the Herman Melville novel. The audience was made to feel as if it were on an 18th-century warship whose machinery dominated the setting. Rigging—sometimes with sailors on it—hung over the heads of the audience. As with *Macbeth*, there was a wooden runway and pipe scaffolding. During a battle scene, performers and action

filled the auditorium, including overhead; sound effects and smoke engulfed the space.

None of this evolved from theory. The term "environmental theatre" had only recently been coined. Hall, in fact, does not refer to the settings as environments but as "atmospheres." *Son of Man and the Family* (1970)—a play created by the company about the Manson Family—for example, was an attempt to recreate the atmosphere of a prison. A visit to a Rhode Island prison left Hall and Lee with the impression that "everything is happening over your head. Men seem to be marching on steel grates above you," said Hall in an article in *Theater* (Winter 1982). The resulting design included steel-mesh catwalks above the audience.

Part of the creation of atmosphere, they realized,

*Ibsen's* Rosmersholm *(Trinity Square, 1977). While two-level sets are not unprecedented, this may be the only multilevel interior ever to include a basement.*

was the creation of an aural environment—not just recorded effects, that can be as phony as the painted scenery Lee deplores, but live sound produced by the setting. The overhead catwalks in *Son of Man* and the machinery in *Billy Budd*, as well as similar effects in later productions, recreated sounds found in the original environments.

Lee and Hall were working to revitalize theatre through "a real desire to confront the audience in the most challenging way," as Hall says. They rejected pictorial scenery as a relic of the 19th century. "I've never been interested in stage design as pictures," states Lee. "I remember seeing *The King and I* in Chicago when I was in high school and I love that kind of scenery—but not for me. It's just pretty pictures passing by." Hall has a similar sensibility. This unique collaboration at Trinity—which Lee likens to the best ensemble theatres of Europe—allows him to do things at other theatres that he might not otherwise have had the courage or experience to try. "No matter what I've done elsewhere," he says, "in theatre, television or film, I always did it first in some way at Providence."

The Providence approach was first seen in New York when Lee designed the Chelsea Theater Center's production of *Slave Ship* at the Brooklyn Academy of Music. He did not merely place scenic elements around the audience but literally rebuilt the entire space, platforming over the raked auditorium of the narrow performance space to create one large space. In the center was a two-level wooden platform built on rockers which, for the first half of the play, represented the ship. Spectator benches surrounded this platform on four sides. Raised platforms where other scenes were played were constructed along the four walls behind the audience areas. A ramp extended from one such platform to the central playing space. The audience was within a few feet of the performers and this proximity was exploited to create terror, tension and guilt, but the actors stopped short of direct contact. Critic John Lahr, in his introduction to the play in *Life Show*, described the set as:

an environment where humiliation cannot be escaped . . . Blacks are chained to the floor, the ceiling is three feet above their bodies . . . nothing is more shocking, revolting or obscene than the fact of the cramped violence of the space. . . . The actors crawl beneath our feet; their shackles clink as they move. . . . They surround the audience with their madness and their despair.

At about the same time, Lee and his former wife, Franne Newman Lee, were designing Andre Gregory's landmark production of *Alice in Wonderland* (1970) with the Manhattan Project. (Through the 1970s, most of Lee's work was done in collaboration with Franne Lee. While the credits generally read "Sets by Eugene Lee" and "Costumes by Franne Lee" the collaboration was usually more complex and not so easily classified.) The company had been at work on the production for about a year and a half when Lee came in. Gregory, inspired by Grotowski's "poor theatre" concept, wanted to create with actors alone a movie-like aesthetic. "It was obvious," explained Gregory, "that there should be no sets, lights or costumes. Eugene's work was to give the illusion of no sets, lights or costumes, while still creating an environment—an environment that would look as if the performers had created it themselves."

The result was a cross between a circus tent and a children's club house—Lee wanted a sense of both circus and claustrophobia. The audience first entered a foyer constructed of wooden doors taken from construction sites. They gained access to the performance space—also surrounded by old doors and planks—by ducking through a 3½-foot doorway. Inside, old wooden chairs with legs sawed off were fastened to a bleacher-like seating area randomly so that the hundred-odd spectators could sit on chairs or bleachers. The original idea was to have all sorts of seats such as barber and dentist chairs to encourage a sense of fantasy—economics prohibited this. Both audience and performance

*Top,* model for last act of Puccini's La
Fanciulla del West; *bottom, production
photo of its first act (Lyric Opera of
Chicago, 1978). The production was
co-designed by Franne Lee and directed by
Harold Prince. The scenic structures were
built to a realistic scale, thus creating
cramped spaces on the large stage.
Performers working on the mountain were
dwarfed by its massiveness. For the finale,
the heroine arrived by handcar.*

areas were covered with a large parachute—like a circus tent—and everything was lit by two bare bulbs. Thus, while intimacy and a sense of participation in the fantasy world were created, there was never any direct contact between the performers and spectators.

Lee's work on *Slave Ship* brought him to the attention of director Peter Brook who invited him to work on *Orghast* (1971), an ensemble-created, ritualistic piece performed in found spaces—mostly tombs and monuments—at the Shiraz Festival near Persepolis, Iran. Lee's contribution was primarily the creation of fire implements, including a ball of fire lowered by a crane in front of Ataxerxes' tomb. As Lee explained, "When you play in a natural environment like Persepolis, you don't need a set. How can you compete with 5,000-year-old monuments? [My job was] rudimentary problem-solving: 'How do we make a fire ball? What do people sit on?'"

The following year Lee created a set for *Kaspar* at Brook's International Centre for Theatre Research in Paris. The set was like a shadow box, but the key element according to Lee was the lighting, which was very flat and eliminated shadows. Lee has strong feelings about lighting. Just as he prefers real materials on the stage, he prefers large, simple lighting instruments like movie lights and scoops that cast flat, white light. He has little use for the standard, mood-provoking and illusionistic techniques of lighting such as slow fades, color mixing and the new computerized dimmer boards. "All of it bores the shit out of me, frankly." He would like to light more of his own sets, and expresses some disgust at a system that allows him to design lights for Peter Brook in Paris but not for shows on Broadway.

Lee enjoyed working with Brook because, like Adrian Hall, "He is interested in more than just the picture." But ultimately there was a degree of frustration: "It was Brook's experiment," he notes. Lee needs the sense of collaboration.

Besides the Trinity productions, one of the best examples of this collaboration was the Seattle Repertory Theatre production of Michael Weller's *The Ballad of Soapy Smith* (1983), directed by Robert Egan. The opening sequence as written "seemed

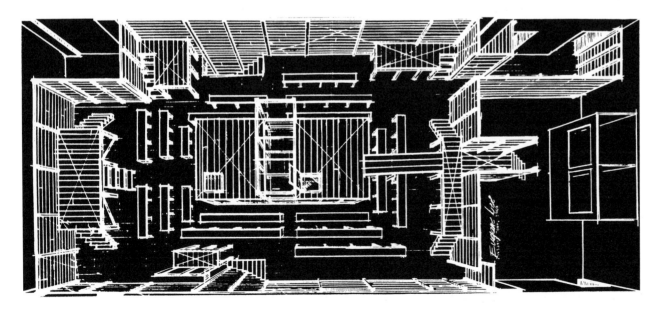

*Top view sketch of the environment for Amiri Baraka's* Slave Ship *(Chelsea Theater Center, 1969). The audience sat on benches around the central playing area, which served as the hold of a slave ship in the first scene and an auction block later on. Lee transformed the entire theatre to create the setting which brought him to the attention of both Harold Prince and Peter Brook.*

too weak" to Lee—it was a narrator describing the discovery of gold in the Yukon. The scene, as it was finally staged, was in part Lee's creation. Lee, who is an avid sailor (and lives on his boat docked at a Manhattan marina when working in New York), remembered the 1983 America's Cup race when the crowds wanted to see the mysterious keel of the Australian yacht. Hundreds of people on the dock chanted "Show it to us!" Lee translated this image into a scene on the Seattle docks:

The scene came alive with a whole stage full of people—a Zeffirelli stage full of people—as many people as we could muster. There was a gigantic steam whistle blasting, big doors opening, a ramp is coming down, you just saw part of the steam ship through the doors—smoke, fog and things. This miner came down, the crowd kind of stopped, and they all started chanting, 'show us, show us, is it true?' He pulled open his coat and it was full of diamonds and gold. He took out a bag of gold and poured it and said "I'll never have to work another goddam day in my life!" A headline came down—"Rumors of Gold in the Yukon"—and the play started as written. It was a good collaboration.

Lee also enjoyed the production because once again the set was allowed to spill out past the proscenium and over the theatre walls. For the New York Shakespeare Festival production of the same play (1984), the set extended along both walls of the Newman Theatre to the back of the auditorium.

Throughout the early 1970s it became commonplace for Lee to reconstruct the interior of a theatre when he designed a set. For the 1972 Broadway production of *Dude*—a rock musical by the creators of *Hair* about a character's metaphoric search through the cosmos—the Broadway Theatre was transformed for a then staggering $100,000. As described by Douglas Watt in his *Daily News* review: "The Broadway has been converted into an arena theatre, the seats sloping down from mezzanine level to a matted round playing area, which is flanked by other seats and beyond which still more seats rise on the former stage. The band is spread out on two levels [along the walls]. There are also runways and lots of gear, including a block-and-tackle arrangement to transport players high into the air, even up through a hole in the ceiling itself." Originally the stage was covered with two tons of dirt, but the dust caused problems and was replaced with felt cloth and eventually plastic. Ticket locations were marked "foothills," "valley," etc.

*Dude* was one of the more spectacular failures of the season, but the following year Lee successfully brought environmental design to Broadway with the Harold Prince production of *Candide*. (Like Brook, Prince had been impressed with the *Slave Ship* environment.) First staged at the Chelsea in Brooklyn, it was a grandiose version of *Slave Ship*. There were seven stages with connecting ramps, aisles and stairs, among which were stools, benches and bleachers for the audience. At roughly the center of the space a pit was created by a raised oval ramp. Spectators sat on stools in the pit. At the center of the pit was a stage built on rockers to create a ship-at-sea effect. In his book *Contradictions*, Prince describes how he thought of staging the play as a circus sideshow with Voltaire guiding the audience from one booth to the next.

I went through the whole trajectory of my thinking process [with Lee], arriving at the sideshow scheme, voicing concern about the schematicness of it. Immediately he suggested limiting curtains to some stages and varying the levels as well as the sizes of them. This suggested to me the possibility of playing scenes simultaneously on stages in opposite ends of the theatre. For the first time I remembered the extraordinary Italian production of *Orlando Furioso* which I had seen in Bryant Park in 1970 . . . .

A trapdoor entered the conversation [for the

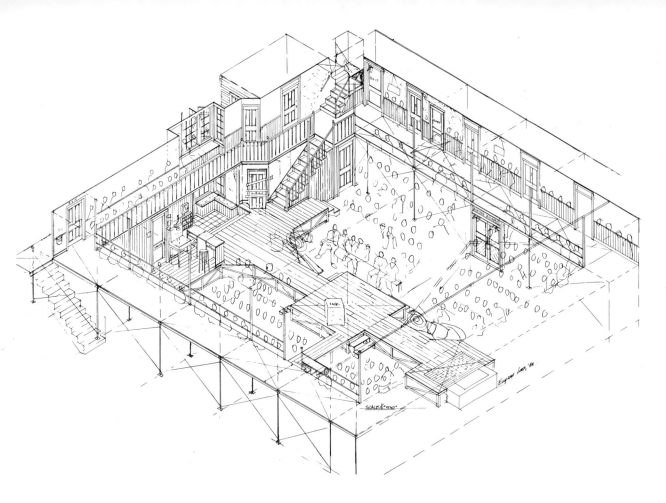

"Glitter and Be Gay" number] and we began breaking the sideshow pattern. Had I any objections to people *sitting* in places other than the center of the environment? Sitting? Well you could hardly expect them to stand for two hours. Hardly. I had no objection. How about all over the set? Did I object to that? No objection.

Lee went off and returned in a month with a model in a shoebox of the set as it would look. The production moved in 1974 to the Broadway Theatre which was once again totally reconstructed. The ceiling was lowered, part of the balcony was closed off and much of the auditorium was platformed. The seating capacity was reduced from 1,800 to 900, which eventually caused economic problems.

Lee and Prince had hoped that the success of *Candide* would open the way for more innovative staging on Broadway. Unfortunately, the musicians' strike, high operating costs and limited seating caused *Candide* to close after only 740 performances. The Shuberts insisted that the theatre be returned to its original state immediately. Prince states that if he had known earlier that the show would close, he would have found something else to put in that space. At around that time, the Vivian Beaumont Theatre was experiencing one of its pe-

*Left, sketch for George M. Cohan's* Seven Keys to Baldpate *(Dallas Theater Center, 1984); right, a photo of the set. Lee created a Victorian residence that surrounded and sliced through the audience in the temporary Arts District Theater.*

riodic difficulties and Prince approached the Lincoln Center board with a proposal for turning the Beaumont into a permanent environmental theatre. He and Lee had worked out a tentative plan for a changeable space that would accommodate 700–800 people. Obviously, nothing came of that proposal.

Lee, in fact, envisioned their next collaboration, *Sweeney Todd*, in that space. The mechanical barber's chair in which the victims' throats were graphically slit before they slid down a chute beneath the chair, was to be on a central stage in the midst of the audience. *Sweeney Todd* was eventually done at the Uris Theatre, the biggest house on Broadway.

Lee was faced with designing a set in the sort of space he likes the least. As he explained in *Theater*, "I just said, 'I have a big, ugly theatre. It's white. I hate it. I'll just make the biggest set that I can.' And that's how the factory happened." The setting, which filled the entire stage and spilled out beyond the proscenium, was a Victorian foundry created in part from scrap metal and mechanical devices from old factories in Rhode Island. There was a peaked roof of grimy glass panes supported on steel trusses and rusted iron beams. Stairways and platforms filled the sides of the stage. The back wall was made of corrugated tin and rose to reveal a painted drop of 19th-century London. There was also a catwalk-bridge suspended from a traveling girder and there were all sorts of moving parts that did little but create an atmosphere. Specific locales were delineated by scenic units on rolling wagons. Prince points out that while the superstructure of the set was huge, the show itself was very small and intimate—"the whole play took place on a nodule and a few stairs."

"Eugene and I agreed that it should be a Victorian factory," recalls Prince, "and that what we were saying, without making a big deal out of it, was that there was a connection between Sweeney Todd and all the people on the stage—what the industrial age had done, not only to the quality of life of so many people in the ghetto just in practical terms, but to the peacefulness and harmony in people's lives—in the environment, the atmosphere. With the industrial age, people could not see the sky for the puke that was flying in the air above them. That's what we tried to do. The whole thing is encased in glass. No one sees the sun except through glass."

By creating what one critic called an "awesome set," Lee was able to overcome the cavernous atmosphere of the Uris Theatre, to overwhelm and "assault" the audience, while remaining essentially frontal and proscenium-bound.

Reconstructing theatre spaces can be costly, and finding producers who will allow this is increasingly difficult. The ideal situation for Lee is a space designed for flexibility. When the Trinity company renovated an old movie theatre into the Lederer Theatre in 1973, Lee designed its two spaces—one flexible, the other thrust—to accommodate his style of design. He also helped convert the National Furniture Factory in Paris for Peter Brook's company, and has designed two spaces for the Dallas Theater Center now under the direction of Adrian Hall. One is a renovation of Dallas' Frank Lloyd Wright-designed Kalita Humphreys Theatre, but he is much more excited about the other—a temporary space constructed in the Dallas arts district. It is a corrugated tin structure, approximately 100' x 100' x 45' high with a compacted dirt floor. "I always wanted a dirt floor," he says with delight. "If you

want a trap, if you want mud, you just bring in a backhoe. We might have a platform consisting of railroad ties or bricks set into the earth." The 1984 production of *Tom Jones* in that space had a gravel lobby area, a pond, a dirt "road" and a real crane.

It was in part Lee's fascination with real materials that kindled his interest in film. Although he had done about a dozen PBS "on location" films, Francis Ford Coppola's *Hammett* (1983)—about mystery writer Dashiell Hammett, set in 1920s San Francisco—was his first Hollywood production. When he talks about the money available for scenery, the crews, research (he had about five file cabinets full of pictures), editing equipment and general facilities, he sounds like a child in a toy store. "You want a 1928 crane, they get you one! You want concrete streets? They bring in the cement mixers and pour them in the studio!" Hammett's house was constructed almost as a real piece of architecture, down to the nameplate on the stove. Lee's job—he was brought in after the film had begun production and then been shelved for awhile—was to recreate San Francisco in Zoetrope's largest sound stage. Concrete streets were poured, the Bay—complete with water—was recreated. Lee called it "summer stock at Zoetrope." He approached it as a type of television scenery, "a combination of *Playhouse 90* and a film set," and described the result as "an homage to telephone wires, poles and streets; but not a lot of detail."

Real material, Lee discovered, is more difficult in television. He had never done television design prior to *Saturday Night Live*. Producer Lorne Michaels hired him largely as a result of seeing *Candide*. "I was looking for someone to create the sort of intimacy of a theatrical environment," explains Michaels. "I was looking for a way to bring the audience close enough in a television studio to be relaxed and comfortable."

Lee created the overall environment of Studio 8H, as well as the individual sets for the sketches on the weekly show. The basic set was a sort of warehouse or Soho garage for which he wanted to use real brick. But as he notes, "on television, stick-on wallpaper reads the same as real veneer." What he succeeded in doing, according to Michaels, was to "restore a certain kind of glamour to New York by showing the beauty in what was run down in urban environments." Given the summer stock atmosphere created by the weekly demands of the live show, Lee learned television technique quickly.

The flip side of Lee's penchant for real and found objects onstage is his delight in tackiness—and that is what emerged on *Saturday Night Live*. The settings for the various skits bordered on kitsch and were often marvelous parodies of sit-com box sets and talk show milieus. This was enhanced by the last-minute approach to the show on the part of the writers and performers. When Michaels left the show after five years, Lee did also; but he has con-

tinued working with Michaels and his production company on films; television specials for people like Steve Martin and Randy Newman; Simon and Garfunkel's reunion in Central Park and subsequent tours; and the short-lived prime-time successor to *SNL*, *The New Show*. Commenting on the Central Park set for Simon and Garfunkel, Michaels said, "I think it worked both for the people who were there and also on television—he tends to bridge that better than anyone I know. He's a genius. The only one I've met."

Working outside of mainstream aesthetics, one might expect Lee's design process to be different as well, but aside from work habits that inevitably reflect his personality, his approach is fairly standard. Lee builds models and is capable of building very detailed and beautiful ones. Given his treatment of

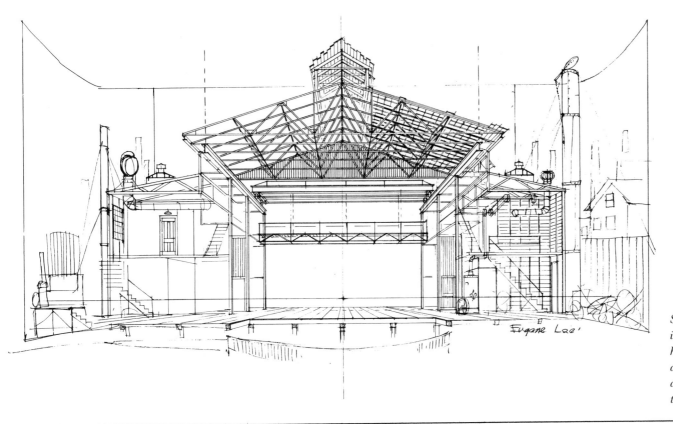

*Sketch for* Sweeney Todd. *Lee is less interested in the polish and "prettiness" of his Broadway productions than in the actual effect. In* Sweeney, *he did not attempt to preserve an illusion by hiding the mechanical contraptions.*

space, models are frequently essential to directors with whom he works. Renderings, even if he did them (he claims not to do them well), would be of little value in an environmental setting. Those directors with whom he works frequently have developed a trust and an understanding of his work so that finished models are rarely necessary, and sometimes they are foregone altogether. Michaels and Gregory, for instance, have on occasion begun work on a production before ever seeing Lee's design.

Lee does much of his own drafting. He works with a few assistants—he calls them collaborators—Leo Yoshimura, Mat Jacobs and Keith Raywood. Perhaps more than any other designer, Lee considers his assistants as equals and discusses ideas, problems and solutions with them. There is also a certain attitude in the work process that can only be described as "laid back." The finished product is by no means sloppy, but the studio atmosphere lacks the discipline, precision or organization of that of most other designers. Lee's lack of interest

King Lear *(Trinity Square Repertory Company, 1977). Director Adrian Hall wanted to convey a feeling of interior and exterior that he felt was suggested by the play. The doors and shutters in the barn-like structure allowed this. For the opening scenes in Lear's court, the stage was covered over with plywood which was then removed to reveal mulch.*

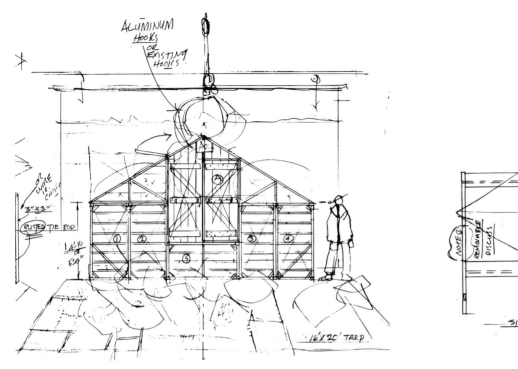

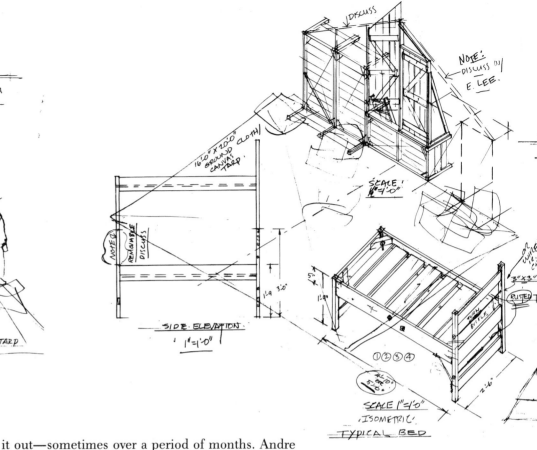

*Sketches for* Of Mice and Men *(Trinity Square, 1981).*

in the usual polish and "prettiness" of Broadway productions, and his seemingly casual approach can be surprising to technicians. Peter Feller, Jr., whose Feller Precision, Inc. constructed the machinery for *Sweeney Todd*, remembers asking Lee about the details of the drive mechanism for the moving bridge. Most designers would be concerned about such things as the visibility of the mechanism, the size or the position. But Lee was interested in the effect and did not care whether the mechanics were visible or not—there was no illusion to be protected and mechanical contraptions were part of the set.

The evolution of a design idea is a very difficult thing to pin down. In Lee's case, images frequently pop into his head that solve all the problems of the show. At other times, it is a long process of talking it out—sometimes over a period of months. Andre Gregory cites his experience in trying to get Lee to design Wallace Shawn's *Our Late Night* as an example of "instant insight." Gregory was having problems arriving at a scheme to accommodate three scenes—a dressing room, a party and a bedroom—in what was essentially a dream play. He wanted Lee to design it, but Lee did not like the play.

I took Eugene out to lunch and I said, "I'm really stuck. Won't you consider doing it?" which is not a good idea with Eugene because he is a poet—either he gets it or he doesn't. He's not a person who can just make something for somebody because they paid him to

do it. So he said to me, "Well, how do you see the play?" And I said, "Eugene, it's a mixture between an analyst's couch, a Chinese funeral, a white coffin and a little child's trolley car going through space." We then spent about 10 minutes in total silence eating our lunch. Finally he said, "It's simple. What you need is to play in a large black space where there are obviously no entrances or exits. . . ."

Lee, according to Gregory, rapidly outlined a whole design scheme. Ultimately, Douglas Schmidt designed the set using Lee's basic ideas.

Lee's work on *Agnes of God* (Broadway, 1982) provides some insight into his approach to a play. He and director Michael Lindsay-Hogg perceived the play as an "acting piece." Ostensibly set in a psychiatrist's office, the play really unfolds in characters' minds and in the past and thus required an abstract setting. "It called for something simple— the show is in the acting and the staging," explains Lee. The playwright told him not to use chairs so, somewhat as a defiant child, "I dealt precisely with chairs. I couldn't see it any other way. I have to have some kind of logic somewhere in myself. I couldn't just design a set of abstract platforms unless the director and playwright helped me a lot more, told me more about the blocking. I can't just do levels and abstractions. Somebody puts out a cigarette—well, you have to have an ashtray."

Beginning with the question of how to stage two people sitting and talking, he envisioned the set as a large sounding board. The result was a raked floor of dark oak, six-inch planking sweeping up to meet a curved back wall of similar construction. Scenes were visible through the planking like a wooden scrim. "It's very simple," he states. "Every time I tried adding to it, it started to become like a room."

Lee has some antipathy toward the commercial theatre and has not designed on Broadway since *Agnes of God*. "It's not a lot of fun, it costs a lot of money. If I can't do that," he says, pointing to the plans for his dirt-floor theatre in Dallas, "I'd just as soon not do it. Fixed, frozen spaces do not excite me." Harold Prince notes that "whenever we can spill over the proscenium or work away from the conventional stage structure, he's a very happy and creative man. The minute he gets jammed into the stage structure he is unhappy and his work shows it." As a result, Lee reneged on transferring *Candide* to the New York City Opera (1983)—Clarke Dunham eventually designed the new settings—and one of Lee's assistants adapted *Sweeney Todd* for the New York City Opera production (1984).

For a while in the early 1980s, Lee was becoming quite discouraged with theatre. The restrictions of Broadway were stifling, and even at Trinity Square he found that once adventurous audiences were demanding conventional seating. The flexible upstairs space at the Lederer became more and more a conventional thrust stage. But recently he has regained a spirit for which the word enthusiasm seems too mild. The dirt-floor theatre in Dallas has sparked his creativity, and the ability to do environmental settings once again in Seattle and New York has engendered a new sense of hope and anticipation. And his new family life—he remarried and had a baby (he has a son from his former marriage)—has rekindled his spirits as well. "What's important," he told *The Boston Globe*, "is that you love what you do, that you have a family life. I have two family lives, one with Brooke and my sons, and one in the theatre. Theatre people are special."

So in a striking about face, while many others are bemoaning the moribund state of the theatre, Eugene Lee happily proclaims, "The future looks bright."

*Facing page,* Sweeney Todd *(Uris Theatre, 1979). Lee's award-winning, massive set filled the vast stage of the Uris Theatre with a 19th-century foundry made of iron trusses and glass, moving bridges and whirling gadgets. Director Harold Prince saw it as a metaphor for the industrial revolution. Despite the size of the set, however, the play itself was staged around a few small rolling units such as the pie-shop unit pictured here.*

# MING CHO LEE

On August 11, 1964, a production of Sophocles' *Electra* opened at the New York Shakespeare Festival's outdoor Delacorte Theater. The setting was designed by the 34-year-old Ming Cho Lee, then in his third year as resident designer for the Festival. With its multi-leveled thrust stage and three highly textured, emblematic scenic pieces hanging from a pipe-batten gridwork, this set marked a turning point in American stage design. No single aspect was, in itself, new—either for Lee or for the American theatre—but the confluence of scenic tendencies and elements began to forge a new style and create a new vocabulary of stage design for the next generation of designers.

Since the mid–1960s, Ming Cho Lee has been the single most influential force in American stage design, both in theatre and opera. Ironically, he has exerted this influence without any truly successful plays on Broadway. Through 1984 he has done a mere 20 productions for the Broadway stage and the more successful ones—*K2* (1983—his only Tony Award), *The Shadow Box* (1977), *Two Gentlemen of Verona* (1971), *Much Ado About Nothing* (1972)—were transfers from resident professional theatres. His most successful designs have been for Shakespearean plays and opera: his design for the New York City Opera's *Don Rodrigo*, which opened the New York State Theatre at Lincoln Center in 1966, virtually altered the American approach to opera design. But in addition to his new approaches and solutions to the problems of design there is an entire generation of designers he has helped to mold. Of the 10 other designers featured in this book, six either studied with Lee at New York University or Yale or worked as his assistants. Of the 30 to 40 individuals who comprise the bulk of working American stage designers, at least 50 percent were trained by him, and almost all the others would admit that they were influenced by his style and approach in some way.

Essentially, Lee combined the sculptural design of Boris Aronson and Isamu Noguchi, the textural quality of Rouben Ter-Arutunian and the conceptual approach of various German designers, especially at the Berliner Ensemble and several opera houses. The result was significantly different from the basically pictorial style of his mentor Jo Mielziner, whose designs had dominated and informed the American theatre since the 1940s. In place of poetic realism with its scrims, painted backdrops and fragmented and isolated bits of architectural reality, Lee and his contemporaries created sculptural settings of "real" materials such as wood and metal. Mood was replaced with texture. Color and ornament were replaced with formality and spatial relationships.

Although influenced by the Brechtian aesthetic, Lee has never totally rejected or abandoned illusionism. He views the stage, however, as a finite space and feels that the design should emphasize that. Furthermore, he wants the audience to experience the performance as directly as possible and is generally uncomfortable with the scrims popularized by Mielziner. "I dislike doing sets that can be

*Facing page, rendering for* Two Gentlemen of Verona *(New York Shakespeare Festival and Broadway, 1971), the rock-musical adaptation of Shakespeare. Lee was well into his collage phase at this point and the set consisted of posters, signs and architectural details hung from a four-story, brightly painted steel scaffold that had been erected as a basic unit for the 1971 Delacorte season. When the show moved to Broadway, the only significant change was the addition of a painted sky backdrop.*

better done by motion pictures," he states in a dissertation by David Nils Flaten. "The stage is *not* flexible and *not* limitless. It is a finite space, and I am happiest when I am showing the finite space. Whenever I try to create endless space I always realize how ultimately unsuccessful it is. So I tend to approach even the suggestion of endless space in a finite way."

To this day, Lee's style is equated by most people with pipe-scaffolding—it has become a cliche, even a joke. But the use of pipe is only one aspect of Lee's designs. Through the years he has been a pioneer in the areas of collage, innovative materials such as urethane foam, beaten metal and mylar (his 1969 design for the Joffrey Ballet's *Animus* was years ahead of Robin Wagner's popularization of the material in *A Chorus Line*), soft-fabric designs, architectural designs and ultra-realism. His work has also included painterly designs, minimalism and surrealism. He has served as a consultant for some half-dozen theatres and designed the Astor Court in the Chinese wing of the Metropolitan Museum of Art (1978). Designer and former Lee student John Lee Beatty has commented that every time he feels that he has gone beyond Lee's work, he looks around and Lee has done something startling and new.

Lee's style is a result of his training and the circumstances in which he has done much of his work. He was born in Shanghai, China in 1930. His father was a Yale-educated insurance company executive. Lee's early education was at various mission schools and he also studied landscape painting with Chang Kwo Nyen. It was this background in painting that provided the basis for much of his later work. Aside from fostering a talent with watercolor, it taught him a particular approach to a subject. Chinese landscape painting is a very simple, yet elegant art that combines formal composition, the texture embodied in the brush strokes, and ornamental detail. Thus, it tends toward the abstract although it is based on real subject matter.

During this time Lee was introduced to opera by

two uncles; and during the Japanese occupation, he saw a great deal of theatre. In 1948 his family moved to Hong Kong where he was introduced to film and for awhile considered a career in movies. He later rejected this because the jobs in film are too specialized—only the director and the cinematographer have any control or means of artistic expression, he feels. In 1949 he came to California and enrolled in Occidental College, at first as an art major, and later in the speech department—since that was where the theatre was. While there, he did a lot of designing, and even acted and directed. He spent a year in graduate at school at UCLA but he was not satisfied. Then, at the suggestion of Edward F. Kook, the president of Century Lighting, he came to New York. Kook introduced him to Jo Mielziner and Lee worked for Mielziner off and on between 1954 and 1958, beginning with the Broadway productions of *Silk Stockings* and *Cat on a Hot Tin Roof.*

Lee got his union card in 1955 and designed two shows at the Grist Mill Playhouse in Andover, New Jersey, before he was fired for making sets too elaborate and expensive. During this period he also assisted George Jenkins, Rouben Ter-Arutunian and Boris Aronson, and did some work at the Metropolitan Opera with Elizabeth Montgomery and Oliver Messel. Other influences included the paintings of Ben Shahn, the stage designs of Eugene Berman, illustrations in German opera magazines and pictures of the Berliner Ensemble productions—a powerful influence on his artistic development.

He began to design what would soon be dubbed Off-Off Broadway, which eventually led to a production of Jean Cocteau's *The Infernal Machine* at the Phoenix Theatre (1958). He also designed Arthur Miller's *The Crucible* (Off Broadway, 1958) but withdrew his name from the credits because of a dispute with the producers. Tharon Musser, who had been lighting designer for *The Infernal Machine*, recommended him to Laszlo Halasz at the Peabody Institute of Music in Baltimore, where he designed sets and lighting for nine productions between 1959 and 1963.

Lee explains that it was not only his love of opera that made him jump at the chance to design for the Peabody. "When I started working for Jo and Boris the theatre was very different. There was hardly any Off Broadway and certainly no Off-Off Broadway and very few regional theatres. So the only serious designing jobs were for Broadway and maybe opera. But I found that Broadway had that whole group of designers—Jo, Boris, Oliver Smith, David Hays, Peter Larkin, Will Steven Armstrong—and it was a little hard to break into. I found that I had to start working somewhere else because it felt like I'd just be an assistant all my life." The president of the Peabody Institute at the time was Peter Mennin, who later became president of Juilliard and created the opportunity for Lee to design operas there. By 1964, Lee had established himself as an opera designer.

The work at the Peabody foreshadowed later developments. First of all, the small budgets created restrictions that he faced again and again working for the New York Shakespeare Festival, the City Opera and various regional theatres. Stylistically, many of his designs employed slatted screens in an attempt to combat the overwhelming nature of the Peabody proscenium. His design for *The Fall of the City* (1960) was perhaps the first to utilize a pole structure as a means of delineating space, anticipating his later work in which poles created a strong verticality.

In 1961 Lee became the resident designer for the San Francisco Opera, only to return to New York in early 1962 to design his first Broadway production, *The Moon Besieged.* Upon his return, he was also asked to design *A Look at Lightning* for Martha Graham, which, because of schedule changes, opened on Broadway before *Moon.* That spring Lee was hired to replace Eldon Elder as resident designer of the new Delacorte Theater of the New York Shakespeare Festival, thus beginning a 10-year association with the Festival. Also, beginning

with *The Tempest,* the second show of that season, Lee began his long-term collaboration with director Gerald Freedman.

The Delacorte was designed by Elder, who left before its completion to take a job at the American Shakespeare Festival. Lee made suggestions to producer Joseph Papp about changes in the general plan, although the stage remained 48 feet wide—too wide, according to Lee. An essential goal of the design was to maintain a connection with the surrounding environment (which includes a lake behind the stage and the nearby Belvedere Castle overlooking the area). The annual three-play production schedule and severely limited budget ne-

*Patrick Meyers' K2 at the Arena Stage (1982). Lee created a towering mountain out of urethane foam. As the need for various ledges or niches became apparent in rehearsal, they would literally be carved out of the mountain. To emphasize the towering height, the curtain rose very slowly, making the revelation of the mountain a dramatic event in itself. The show moved to Broadway in 1983 and earned Lee his only Tony Award to date.*

cessitated unit settings that could be adapted to each play.

The first play was *The Merchant of Venice*, whose setting consisted of a bridge unit that moved on tracks, two tapestries that rolled up from the stage floor and two light towers faced with venetian blinds. This latter device created a slatted background effect while allowing the natural environment to come through. Variations on this approach were used for the other productions of the season.

In the second summer, which began with *Antony and Cleopatra*, Lee introduced a permanent balcony with staircases at either side, similar to those implemented by Tyrone Guthrie at the Stratford Festival in Ontario. Lee subsequently visited Stratford and this influenced his move toward sculptural scenery, epitomized in the *Electra* directed by Freedman. Lee described the set in a 1971 interview in *Theatre Design and Technology*:

Not all of the design was a conscious thing. In Greek tragedy the unities are very important. Greek tragedy has unities of place and time, and, therefore, there is no problem of moving scenery to be solved—there is only one visual

*Lee's set for Molière's* Don Juan *(Arena Stage, 1979). Left, a below-stage room; right, the set as seen from the audience. Director Liviu Ciulei wanted to set the play around 1915-1920, and they agreed upon an Art Nouveau design. Lee, who claims always to work with straight lines, remarked, "I was ready for it. There was not a straight line in the set." Lee wanted a 1920s poster look, but Ciulei conceived the first scene very realistically. The result was a plexiglass stage floor through which could be seen a fully furnished, verdant atrium.*

statement to be made. Furthermore, there is but one theme. Electra is a daughter who wants to revenge her father. It begins with that and it never stops moving. There is this *thrust*, this tremendous *hatred* within the play, contained in a very neatly controlled classical form. . . .

We felt that the materials and the texture should all be stone; whitish stone in the sun. We also felt that the set should not be strictly architectural because that would have little to do with the sense of a single thrust: one place in front of the palace of Atreus, a palace that happens to be falling apart. So we made three very big and very strong stone sculptures, and set them off the floor so they didn't simulate a real building but were really just three panels to show that *this is the wall of the palace.* The one literal thing we needed was the big door that opens for Clytemnestra's entrance.

It is my feeling that the set would have worked in broad daylight. I'm very conscious of the material in relation to the play. If you are doing *Electra*, and you use a metal, say bronze—that is one kind of *Electra*. Stone is another kind of *Electra*. We chose to use three panels of stone.

The groundplan of *Electra* was symmetrical, but the irregularly shaped, raked ramps, slightly differing levels and steps, and the irregular shapes of the sculpted foam "stone" pieces created an illusion of asymmetry. The pipe structure—which provided a framework on which to hang the sculptures, as well as a much-needed vertical thrust to offset the stage floor—was also textured. The set was very definitely presentational, not representational. "The elements each had their own design and formalistic function," he explains. "I had panels because I wanted to present panels. I didn't want them becoming walls."

Lee admits that he was consciously reacting to the pictorial style of Mielziner and Larkin, replacing it with a formal, presentational approach. "During that period, whatever I did, I was very clear about the approach. It was the right thing, for the right time, for the right material."

The pipe structure he has used quite often over the years is simply a practical solution to the demands of the theatre, he explains, although he admits a fascination for scaffolding. "Traveling around the world, construction always fascinates me—I'm fascinated by the difference in scaffolding. Scaffolding here is all pre-made frames. That has one look. In Europe, it looks like they just have a lot of pipes and clamps and there's an improvised look. Then you go to Hong Kong and it's all bamboo lashed together and you wonder how they can build skyscrapers. Lines cutting across planes are interesting for me."

At the Delacorte, scaffolding allows a single structure to change simply by recovering it with different materials. "If you want to do history," explains Lee, "and you want wooden posts and beams, you can always sleeve a wooden thing over the pipe. But if you use wood, you can never get as small as the pipe. So that seems to be a very obvious approach. It also made sense for *Electra*. I wanted a structure that looked totally functional on which to hang or present the panels. Nowadays, when you think of something that is totally functional it is metal framework. Therefore, I started using metal framework on which I hung these obviously Greek,

stone sculpted panels. That was the beginning."

Related to Lee's use of pipe scaffolding is his use of verticality—strong vertical shafts set against, or rising from, a horizontal plane. The wide stage of the Delacorte and park environment beyond required a high scenic background to concentrate and focus the action. The pipe structure, of course, was ideal for this purpose. "In order for the immediate environment to really control the action," explains Lee, "it has to be very tall. When people sitting in the front row look up at an actor, if they see the park, Fifth Avenue and the sky, they lose all interest. But if they look at the actors' faces and there is some surface or line or whatever that belongs to the environment of the show—through which you see the sky—then you feel the performers are acting within something. At the Delacorte, anything lower than 30 feet is not good. We started out at 21 feet, which is normally very high, then we went to 24 feet, which was still too low, then to 28 feet and finally to 30 and 32 feet. It was then that it felt as if the play were happening on the stage and that the environment was really in control. David Mitchell and Santo Loquasto have since gone even higher—40 feet without batting an eyelash."

In subsequent productions at the Delacorte, Lee continued to develop these concepts and explore new ones. He used emblematic units in the form of panels, shields and heraldry often throughout the 1960s, one of the better examples being the 1966 *Richard III* with hanging, textured shields. *Measure for Measure* (1966) incorporated real materials including fire escape-like stairways and a simulated whitewashed brick wall to create a prison environment. *A Comedy of Errors* (1967) marked one of his first uses of flat imagery and bold color schemes:

Instead of trying to make sculptural pieces with a great deal of depth, we deliberately made the walls very flat and the colors very bright and flat—almost like a poster. This particular set had two towers, one on each side, that revolved, as could the centerpiece. The

*Facing page,* Hamlet *(Arena Stage, 1978). Says Lee, "We [director Liviu Ciulei and I] never talked about the set—we kept looking at pictures of people. We agreed that I would take the floor out. That was the first time I took the floor out so that the platform was higher. We lined the wall around the arena with plexiglass. The floor of the platform was very beautifully finished dark, stained wood in a parquet pattern. Underneath the floor, going into the pit, was brick vaulting. The audience saw the brick vaulting through the plexiglass. On the surface it was clean, neat, elegant, warm; underneath it was a labyrinth. It was a little like K2—I thought we should take the audience on a tour."*

roofs were terra cotta and the walls were painted white. It was essentially very bright, not at all multi-layered. We tried to do this play in the commedia form, so there was a wooden platform, and we even simulated footlights (which actually hid microphones). For interiors, we painted an entire room on the curtain in very faded colors. (*Theatre Design & Technology*.)

Just as Lee's aesthetic shaped the look of the New York Shakespeare Festival's productions—and ultimately much of mainstream theatre—his design for Alberto Ginastera's *Don Rodrigo* and subsequent productions set a style for the New York City Opera and eventually reshaped much American opera design. Through the 1950s, most design at the Metropolitan Opera was in the 19th-century style of painted Romantic Realism. Into the 1960s, many otherwise reputable companies relied on stock scenery as background for their productions. But an increasing acceptance of opera as a legitimate theatrical form and as an outlet for serious design, combined with the tight budgets of most regional opera companies, led to increased experimentation and the cross-fertilization of theatrical design with opera.

For *Don Rodrigo*, the first of his many collaborations with director Tito Capobianco, Lee made an admittedly conscious effort to break away from pictorial Romanticism and to create "a visual statement that was less literal and less Romantic. We were looking for a City Opera 'look' that was different from the Met 'look.'" Lee acknowledges that he drew on what he had seen in German opera magazines and on European design in general. "It was not new at all," he explained. "I remember German designs that used floating sculptural pieces, people acting in front of engravings, and so forth. At the time it was a matter of having a subscription to *Opernwelt* and saying, 'This is what I must do,' and taking the opportunity to do it."

What Lee created was a unit setting that began with a look of great splendor and opulence and, as the opera progressed, was stripped down to a final stark, fragmentary setting. The use of "collapsible" scenic pieces (actually, the set split in pieces, somewhat like pavement ruptured by an earthquake) also allowed a progression from an essentially vertical space to a horizontal one. Lee described the design in an interview in Lynn Pecktal's *Designing and Painting for the Theatre*:

*Don Rodrigo* [was] an opera about Spain. I always felt that Spain is full of white, great big stone sculpture and walls, and golden sky and mosaics—and that is pretty much what I did.

The set consisted of a raked platform surrounded by a gold mosaic sky and tall lean statues on gold pipes lining both sides of the platform. Pieces of white stone wall came in for specific scenes. I think it had a real look.

The set incorporated much of the design vocabulary that Lee had established at the Delacorte. As in *Electra*, the lines, textures and emblems of *Don Rodrigo* were suggestive, yet presentational. The singers were not acting in front of a two-dimensional scene as was common in opera, but were contained within a sculptural space—a theatrical environment. The raked stage seemed at times to project the performers forward, as if they were on a thrust stage.

Lee feels that one of the great strengths of the design was its ability to utilize a unit setting without neutralizing the space in the way he feels Mielziner's unit sets did. "I think *Rodrigo* was the first of the opera productions here that did not become characterless and still managed to have a unity that went through the whole performance. Now, of course, that approach is overused—including my own overuse of it—but at the time, at least, I thought it was relatively groundbreaking."

For Lee, the key to opera design is a feeling for the "weight of the music" and an understanding of how to translate this into visual terms. In an essay in *Contemporary Stage Design U.S.A.* Lee wrote:

A large, unbroken expanse of space suggests one musical quality. The same space, broken into small areas or patterns, suggests another. A room painted completely in frescoes gives a sense of lightness and airiness, while an elab-

*Model for Moussorgsky's* Boris Godunov *(Metropolitan Opera, 1974). This was Lee's Metropolitan Opera debut and he spent a year and a half on the project. Critics were impressed by Lee's ability to rapidly shift the many scenes of the opera, as well as by the set's apparent lushness and richness. The director August Everding was quoted in* The New Yorker *as saying, "I chose Ming Cho Lee as the designer because he is very good at making skeletons that hint at places and situations. He knows how to abbreviate, and I know how to fill up a stage."*

orately carved and heavily coved space gives a sense of opulence and weight. Different materials also suggest qualities, reflecting even the sound of the orchestration. Stone suggests the bass instruments; metal a percussiveness and sharpness; wood is closer to the lighter warmth of the lower strings, whose tones do indeed emerge from a wooden soundbox.

In opera, he suggests, the music and the libretto do not always have the same feel—as in Verdi's *Macbeth*—and the designer must decide which aspect of the design to fulfill. Lee notes that criticism of his design for Mozart's *Idomeneo* (New York City Opera at the Kennedy Center, Washington, D.C., 1974) was that it was not traditionally Neoclassical (i.e., ruined temples). "The music," he explains in the same essay, "is clean, pure in line, lean—and my design reflected this. I used a simple, formal arrangement of cantilevered platforms and two-dimensional wire sculptures to give a sense of place: an open terrace, a harbor, a sacred place. . . . As long as the visual weight does not violate that of the music, you *can* go against the style—even abstraction for neo-classicism—in favor of other values in the work."

Lee has designed well over 60 opera productions including notable productions of *Bomarzo* (Opera Society of Washington, 1967 and New York City Opera, 1968), *Le Coq d'or* (NYCO, 1967), *Faust* (NYCO, 1968), *Roberto Devereux* (NYCO, 1970) and *Boris Godunov* (Metropolitan Opera, 1974). Nonetheless, Lee, who is forever reevaluating his own work and finding weaknesses and flaws, now has doubts about most of his opera work. "Even *Boris Godunov*," he sighs. "It was good, but it was not a definitive design." The problem, in his eyes, is that the various approaches have become overused and cliched—by him and others—so it is difficult to evaluate the work. His current opera project is Moussorgsky's infrequently performed *Khovanshchina* for the Met's 1985 season. There is opportunity for spectacle—the climax is a great fire in

which a chorus of 90 burns to death. The opera begins in Red Square and Lee is playing with the vast space and horizontality of the locale. As it progresses, the sets become increasingly vertical. He hopes that it will have a new look: "more photographic."

Lee has expressed great admiration for the designs of French director-scenographer Patrice Chéreau who staged the centenary production of the Bayreuth *Ring* (1976). After seeing photos of that, Lee remarked that he might want to develop an approach in which "the work has a look." He describes Chéreau's look as a "very hard-edged, photographic realism that feels unreal" but he feels uncomfortable attempting that style.

I have a hard time doing that, perhaps because when I began in the theatre American design was just breaking away from realism and getting into the Mielziner style. I reacted against that. I latched onto an American Brechtian approach. I'm dying to find a way to do that Chéreau or Robert Wilson approach. In one

*Rendering for Donizetti's* Roberto Devereux *at the New York City Opera (1970). Lee employed his basic vocabulary of a skeletal unit set and a raked stage which in this case was intended to be used for subsequent productions of* Maria Stuarda *and* Anna Bolena. *(It was used for the former with some variations, but a new setting was designed for the latter.) The space was carefully articulated through the use of upright posts on either side of the stage. Elegant scenic pieces created the locales of the opera within this framework.*

way I'm very tired of using pipe and a very spare and stark kind of design. I tend to eliminate, rather than to do opulent things. But when I try to be Romantic it tends to be fuzzy—a watercolor type approach, which is my training.

Another Lee trademark is collage. It first appeared as a minor aspect of a set—a collage of signs incorporated into a setting for the Joffrey Ballet's *Night Wings* (1967)—and then emerged as a dominant approach in the original New York Shakespeare Festival production of *Hair* (1967), directed by Gerald Freedman. Lee's design for the first rock musical was dominated by a steel scaffold that filled the height of the Anspacher Theater. The structure was symmetrical but the symmetry was offset by a collage of posters hanging from the scaffolding and the grid above. Ironically, there were no images of the Vietnam war, despite the play's theme and the fact that Lee had incorporated seemingly anti-war emblems into some of his other designs at that time.

The evolution of the design and the production in general fell prey to chaos as, Lee recalls, first his assistant and then Freedman "turned hippie." There were complications resulting from a scenic artists' strike and disputes over directorial control between producer Joseph Papp and the authors Gerome Ragni and James Rado. As Lee describes it:

I thought the original design was good. I had done collages, but I had never done such an enormous amount of collage or color before. Before *Hair*, all musicals were narrative; *Hair* was a collage. We were opening the Anspacher Theater and it was a really bumpy trip. It was a week before rehearsal and the script wasn't finished and I hadn't seen it. I called Gerry [Freedman] and said, "if I don't see a script there won't be any set." He said he would like to improvise into it—it was all terribly '60s—and I said, "I don't know how to improvise into

a set." I got a script, but it was very hard to make head or tail out of it. Obviously it was about—what do you call that group of people?—hippies. But should we create an environment that caused the hippies to happen—war and injustice and so forth? With Gerry and Rado and Ragni we went and looked at the Village "head shops," the Electric Circus, light shows. And I bought the *Life* magazine with all the hippie things, cut it up and started doing a collage. It took much longer than I expected but I finally managed to finish the sketch. At that time I tended to make models more than sketches. I would make initial sketches then jump into the model very quickly.

I finished the sketch and Gerry and Rado and Ragni loved it. But the show was becoming less and less in control. There was a change of directors but finally Gerry took over again at the first preview. We thought it was going to be the greatest disaster of all time. A week before opening, the scenic artists went on strike. At the dress rehearsal, stage right was finished but stage left was not.

To everyone's great surprise, the show became very popular but, as Lee recalled, the creative team felt "very idealistic" and scorned the idea of moving to a commercial house. Instead, the show moved to Cheetah—a disco—but "the acoustics were horrible, the space was wrong, we all had other things to work on so we never went to look at it." As a result of this attitude, when producer Michael Butler moved it uptown, he hired new creative personnel. Lee says that they all learned their lessons and when the Shakespeare Festival's rock version of *Two Gentlemen of Verona* (1971) moved to Broadway, they were all actively involved.

Much of Lee's work through the 1970s, such as *Much Ado About Nothing* (1972), used a collage approach as a means or system for dealing with low budget productions. As with the scaffolding, Lee began to treat collage as a design system and forced

*Facing page, model for the landmark production of* Electra *(Delacorte Theater, 1964). The hanging, textured, emblematic scenery and the articulation of space marked a strong break with the poetic realism of previous decades.*

productions to fit the scheme. But his attitude has been changing in recent years. "I think collage was the right approach for the time," he explains, "because people were more interested in a visual statement than in creating a place. We were in a period when we didn't want anything to be literal. And the whole collage thing fit into my training as an artist very well. It came very naturally. But my whole collage era is over." In an article in *Theatre Crafts* (February 1984) Lee explained, "Earlier, my approach was that by changing things—changing the collage—the whole play or opera could fit in the set. No more. It's not good. People are getting bored with it. I'm getting bored with it. The sets have to do something else. Something that has a bit more integrity. Something that treats the work more seriously. The design should be for that work alone, instead of trying to fit the work into a scheme."

Lee's influence on design for dance has been minimal and more often it was the medium that exerted its influence on *him*. Much of his work, for instance, was strongly influenced by Isamu Noguchi's designs for Martha Graham. But the dance world has frequently been a proving ground for Lee, with certain of his tendencies and aesthetics first appearing there. It is also his favorite form of design. "Designing for the dance," he says in the Pecktal interview, "is the most enjoyable because it is designing in the purest sense. You are designing a visual statement in a space that is compatible with a human form moving, expressing a theme, and that is pure set designing and is most enjoyable. It is totally nonliteral because dance itself is nonliteral. It is theatre expressed through movement; therefore, if your form is compatible to the movement, you have achieved the impact of the piece of work."

Aside from the already-mentioned introduction of collage and mylar in various dance designs, Lee's use of multi-media first appeared in the Joffrey's *The Poppet* (1969), co-designed with Robert Yodice. He acknowledges the influence of Czech designer Josef Svoboda at that time, especially in relation to

the use of mylar mirrors. The use of tensile structures—scenic pieces suspended by tension wires or ropes—first appeared in Martha Graham's *Myth of a Voyage* (1973) based on the story of Odysseus.

Lee has never designed story ballets. "My fuzzy Romanticism may be right," he says, "but I feel that Desmond Heeley and Santo Loquasto are much better at it than I." And despite the significant number of modern dance designs he has done over the years, Lee still feels uncomfortable with it. "At least for several years," he notes, "I found it very difficult to design for dance because the work itself is already so visual. Unless the dance needed a visual element to pull it together, I always felt that I was adding something to it. Designing for a play or op-

era you are dealing with words or music and giving them a visual counterpart. But in dance the whole thing is visual already and I'm not sure what more I can offer."

Recently, however, Lee's attitude toward dance has changed. He has become interested in Matisse's cutouts and he was impressed by artist David Hockney's use of pure color in designs for the Metropolitan Opera. "Suddenly, dance design seemed to open up a little. For *The Rite of Spring* [Ballet West, 1984] and *The Dream of the Red Chamber* [Cloud Gate Dance Theatre, Taipei, 1984] I'm treating the space in a much more bold, visual pattern—a little bit op-art, which I hated for a long time. I began to feel that I had become too literal-minded and it was

*Model for* The Gnadiges Fraulein, *the second of two Tennessee Williams one-acts in a Broadway production entitled* Slapstick Tragedy *(1966), and one of Lee's most famous designs. Lee has described the set as "extremely grotesque, with the house leaning and the perspective distorted in an attempt to reflect the distortions in the characters themselves." It was an early example of Lee's combination of painted backgrounds with architectural elements.*

good to get away from that and just deal with shape and color."

Lee calls *Red Chamber* a "breakthrough" for him. "Suddenly," he says with delight, "I was using a very horizontal shape for its own sake." The setting is a 60-foot scrim stretched across the back of the stage in front of a backdrop with horizontal bands of color. The floor is also painted with horizontal bands. Frames of colored fabric move up and down against the backdrop, passing each other to create differing colors and patterns. "It's all panels," explains Lee. "A white panel, a green sun, a green panel and a red panel. It's truly abstract. I don't think I had ever done a dance or a show that was just a big swatch of color." He compares it to a Jim Dine painting.

Lee had done some work with fabric as a design element before—a soft-fabric flower in *For Colored Girls . . .* and a fabric landscape banner in an unproduced Graham project in 1977—but the inspiration for this came from seeing fabric used in other dances by the Flying Cloud Dance Company. He says that the dance and the music just "felt very much like horizontal bands—you look at Chinese painting and it's all mist and horizontal bands." Lee also enjoyed solving the technical problem of how to stretch scrim for such a length without sagging. Former assistant Leigh Rand notes that Lee really seems to enjoy being in the theatre during put-ins and dealing with the minutiae of technical problem-solving.

Since so many designers have been taught by Lee, his work process is of more than passing interest. Everyone who has ever assisted him remembers

Dog Lady *by Milcha Sanchez-Scott (Intar Theatre, 1984). This perspective vista of a Los Angeles barrio street demonstrated Lee's ability to create stunning perspective settings on a limited budget and in a small space. In the companion piece,* The Cuban Swimmer, *he created the Pacific Ocean complete with a boat and helicopter.*

rebuilding models over and over that were off by as little as 1/32 of an inch, or redrafting to get just the right weight to a particular line. "I like to think that I really appreciate the craft for its own sake," he notes. "I appreciate careful model-making. I hate even rough model-making if a straight line is not straight—it drives me up a wall. I like clean models."

Lee's precision is perhaps unmatched in the design world. This is nowhere better demonstrated than in his response to the Broadway production of Patrick Meyers' *K2*. After the mountain was moved from the Arena Stage to the Brooks Atkinson Theatre, Lee discovered that it was *15 inches* too far stage right, causing him to lose sleep for a whole month. He claims to be able to tell if a set is off by even an inch-and-a-half. The result, says Lee, is that the mountain became too centered and the audience saw a little too much of it and not enough sky. "It's better if it's either to one side or the other. If it's dead center it divides the stage in two and you don't see the middle."

Lee typically reads a play or listens to an opera or a ballet only once to get a feel for it, and then sets it aside and begins sketching out ideas. Only after he has some concept does he come back to the script or score. He does this in order to evolve a design that encompasses the entire production. He designs, he explains, for the whole play, not for individual scenes. The details are filled in later. This early phase of design is the most fun for Lee, "because the choices at the start are so endless. Once the approach is decided, then you begin narrowing in, throwing away, refining. Theoretically, I like to think I at a design through drawing—using drawing as a thinking process or exploring process—rather than setting down facts. Then eventually through drawing I arrive at a finished piece of work."

Once an approach "has some validity," Lee usually makes a ¼-inch or ½-inch white model. He may do some painting on the rough model. "I really distrust paint elevations unless it really is a paint elevation," he explains. This, ideally, is followed by a finished model from which the drafting is done. "It never really quite happens, though," he sighs. "I spend a lot of time on proportions—maybe to the detriment of the design. Maybe everything looks a little too tasteful, or there is not enough vulgarity, or it may not be extreme enough. So I spend a lot of time ditzing around in terms of proportion."

In dealing with directors with whom he has an established relationship like Freedman or John Hirsch, Lee can communicate through sketches. Other directors really need the aid of a three-dimensional model. Lee's first rough sketches are usually done on yellow legal paper or tracing paper, in pencil and with Gesso if color is needed. They are usually in correct perspective and often suggest not only the set but a sense of the light as well. Once the initial design is approved, Lee does a lot of research. While the general imagery, style or look of a production may evolve from a feeling he gets from the script, Lee believes strongly that in terms of detail, nothing can be made up: "If it's real, it's real." Research includes not only books and pictures but travel when possible.

Obviously, this approach does not lead to literal realism. Lee often combines realistically based images with ideas that come out of conceptual discussions with the director rather than simply recreating the apparent locale indicated by the script. The design for *Romeo and Juliet* (Circle in the Square, 1977), for instance, was a room based on Lee's memories of frescoed rooms he had seen in Italy—but recreated from paintings by Giotto.

Lee generally does his own rough drafting if time permits, in part because he considers drafting an extension of drawing. But, says former assistant Douglas Schmidt, "Ming's 'rough' drafting is everyone else's framable plate." During busy periods he employs up to three assistants. Lee truly enjoys taking in young designers who are "unformed," but who have "a potential for drawing well and whose conversation is exciting and articulate," and training them over a two- or three-year period to draft, build models and become "great designers." He has even taken on extra design jobs in order to keep his assistants busy.

Schmidt, who worked in Lee's studio for three or four years, describes the teaching process as both rigorous and casual at the same time. The assistants learn how to do things by being handed projects. Schmidt somewhat facetiously describes a typical conversation:

"Here, do this."

"How?"

"Oh, you just glue this, and cut and paste this, and draw this. Sorry, I have to go now."

But at the same time, Lee's critiques are stern and, says Schmidt, "Everyone who works there benefits from that rigor." If there has been any criticism of Lee's teaching, it is that he imposes such a strong style on his students and assistants that it sometimes buries their own individuality.

Many designers work out of their apartments, but few, if any, have so thoroughly integrated their life and work. Lee's studio is also the bedroom he shares with his wife Betsy, who essentially manages the details of Lee's life so that he can concentrate on design. They have three children. The bedroom/studio holds three drafting tables, mounted models, piles of books and collections of art supplies. Some of this frequently spills into the living room. His

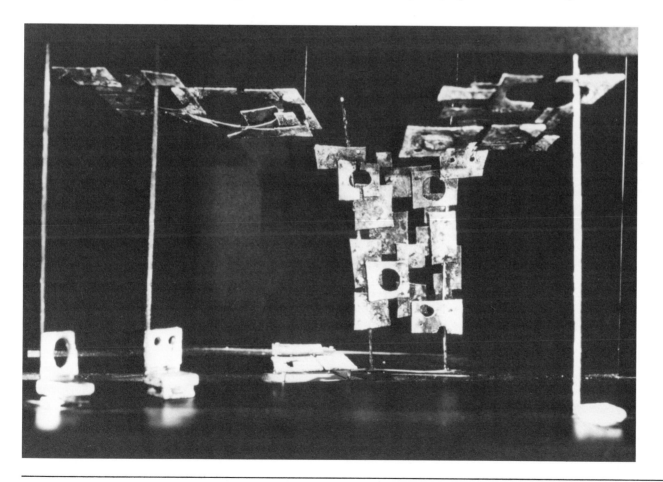

*Model for Martha Graham's* The Witch of Endor *(1965), based on the biblical story of King Saul. Lee's early dance design was heavily influenced by the work of Isamu Noguchi and the similarity to his design for* Electra *the previous year is readily apparent. In the final design, the overhead pieces were cut because Lee felt that it made the dance heavy and worked against the movement of the dancers. The upstage unit came forward like a steeply raked drawbridge for a scene with Saul, Samuel and David.*

Tony Award stands amidst piles of papers and books on a dining room sideboard that also seems to function as a repository for items with no defined storage space.

"When we were young it seemed easier," says Lee. "You immersed yourself in the work. Immersing yourself is good, but the fact that you can't get away from it is a little devastating. Now I've gathered such a body of work that it's taken over. We just don't have enough room. We're forever stepping over models and books. We take them off the table to work and put them on the bed, and then have to move them to sleep." He talks about moving the studio into the childrens' bedroom now that they are in college, but one gets the impression that the

seeming chaos will simply spread to fill the new space.

While Lee is generally acknowledged as the dean of American designers, he is self-effacing and curiously insecure. A perhaps apocryphal story is told by a former assistant: For years, Lee has had a drafting table with a bad wobble. It is very difficult to work at. "Why don't you replace it?" he was asked. "Because," he supposedly replied, "if I get rid of this table I will never get another job."

Being such a perfectionist, he is seldom satisfied with his work. Often, he says, he feels bad about taking a theatre or producer's money because the design is not good enough by his standards. He is aware of his limitations and worries that certain

*Samuel Beckett's* Waiting for Godot *(Arena Stage, 1976). Lee is able to achieve great variety in the most minimal designs. Here, the polished pine-board floor used different grains and was laid in various directions, thus dividing the space through nothing more than the interplay of woods. He also lowered the lighting grid to help confine and theatricalize the space.*

trends might leave him behind. "When I look at a lot of Robert Wilson's stuff, some of Michael Yeargan and Andrei Serban's work, Santo Loquasto's designs and, recently, some of John Conklin's stuff, I get nervous. I certainly don't want to be left behind but there are things I cannot do. Robin Wagner loves to work on an unformed script; Eugene Lee likes to rebuild theatres. I can't do that. I have to take on something that I consider a constant—I take the theatre as the constant, I can't rebuild it."

The one piece of his own work that continues to impress him is that seminal *Electra*. "I never expected that something that impressive could happen out of me. For a long while I thought that I would never be able to do anything that impressive again. Thinking that I had done my greatest work at age 34 was very frightening." When asked what he thought subsequently equalled that design, Lee replied: "I don't know that I have equalled that. I have done things with strong points and less strong points but I never quite get the satisfaction of *Electra*. Except that I now look at the same kind of material differently, and I think differently about the relation of the set to the work and the actors. In a way, I've moved past it. I'm no longer trying to do the same thing better. I just design differently. And in different ways there are designs that feel good. I just grow older and think differently."

*Rendering for* Jack MacGowran in the Works of Samuel Beckett *(New York Shakespeare Festival, 1970). Many of the sets Lee did in the Anspacher Theater echoed the verticality of the space. It was in this production that Lee first used a floor curving into a wall.*

# SANTO LOQUASTO

Santo Loquasto is a designer in the tradition of Ming Cho Lee and Boris Aronson, and he has earned the respect appropriate to that company. His settings tend to have a distinct style and make strong artistic statements through a careful and deliberate manipulation of space, line and color. While he is generally associated with semi-abstract, sculptural and conceptual designs, he has done an equal number of realistically based interiors, especially at the Hartford Stage Company. Loquasto is also one of the major designers for modern dance and ballet, having designed for choreographers Mikhail Baryshnikov, Glen Tetley, Jerome Robbins and Twyla Tharp, although his work for dance is primarily as a costume designer. Robbins was not even aware that Loquasto designed sets when he first hired him. His costume design has also taken him into film, most frequently with Woody Allen, and his costumes for *Zelig* (1983) earned him an Academy Award nomination.

Loquasto has achieved recognition without ever having had a true hit play. Admiring reviews do not translate into money. "I'm sick of being respected," he jokes. This situation has frequently resulted in his taking on many projects simultaneously, creating a hectic schedule on which he seems to thrive. He claims that he does not like the long hours, the occasional all-nighters, and "the entrance to my apartment looking as if I were about to load out three shows," but the animation with which he discusses this lifestyle belies the statements. His excitement mounts as he describes his burgeoning film career: the pressure, he notes, is exhausting,

and the pace hectic, but the overall process, he concludes, "is quite marvelous."

Loquasto does not approach set design from any theoretical basis. While he talks quite articulately about space and places himself in the "sculptural tradition" of theatre design, he is unable, or unwilling, to discuss stylistic elements. He claims not to be a colorist despite his skillful manipulation of mood through color, especially in such productions as Nikolai Erdman's *The Suicide* (Broadway, 1980). And he seems almost surprised to discover a consistent use of line, angularity and verticality in his sets. "There are certain things I like," he admits, "so I know they are probably there in the designs. And there are probably ways I go about things which are predictably the same." But when pressed, the only example he can offer of such a stylistic element is his method of finishing the fascia of a staircase.

Loquasto discusses his work distantly, almost as if he were talking about the work of a stranger. Describing his stylistic approach to space he commented: "In [Woody Allen's] *Floating Lightbulb* [Vivian Beaumont Theatre, 1981] and [Martin Sherman's] *Bent* [Broadway, 1979], I saw a similar kind of break-up of wall space and how it allowed for the abstraction of rooms without ceilings." Regarding style, he concludes that, "Designers who have particularly vivid styles are either those who come out of a painterly tradition, or those who do the same kind of show over and over again, and are asked to do, and choose to do the same thing over and over again." Neither of these descriptions applies to Loquasto.

*Facing page, Act II of Martin Sherman's* Bent. *The scene was a Nazi concentration camp. Loquasto used a white surround of textured walls as a constant through both acts. The barbed wire grid created not only a sense of place and mood, but also an abstract element to focus the spectators on the performers. It also provided a sense of confinement in an otherwise open space.*

One of the distinguishing elements of his work is the apparent combination of the contemporary and the traditional. At first glance, his early sets reveal the typical stylistic elements of the 1960s and 1970s—textured surfaces, materials such as erosion cloth and rough wood, and Constructivist elements such as pipe scaffolding. He is quick to point out that the presence of these elements is not the result of intentional copying, but an inevitable similarity that develops among designers in a given period. Any use of pipe, for instance, is immediately compared with Ming Cho Lee. Loquasto recalls that Lee once assured him that their use of pipe was different.

It is Loquasto's use of line that is distinctive. While the standard practice is to set walls on a di-agonal line and to break up long expanses with jogs or extrusions of one sort or another, Loquasto tends to set flat walls at right angles to each other and to create a sense of great height through his use of vertical line. Many of his designs, then, are not so much box sets as they are immense cubes. There is something almost classical about his angularity.

A look at the groundplans alone might suggest a certain starkness in such sets, but relief is provided by rich texture, such as the rough-hewn wood of *King Lear* (New York Shakespeare Festival, 1973). In *Bent*, he notes, the back wall "was broken up, not in any representational way, but simply as texture." Sometimes he thwarts this symmetrical-angular approach for specific effect. *Richard III* (New York Shakespeare Festival, 1983), for example, was de-

*Richard III at the New York Shakespeare Festival's Delacorte Theater, (1983). Although his designs are frequently linear and angular, for this production Loquasto created a "skewed space" for a sense of "improvised theatricality." This design also demonstrates his use of great height at the Delacorte, in which his sets often soar upwards of 40 feet.*

signed with a "skewed space—just enough off that it was kind of an irritation. It had an improvised theatricality about it."

Loquasto balks at any categorization like "classical" unless there is a specific intentional reference within the design, but he acknowledges that there might be some classical approaches in his style. He admits a liking for certain Postmodern architects like Aldo Rossi who have strong classical references in their own work.

The key to Loquasto's style is rooted in sculptural design which he defines not only spatially, but in terms of the interaction between the space and the performer. "If you think of stage design at its most formal level," he explains, "it is really a frame and a backdrop, as in fundamental design for dance which one thinks of as legs, borders and a backdrop. Whereas sculptural design, I think, cuts through the space. It's an invasion, or it intercepts in some way. It demands that the performers deal with the scenery. It's not simply that it's textured; it's that it really moves into the space. It can be a Noguchi-like suspension overhead, but nonetheless it is there to be dealt with. It demands interaction. Design should ask for an exchange between the performer and his or her environment, just as acting does."

As Loquasto describes a set, his hands and arms move expressively, slicing the air with definite vertical and horizontal strokes as if sculpting a set in the air. These same horizontals and verticals appear in many of his pencil sketches such as those for David Halliwell's *Hail, Scrawdyke!* done at Yale in the late 1960s, and David Mamet's *American Buffalo* (Broadway, 1977) which hang side-by-side on the wall of his cramped studio—a room in his Riverside Drive apartment. Both designs are relatively square and linear. He jokingly suggests that these two sketches demonstrate his true stylistic trademark—the cluttered set. The two rooms are similar but *Scrawdyke*, he points out, is fairly spare, while *Buffalo* is very cluttered. "I keep them up as a sad reminder," he says a bit facetiously. "There is a 10-year separation between them during which time

that room [*Scrawdyke*] just filled up with junk and became that room [*Buffalo*]."

*You Can't Take It with You* (Hartford Stage Company, 1973) also dealt with clutter and "the relationship of the object to the person." In an article in *ARTnews* (February 1981) Loquasto noted, "It's very American, I think, this fascination for saving, accumulating, turning spaces into shrines to acquisition. [In *You Can't Take It with You*] I was interested in the unfinished quality, the do-it-yourself project that never gets completed, the rough edges in people's lives."

Stage managers say that they can spot his sets instantly. "I don't know whether that means that the designs are similar," he responds, "or simply that they are all similarly littered with piles of garbage." More seriously, he notes that the "clutter" helps to soften the angularity of a set. *American Buffalo*, he explains, "worked off grids of debris and I broke down the sharpness of the space with the junk."

Loquasto talks fluently about the subtleties of space. He believes that his feel for space developed in response to his frequent work on arena and thrust stages such as those of Hartford, Arena Stage and the Beaumont. "It demands that you be involved in pushing action forward," he explains. Most of the plays he has done at the Beaumont, a space with very specific design problems, have been intimate shows for which he feels the theatre is totally unsuited. The actors, he explains, are forced to deal with the sweep of the house and the vast overhead space. "I was always trying to bring the focus down to a human proportion, but the pitch of the house is so great that you always feel that you're looking down on this little playing area." This is further complicated by sightlines that do not allow the performers to use the whole space, and a stage height that blocks the first few rows of the audience.

These problems seemed acute in designing *Floating Lightbulb*. "It was a play that needed to be looked at in a small space," states Loquasto. "But at the Beaumont you always felt the space *around* the acting area." To create greater intimacy he thrust

the stage forward slightly more, taking out almost two rows of seats; reduced the playing area to a "comfortable, almost realistic proportion" of a bedroom, living room and kitchen; and created a surround (a background that envelops the set) of brick apartment buildings with windows and fire escapes. His intention was to create an atmosphere and fill the space without detracting from the visual focus.

"It was middle-class Canarsie in 1940s Brooklyn, but unfortunately it looked a bit like a tenement," he admits.

Because so many plays present similar challenges, designers are always seeking better solutions to recurring problems. Loquasto feels that he finally achieved an effective method of dealing with the *Floating Lightbulb* problem—"focusing on an

*Chekhov's* Uncle Vanya *at the La Mama Annex (1983). Loquasto and director Andrei Serban wanted to create a set that caused "unnatural spatial relationships among people." Space was articulated through levels rather than walls, but the set had familiar Chekhovian textures— wood, candles, wicker.*

interior room while allowing a surround to come to life"—in a 1983 production of *The Glass Menagerie* at Hartford Stage. The surround was created of light boxes suggesting windows and fire escapes. In front of that was a scrim painted to suggest a brick wall. There were several layers of scrims creating an "atmospheric and lush" image. A large fire escape cut across the top of the space which forced the lights to be hung unusually close to the actors. Thus, instead of long shafts of light illuminating the actors as is usually the case, the performers were

more isolated—"It was rather like a television studio," explains Loquasto. The arrangement allowed for both a large and an intimate playing space.

On the whole, Loquasto probably designs taller sets than any other working designer, which may be partly due to working at the outdoor Delacorte Theater in Central Park in the mid–1970s. In order to achieve any sort of focus in that space, the back wall of the set must block out the natural background of the lake. Standard flats in proscenium theatres tend to be 12 to 14 feet tall. When Ming Cho Lee was

THE SUICIDE. —LOQUASTO '80

*Pencil sketch for Nikolai Erdman's* The Suicide *(ANTA Theater, 1980). Made largely of doors, the set was almost a paradigm of Loquasto's frontal, angular style. It was a cube, although the "fourth wall" was shattered by catwalks that extended into the auditorium, and tattered banners hanging over the audience. Along the upper back wall was a "shooting gallery" of political and literary figures that periodically lit up.*

resident designer for the Shakespeare Festival in the 1960s he regularly used 18- to 24-foot units at the Delacorte. Loquasto's sets became 30 feet and more. "I certainly was comfortable working out there under the sky," he laughs. "I think it comes from working with Michael Annals on *Prometheus Bound* (Yale Drama School, 1967). We went right up to the grid. I've always liked high trims—Gordon Craig and all that."

Much of Loquasto's work consists of single or unit settings, but since *Bent*, he has experimented more with the manipulation of space through the use of moving scenic elements. The rear wall in *The Suicide*, for instance, moved up and down stage, the play beginning with a shallow space which deepened throughout the production. He employed moving scenic pieces in *Bent* to provide a unifying element to the episodic script—its two acts seemed like separate plays. "The problem was to provide the piece with a visual continuity," explained Loquasto. "You should feel as though you have traveled through the first act and come to this unfortunate resting point in the second. That was the crux of the design." As Loquasto describes the set, some sense of his approach to design, color, line and texture becomes apparent, as well as the rationale of the transforming sets.

There was a white surround of textured walls which remained constant through both acts. It was clearly an abstraction—it was not specific but rather it was sympathetic to the various locations required: a city park, backstage at a cabaret or the unremitting confinement of a concentration camp. It was also segmented in a way that not only allowed it to pass through the doors of the theatre, but to be clarified in its abstraction. In the second act, barbed wire crossed against the surround, forcing us to view these men against a grid. You really felt a scrutiny of the human condition. This effect was achieved, I hope, rather subliminally. The production was postponed, and during that time I continued to think about the play and to change things—sort of cut things down to basic elements. The set was quite stark but maintained a rather Broadway-Brechtian format with exposed lights and all. Ultimately, I worked with small, tight elements defining each scene, the space being fully revealed in the second act with only the barbed wire in the back. It was at once its most open and yet its most confined.

Loquasto's use of color is distinctive, although he protests that it is "all rather low key." During the design process he works almost exclusively in black and white; he does little if any color rendering and works largely with white models. But his use of color is frequently singled out by the critics. The set for *Sarava* (Broadway, 1978) "hauls us instantly into a suspension of disbelief; and the hazy turquoise backdrop of the scrim locates this suspension precisely in a decaying tropical city," noted *New York Times* critic Walter Kerr. Kerr also remarked of *Bent*: "The blazing reds and yellows with which designer Santo Loquasto has made a hothouse of the passage are directly followed by the cool grays and muted blues of a vast public park equipped with a lone bench." Loquasto admits that *The Suicide* was very colorful and that its mood was manipulated through a subtle use of reds. The design for that play is almost a paradigm of Loquasto's techniques.

The Soviet play by Nikolai Erdman takes place in a nightmare world representing the Communist dream gone awry. It is ostensibly set in the bedroom of a house taken over by the state. The set was an open cube, the high back and side walls set at right angles to each other, and it was made of doors. "It was like a tenement," explains Loquasto, "only the doors were like Russian icons and antiques." The moving back wall was a shooting gallery lined with faces of writers and other historic figures which periodically lit up. Across the top of the back wall and along the sides were catwalks that extended into the auditorium as far as the balcony. Scenes occurred over the audience on these catwalks. There were tattered political banners on dropcloth-like material hanging from the auditorium walls, and rusty pipes and old rags visible throughout the set. He worked with "dark icon colors" to achieve an old, but rich-textured feeling. All the doors were painted red beneath their surface colors and the surface paint was allowed to dry and crack so that the red showed through. "You felt that this rich age had been splattered by a sort of decadent contemporary world," explains Loquasto.

More than most of his contemporaries, Loquasto is a conceptual designer, seeking strong visual and spatial metaphors for the themes and ideas in the plays. He refers to design as a process of translation—from idea to design, and from design to finished product. Significantly, he seems more familiar than his colleagues with the work of Europeans like Patrice Chereau, Peter Stein and Giorgio Strehler—people who combine the roles of director and designer in highly visual, conceptual productions. "Strehler's production of *The Good Woman of Setzuan* in Milan, for example, was probably the most extraordinary thing I've seen in the theatre—as moving as Peter Brook's *A Midsummer Night's Dream*," comments Loquasto. His affinity for conceptual staging has led to collaborations with such Eastern European directors such as Andrei Serban, Liviu Ciulei and Jonas Jurasas, the director of *The Suicide*. "I've always loved the larger-than-life quality of the Eastern European—the passionate commitment that battling with repression can give rise to," he states in the *ARTnews* article, and notes laughingly that, "Someone once called me 'the dissident's designer.'"

His interest and admiration for the theatricalist approach is undoubtedly related to his desire for control and precision in his designs. He loves the collaborative process and has a good working relationship with several directors, as well as with lighting designer Jennifer Tipton. Yet occasionally and indirectly, he expresses a desire for an experience in which there would be no compromises, in which he

could create something truly his own. He says that he has never been interested in directing because it "seemed a vast undertaking . . . . I often thought there was actually less control in directing than in designing, which made directing less interesting and less attractive, although far more vital." Given this outlook, it is not surprising that Loquasto is an avid patron of avant-garde theatre and tries always to see the work of Richard Foreman, who generally writes, directs and designs his own productions.

It is in part the desire for greater control, as well as his interest in the European theatricalist approach, that led him to do more and more costume design in conjunction with set design. "When you're doing something like Shakespeare," he notes, "or working with a kind of open expanse of space, the way in which it is articulated with people becomes very important to you and you can orchestrate visually more effectively when you do both." An added benefit of costume design is the contact with the performers, although he admits there are occasional problems of temperament to deal with that do not exist with scenic design.

Much of his conceptual approach to design came together in two 1983 productions directed by Rumanians. One was Ibsen's *Peer Gynt* directed by Liviu Ciulei at the Guthrie Theater, and the other was Chekhov's *Uncle Vanya* directed by Andrei Serban at La Mama E.T.C. in New York.

Ciulei's conception of *Peer Gynt* was quite specific and, in a sense, limited Loquasto's possibilities. Ciulei became fascinated with the idea of using

*Act I of Harold Pinter's* Old Times *(Mark Taper Forum, 1972)—an unusually spare interior for Loquasto. For Act II, the bookcase unit was replaced with louvered closet doors, and the chairs were replaced with two very geometric beds.*

mirrors, partly as a result of seeing Serban's mirrored production of *The Marriage of Figaro* earlier that season. Loquasto eventually designed a unit set with a mirrored surround. Sections of the left and right mirrored walls could slide in order to allow props to be brought onto the stage. The rear mirror, made of stretched vinyl (popularly known in theatre as the *Chorus Line* mirror), was hinged and could tilt up. (The side mirrors were plexiglass and tended to create distorted, funhouse images which did not please Loquasto.)

Mirrors become an immediate scenic metaphor. Therefore, we created this space that was surrounded by moving mirrors allowing the space to yawn at the audience at times and become a great mysterious void. It both confined the space and at the same time created a distorted reflection of the space. It also took the action and made it far more exciting because you could see the actors tipped up at a 90-degree angle. It was all housed in a steel 19th-century type structure. I was not so much concerned with a sense of Crystal Palace architecture as with keeping the reference to the 19th-century mind and 19th-century fantasy of the play. I presented the necessary scenic elements just as elements, all housed on scaffolding structures which allowed them to seem almost like shards in a museum pinned together with steel bolts. Anitra's tent was a 19th-century Romantic vision of the East complete with tassles, but not at all like a side show—it was all rather colorless, like cool sand. The horse in the desert was a beautiful silky horse, but on a platform of steel and simple planks.

Although the production utilized 20th-century technology and materials, such as air casters to move platforms, and the stretched-vinyl mirror, it was filled with images that referred to or "quoted" the 19th century. Loquasto researched the period using, among other things, photos of period construction sites. This formed the basis of the grills on the stage floor which functioned as traps for actor entrances and exits, as well as a source of smoke and light.

The production also embodied another Loquasto trademark: an almost Brechtian exposure of the mechanics of the stage by which, he explains, he is acknowledging the limitations of the stage. "It's not illusionistic, it's not about fooling the eye," he declares. But Loquasto is also fascinated with 19th-century gimmickry which is intended to be *completely* illusionistic. So he equivocates: "The purpose of the designer is to either deceive or clarify."

For all its conceptual imagery, *Peer Gynt*, especially the second part (the production was divided into two separate evenings), was filled with devices lifted right out of 19th-century stage craft, including a shipwreck at sea. The lights came up on a 12-foot boat "floating" in a sea suggested by parachute silk covering the entire stage. Stage hands under and around the silk, together with fans, and aided by Jennifer Tipton's dappled, "mysterious" lighting, created the illusion of a stormy sea. The parachute silk rose up to cover the boat which protruded through a slit thus completing the illusion of the sea swallowing up the victims of the storm. Other effects in the production included an explosion and flames. Loquasto feels that using these "old-fashioned devices" in a self-conscious way eliminates any need to "apologize."

*Uncle Vanya* provides an insight into the process of design under non-commercial circumstances. In a September 1983 *New York Times* article, director Andrei Serban discussed his approach: "There's a line in the play about the big empty house being 'like a maze.' All the productions of 'Vanya' that I've seen have been small. This one has the reality of film. The [La Mama] Annex has become like a wasteland barn." Loquasto and Serban talked every day for a week about the production, considering the "familiar list of Chekhov metaphors" Loquasto explains. The basic space they decided on was to be "seemingly simple but long, creating an unnatural spatial relationship among people. The characters

talk to each other in a normal way, but they may be 30 feet apart." Rooms and spatial divisions were defined by differing stage levels rather than walls. There was very little furniture. "It was very Ronconi," laughs Loquasto, referring to Italian director Luca Ronconi. But we needed recesses here to break up the space—for psychological shelter. It was Andrei's notion to really go down into the floor and make Vanya's study into a kind of hollow. He wanted the sweep of a Beckett landscape, but one where you also had warm wood and familiar Chekhov textures of candles and wicker. But by stretching the space, it took on the ascetic serenity of an Oriental walkway as well."

The set was built and altered during the rehearsal period. "It was really like building a full-scale model," explains Loquasto. "We could see what worked in the space and what didn't." Few production situations, of course, allow for that kind of flexibility.

Most of Loquasto's design for dance has been costumes, although for story ballets such as Baryshnikov's staging of *Cinderella* for American Ballet Theatre (1983), and such contemporary works as Twyla Tharp's *The Catherine Wheel* (1981) he has also created some elaborate settings. His most successful ongoing collaboration in dance has been with Tharp, with whom he first worked on *Sue's Leg* in 1975. Mary Clarke and Clement Crisp in their book *Design for Ballet* credit Loquasto with virtually

*Two dance designs for Twyla Tharp. Left, Sue's Leg (1975). Loquasto's costume design for this dance altered dance costuming and even affected fashion by glamorizing standard rehearsal clothes, creating unisex outfits of satin and crepe de chine. Right, The Catherine Wheel (1981), for which Loquasto created a mechanized abstraction of a torture device that moved about the performers and cast shadows on the silk backdrop.*

creating a new form of costuming for dance—"elegant and wildly relaxed . . . essentially of their time and very chic."

"Ballet dancers all wear rehearsal garbage," notes Loquasto, and Tharp was not interested in "unitards or the modern dance look which, regardless of what it costs, looks bedraggled." Loquasto had previously done little design for dance and simply took rehearsal clothes—legwarmers and loose-fitting clothing—and glamorized them, creating monochrome, unisex outfits of satin and crepe de chine. In the process, he inadvertantly created a new clothing fashion that went beyond the stage world (something that he nearly did again with the jeans he designed for the film *So Fine* [1981] with see-through panels on the buttocks).

Tharp claims that every time she discusses a new design with Loquasto she shows him the same picture from a book of paintings by Munkasi and says, "Just do something like this. Each time, of course, he comes up with something original, but it has that sensibility." Interestingly, many of Loquasto's designs for Tharp start out much more elaborately than the final product indicates. *Fait Accompli* (1983) had very elaborate costumes in its Texas premiere but was eventually greatly simplified. "The costumes, which we all loved, probably wouldn't have contributed very much in what we wound up doing which was extremely simple," relates Loquasto. In the final version "you just see the movement of these superb dancers. We finally hit upon the simplest kind of costume that suits her company. It's neither a unitard nor a leotard."

*The Catherine Wheel*, with music by David Byrne,

is one of Loquasto's favorite settings for dance, but even that was eventually cut back by Tharp. The dance tells a story about the disintegration of a family, but there are parallel references to mythology and St. Catherine. There were large silk drops to allow for the play of shadows and "a nasty environment of steel and rather crude or menacingly formed devices which all had a sense of torture about them. They were made of mechanized wheels, and suggested claws and instruments of torture which came in and clanged about the dancers during certain portions of the piece," as Loquasto describes it. "Along with its brilliant score," he continues, "the piece had such authority in how it was presented that it completely overwhelmed the audience. I have never, in a dance performance, except *Fait Accompli*, seen or felt an audience gripped in such silence."

When asked what it is she likes about Loquasto, Tharp simply replies, "He's such a perfectionist." But, Loquasto believes that Tharp was ultimately dissatisfied with the design for *The Catherine Wheel*, and the performance has subsequently been presented only in excerpt form against drops.

Loquasto has done few story ballets and is still fairly uncomfortable with what he calls "decorative" design. "Because I am not a painterly designer," he explains, "there is a real insecurity that does not allow me to move into that form of design with great ease." He expresses an admiration for easel painters who work for the stage, from Picasso to the "simplicity and authority of David Hockney which takes your breath away." He feels that for painters working in decorative design, there is a directness. "The translation [from design to stage setting] is just an enlargement; it is very much a personal expression." But for someone trained as a stage designer working in that tradition, Loquasto feels, "you are working out of so many references that the work begins to deteriorate. You almost know too much about what it is you are doing! You are denied a simple impulse. You have so much to draw on—art, architecture, the music, and movement itself that you have lost your spontaneity. It saddens me that I see in Boris Aronson's *Nutcracker* that struggle right to the end of his great career. He wanted very much to be an artist at work in the theatre, not simply a designer. But the parts of that ballet that work best are the parts where he was doing what he did best: wonderful stage magic."

Despite his own reservations, Loquasto received accolades for *Cinderella*. While criticizing the gaudiness of some scenes, Joan Ross Acocella in *Dancemagazine* (March 1984) talked about gowns that were "truly poetic creations—cotton candy spun of amber and verdigris. God knows how he imagines such a thing."

How his imagination works, of course, is something that he himself is hard-pressed to explain. But Loquasto does comment that, "We are inundated with images and we accumulate so much. My mind is a file cabinet of designs." He claims that he cannot walk past a dumpster without glancing inside "just to see if there might be a piece of wood or a chunk of plaster that suggests something to me, and that I can carry away in some sort of triumph." His actual process of creating a design, though, is fairly routine.

For theatre projects he begins by reading the script, but he does not like to do so until the director has been chosen, since he feels that the basic concepts must come from the director—"it's usually the collaboration with the director that is the fun of the project and that attracts me the most." In general he wants to do plays that provide "an opportunity to do something important—not important in terms of fame or fortune—but important to my development." What Loquasto seems to want most from a director is the creation of a positive working atmosphere that allows ideas to develop, to be tossed around, to "gestate and change." Nikos Psacharopoulos, artistic director of the Williamstown Theatre Festival and a former professor at Yale is, according to Loquasto who designed dozens of productions for him through the late 1960s and early 1970s, ideal in this respect. He "allows you to search out production values in a play. He points out ways of exploring a play that give it a kind of physical and visual energy. He sets up an atmosphere in which the designer can pursue an idea."

This seems to be the key to Loquasto's method. Rarely does an idea spring full-blown into his head. He likes to pick a director's brain, mull over ideas, let things evolve and change. Frequently he builds several models, changing elements or whole concepts each time as he did with *Bent*. A ballet he did for Glen Tetley is typical. Several models were constructed, each one a pared down version of the previous. "He's choreographing," Loquasto explains, "and you've designed it—but you're still finessing the design, so you're all working together. That, of course, is quite exciting." But dance can frequently be frustrating for someone who thrives on collaboration since the designer is sometimes not brought in until the work is otherwise complete.

Film can present similar problems. "It's really the director and the cinematographer's world," he says. Your job [as production designer] is more of a service. You are there to surround the director with appropriate choices." His work on the film *Falling in Love* (1984), directed by Ulu Grosbard, however, was much more collaborative. (He had previously

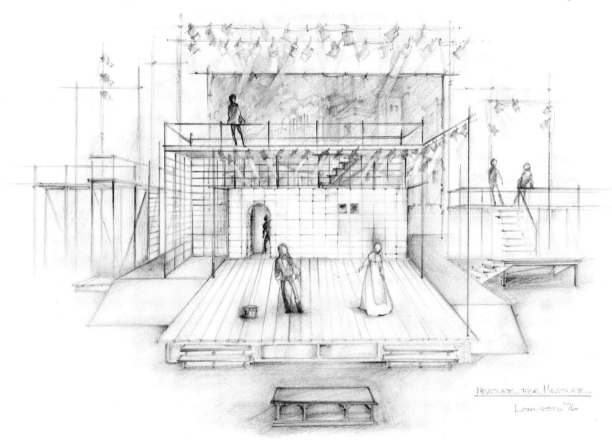

*Pencil sketch for* Measure for Measure *(Delacorte Theater, 1975). Although typically angular and frontal, the set was asymmetrical so as to create a degree of physical and spatial tension.*

worked with Grosbard on several stage plays, including *American Buffalo*.)

"Process" is a word that comes up over and over as Loquasto describes his work, and it seems that the process is as exciting and important for him as the finished product. For this reason Sam Shepard's *Curse of the Starving Class* (New York Shakespeare Festival, 1978) was one of his favorite productions, primarily because of the relationship he established with director Robert Woodruff "who allowed the design to evolve in a totally individual manner." This set was also remarkable for its starkness—an almost bare stage with a refrigerator (which Loquasto referred to as an "icon").

Because of his enthusiasm for collaboration, he truly enjoys working in the resident theatres which provide more opportunity for experimentation and exploration in a relatively unpressured environment than the Broadway theatre. He is also impressed with the wealth of "talented, skilled young technicians and the great spirit with which they work" at these theatres.

The most successful designs seem to happen quickly but "sometimes the process goes on forever and you never feel at rest. Productions that have worked I don't think about, but the ones that have been tortured or twisted are always with me and I'll continually see something and say, 'That's what I should have done!'"

Because Loquasto does both sets and costumes, and because he is often working on several projects simultaneously in various media, he maintains a larger staff than many of his colleagues. His assistants generally consist of a draftsman/technician who also works at the shop, and a production assistant who deals with props, set dressing and the like (although Loquasto usually selects the set dressing himself). Costumes usually entail two more assistants who shop, dye, age costumes, alter and so on. For Woody Allen's *Zelig*, Loquasto had a whole team of assistants searching New York City and environs for appropriate period clothes that would match those in the black-and-white photos and films incorporated into the movie. "My work habits are expensive," he states. "I am blessed with loyal assistants, many of whom work with me when they can and who will work for less when the job pays less. But they shouldn't have to suffer for my sins."

Like most successful designers, his days are long, generally starting at 8:30 a.m. and going to midnight. When working on a film they are even longer. The filming of *Falling in Love* and the New York premiere of *Cinderella* were happening simultaneously and it was not unusual for Loquasto to be decorating Saks Fifth Avenue for a film scene until 2:00 a.m., and then be in the American Ballet Theatre scene shop at 8 a.m. Such a schedule allows for little personal life. "I'm a pretty boring person," he jokes.

Loquasto was born in Wilkes-Barre, Pennsylvania in 1944. He became interested in theatre in grade school and by age 15 was an apprentice at the Ross Common Playhouse in Wind Gap. During his second summer there he designed his first shows: *Gigi* and *Picnic*. He subsequently designed for other community theatres and did some acting at nearby Lafayette College in Easton when youngsters were needed. He attended Kings College in Wilkes-Barre where he was an English major. "I really wanted a liberal arts education," he states, "even though it was very apparent to me that I wanted to work in the theatre. I knew that if I didn't force myself to become familiar with other disciplines, I never would."

Loquasto feels that the strongest influence on his career was his work at the Williamstown Theatre Festival in Massachusetts where he worked in various capacities on and off for 11 summers beginning in 1965. It was there that he met Nikos Psacharopoulos who was influential in his attending Yale, and John Conklin, who was the resident designer then, and for whom he expresses the greatest respect and admiration. He envies Conklin's knowledge of art and literature, and his ability to draw upon and incorporate that knowledge into his work.

Loquasto says he patterned his basic approach to design on Conklin's process and learned "more about design from him than anyone."

He speaks with great enthusiasm of Yale and singles out Donald Oenslager and Michael Annals as especially influential. Loquasto attended from 1966 to 1969, the first years of Robert Brustein's reign, and remembers the general excitement created by such artists in residence as Jonathan Miller, Robert Lowell, Irene Worth and Kenneth Haigh, and the stimulus and provocation of the political and social upheaval of the period which engendered a generally creative atmosphere.

While at Yale he began to design for the Hartford Stage Company and the Long Wharf Theatre, and later for the Yale Repertory Theatre. It was through Conklin and such fellow Yale directors as Jeff Bleckner and A.J. Antoon that Loquasto made the move to New York and became associated with the New York Shakespeare Festival. His work in dance and film came about almost accidentally, the result of choreographers or directors seeing his theatre work. Lighting designer Jennifer Tipton recommended him to Twyla Tharp. He never expected to work in these fields and, in fact, remembers as a student thinking about classical ballet costume, "God, who would want to do this?"

He has done few operas and admits to being somewhat intimidated by the tradition. "You don't simply do a *Traviata* or a *Bohème* without knowing those operas inside and out," he says. Opera, he feels, should be left to those who thrive on it. "Dance has replaced what would probably have been my desire to work in opera."

Given his conceptual designs and his affinity for European directors and designers, one might expect Loquasto to long for some sort of European repertory situation and a season of classical European plays. But what he really wants to do is more American classics—not the somber, weighty plays

of O'Neill but something like *Arsenic and Old Lace*. "I want to do that desperately." In 1977, when he was primarily known for his realistic sets like *That Championship Season* and *American Buffalo*, he told a *New York Times* interviewer, "I suppose I've always had a flair for that kind of busy, chochka-filled set." Despite his subsequent work with Serban, Ciulei, and the ballet, he still does. His style may be in the tradition of Ming Cho Lee and Boris Aronson, but his heart is with Raymond Sovey—the designer of the original production of *Arsenic and Old Lace*.

*Act II of* The Cherry Orchard *(Vivian Beaumont Theater, 1977) directed by Andrei Serban. This non-traditional, conceptual production of Chekhov upset many critics. Loquasto's design incorporated the iconography of Chekhov but none of the texture or mood associated with him. The setting seemed surreal: scenic elements stranded in the midst of a vast, white space.*

# DAVID MITCHELL

"To earn a living in this business—in order to survive—you must do a great variety of things. I don't feel I have the luxury of taking a philosophical stance. Although I take what I do very seriously, I don't take being a designer that seriously. Basically, it's an interpretive and derivative art rather than a truly original or seminal one."

For David Mitchell, stage design is more craft than art—he compares it to graphic and commercial art—and he considers theatre a business. It is what he wants to do and he considers himself lucky to be able to do it. Still relatively young—he was born in 1932 in Honesdale, Pennsylvania—he is among the senior generation of working designers. He is also one of only a handful who have become financially comfortable, although this came after some 20 years of hard work doing dinner theatre, Off and Off-Off Broadway, Shakespeare in the Park, ballet, the occasional Broadway production and even opera in Chile.

By the mid–1970s he was a respected, steadily employed designer, but with no real hits to his name. Suddenly in 1977 he had three shows simultaneously on Broadway: *I Love My Wife*, *The Gin Game* and *Annie*. Seemingly overnight he became a major Broadway designer and, more significantly, as a result of *Annie* he became known as a master of multi-scene musicals. Since then he has designed *Barnum* (1980), Neil Simon's *Brighton Beach Memoirs* (1983) and *La Cage aux Folles* (1983), among others, while also branching into film and television and continuing to design occasionally for the New York Shakespeare Festival, the New York City Ballet, Off-Off Broadway and the regional theatre.

*Annie*, of course, was the "big break" that so many designers wait for and Mitchell retells with amusement how he almost passed up the chance to do it for fear of losing his position as resident designer with the New York Shakespeare Festival. When he finally agreed to design the show, producer Mike Nichols told him, "It's guaranteed annuities, you know. You've made the right decision."

Given the range of media and variety of theatrical forms in which he works, there is, not surprisingly, a certain eclecticism in Mitchell's designs. Nonetheless, there are stylistic consistencies. By his own admission he prefers what he calls a classical use of forms, shapes and space. By this he means that his designs are frequently frontal, use right angles and parallel lines, and are fully contained within the frame of the stage space. This latter point seems most crucial to Mitchell. He generally dislikes settings that are angled in such a way as to imply that they continue off stage or project through the proscenium—he wants the stage picture to be complete and self-contained or, as he puts it, "to seem comfortable." "I like settings to have a certain strength by seeming to work within a stage space, rather than having sets that angle off and out of a stage picture, implying that some horrible distortion must occur right offstage. I would rather have you believe, as you look through that picture frame, that there is a complete universe there. I like French classical painters, like Poussin, and certain Victorian painters too. I like that sense of space. Forced, phony

*Facing page, model of* La Cage aux Folles *(Palace Theatre, 1983), showing its opening sequence. During the overture, the set moved in imitation of a cinematic dolly shot, taking the audience from the street to the inside of the nightclub.*

perspective frequently disturbs me, although I certainly use it. It can become very mannered. But then," he laughs, "my preference for frontality becomes very mannered."

In fact, many of Mitchell's sets are compositions in rectangles. One of the starkest examples is the setting for Miguel Piñero's *Short Eyes* (New York Shakespeare Festival, 1974). Although played on the curved thrust of the Vivian Beaumont Theatre, the floor of the prison set was rectangular. The back wall, the doorways, the wire-mesh catwalk, the bars, the gates and even the bricks created a collage of rectangles—intersecting vertical and horizontal planes.

Although stark and sinister, the *Short Eyes* set was not that far removed in composition from *Brighton Beach Memoirs* or *La Cage aux Folles*. The latter, especially, is a study in rectangular planes gliding on and off the stage, constantly intersecting. Certain scenes in *La Cage*, such as the dressing room and the interior of the nightclub, are compositions of rectangles within rectangles, all parallel to the audience. The inevitable horizontal and vertical movement created by the constant shifting of the drops, flying scenery and wagons is echoed in the shapes of scenic and decorative units. Although well aware of his preference for frontality, Mitchell believes that the use of rectangles is essentially unconscious on his part and evolves out of the basic demands of the design.

In the realistically based plays that Mitchell has designed, he combines this sense of formality with intricate, realistic detail, resulting in a sort of surrealism—or what might even be called "abstract realism." "I feel that detail, if set off against other things, is enriching," he explains. "I like to have a subtle, surrealistic quality—things that are very clearly felt and seen surrounded by a sense of space that is perhaps unreal." He believes that such tangible details create the opportunity to take liberties with the rest of the setting. "It's as in a dream," he continues. "You think you can touch a certain object—you know it's there—and then the space dis-

solves in a curious kind of way. That's always fascinating to me."

The result is a setting with realistic textures, yet one that is not naturalistic. A striking example was the set for Vincent Canby's *The Old Flag* (George Street Playhouse, 1984), set in the Andersonville prison camp during the Civil War. It consisted of a mound of dirt (real dirt built up over platforms, erosion cloth and carpeting) in the center of the stage surrounded by rows and rows of tents greatly scaled down in size to suggest a vast camp stretching into the distance. There was a scrim cyclorama with a vague suggestion of an American flag behind it and a framework of wooden slats around the outer edges of the thrust stage. The result was a setting of real textures—dirt, canvas, wood—but with a nearly abstract geometric design. The abstraction and the texture worked as mitigating factors, creating a visual tension between the real and the abstract. "When properly done," explains Mitchell, "the play should have an austerity that one associates with Beckett. Set pieces and movements have to be stylized. You have to have a sense of the prison without being totally real, and a sense of the landscape with the three characters isolated as if on a raft in the middle of this ocean of death and disease."

The best and most elaborate example of this mixture of detail and abstraction was in *Foxfire* (Broadway, 1982—an earlier version with sets by John Lee Beatty had been done at the Guthrie). The set reproduced the exterior of a cabin and yard of a farm in Georgia. The details of the building were painstakingly recreated from a variety of sources, yet there was a painted scrim backdrop, an overhead scrim for gobo projections and the floor was made of wood planks with some leaves spread over them. Mitchell and director David Trainer felt that they had to make the space slightly abstract. "By making a platform for everything to sit on," says Mitchell, "you imply the space without being entirely literal. Instead of a mound of dirt you have a sense of the ground, but not quite. The scrim overhead was necessary for atmosphere."

*Pencil sketch for Bruce Jay Friedman's* Steambath *(Truck and Warehouse Theatre, 1970). Until this time, most of Mitchell's work was strongly influenced by Ming Cho Lee. This was, he says, his "first strong construction and physical presence." Many of his subsequent sets moved in the direction of strong, realistic detail, and the square frontality demonstrated here.*

Despite these abstractions Mitchell felt the need for a grounding in reality. The play was based on material from the *Foxfire* books which detail the culture of the people of Appalachia. "It was so grounded in specifics," explains Mitchell, "and there is such a strong graphic style associated with that work—the specifics of every step of making those chairs, tables, houses. In order to do justice to the origins of the material, you'd better be damn sure that the things put onstage accurately reflect that way of life, that way of putting things together. It gave the play a certain visual integrity." The setting, therefore, was intensely researched.

David Trainer and I flew down to Georgia and drove around in a pickup truck for two or three days with the *Foxfire* book people. We looked at barns and houses and I took lots of pictures—we were even shot at by someone who didn't like strangers taking pictures. The details were things you cannot imagine. I took about 10 pictures of sections of a chimney close up, using a zoom lens. Then I had the pictures blown up to almost full scale and put them on the wall of the scene shop. I had each one of the stones carved individually in the shop [out of styrofoam] matching the ones in the pic-

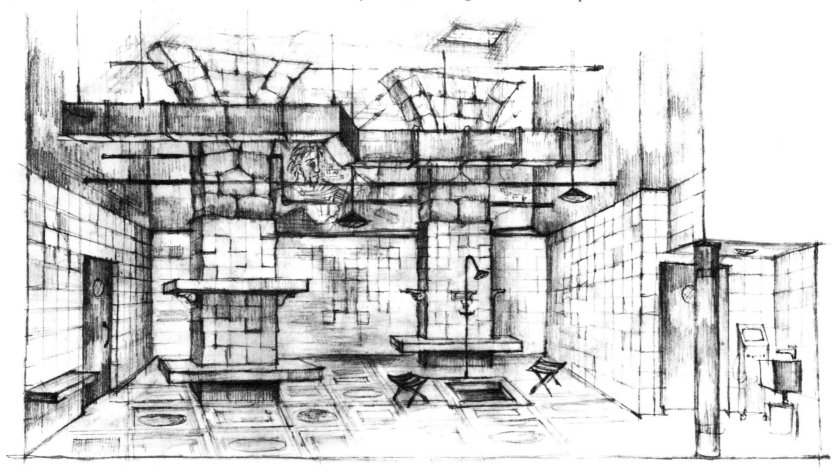

tures, and then it was put together as a real chimney.

There is a kind of entropy in executing a design—everything going toward the easiest way, the way you've always done it: the way you do stones, the way you do bricks. You have to constantly resist the cliches that creep into the craft as a result of money pressures or craftsmen relying on certain techniques to turn things out quickly. As a designer you have to find ways to give things a fresh, authentic look. In this case, I knew I wanted the stones individually carved so I had it built into the shop bid. It had a feel about it that I think was important. It was a set of details.

A wagon was built in the shop from directions in a *Foxfire* book. Elements like shingles, siding,

chairs and hardware were located in Georgia by an assistant, and the house was built from real split logs.

All the realistic detail, however, functioned primarily as texture and environment rather than as a naturalistic setting. Although it was a permanent exterior, many of the scenes occurred inside the house and would somehow have to be played in front of the house. The director, and author Hume Cronyn, considered inserting lines to explain this, but Mitchell felt it was unnecessary. He felt that by sitting at a table with the proper lighting the locale would be conveyed: "You could believe it was inside or outside, it didn't matter. You shouldn't have to feel yourself bound to quote lines from the script to explain which scenes are outside and which are inside."

Part of this approach comes from a Brechtian aes-

D. L. Coburn's The Gin Game *(Long Wharf Theatre and Golden Theatre, 1977). Once again, the detail and frontality are evident. Theatricality derived from the size of the set, which was high and deep and yet succeeded in creating a kind of intimacy necessary for the two-character play.*

thetic regarding props. "I like that aesthetic," says Mitchell. "A well-made prop can create a whole world and you don't need very much else. A properly executed table and chair can give you a whole room. Objects, if carefully observed and reproduced have a certain power, a certain way of supporting—they radiate certain memories, they have important resonances. I think you have to have, particularly around actors, a kind of conviction—feelings that there are moments when these things really do exist, that they have a history with the environment, even though other elements in the space are not real. The variation of very accurately observed detail plus the communication of the unreal makes a rich, interesting combination."

Mitchell's attention to detail carries over to the way he works. He is a tenacious perfectionist and has a reputation among technicians for sticking with a problem longer than most other designers in order to get the image or effect that he wants—a quality noted by Peter Feller, Jr. of Feller Precision, the shop that builds many of the mechanical systems for Broadway shows. "David Mitchell is most apt to fight very hard to stay with a certain design, even if it's going to create problems. That's just the way he is," explains Feller. "He feels that if you just don't give up and persist a little longer, the problems will be solved. Some are and some aren't. The only problem with that approach is that if you don't come up with a solution you are three more weeks down the line." Scenic artist Arnold Abramson, who has executed most of Mitchell's drops over the years, echoes this view. "He may seem casual at times," notes Abramson, "but he's very insistent on getting what he wants."

All designers are, by nature, particular about details, but Mitchell seems more so. In *The Old Flag* there were two notched tree branches stuck in the top of the mound of dirt with another branch resting at an angle between them; in the second act it served as a makeshift tent support. Mitchell spent a couple of hours adjusting the position, height and angle of the sticks. He matter-of-factly explains, "I

fooled with it because it was a big visual element. We had to make sure it wasn't too high, but was supportive of the action in front of it, while working with everything else. It became a key element in the design."

Despite some 20 years of this sort of approach and despite the fact that he has done few large-scale shows (compared, say, to Robin Wagner or Douglas Schmidt), Mitchell finds himself known in the 1980s as one of the premiere designers of the fluid—almost cinematic—style of moving scenery. "When I started doing musicals," he says, "the fascinating thing for me was kinetic scenery—when you did a musical, that was what you did." Mitchell's designs for *Annie* and *La Cage aux Folles* have recaptured the spirit of a musical production style that seemed to disappear after the 1950s. What is significant about these designs is not merely the spectacle or look, but the rhythm, pacing and style that Mitchell imposes on the productions. It is arguable that the success of those two shows is more to Mitchell's credit than critics and audiences realize. In all probability, neither would have succeeded as

*Model for* On the Waterfront, *a stage adaptation of the 1954 movie scheduled for a 1985 production. In an attempt to create both the fluidity and realism of the film, the setting will be one of the most elaborate and mechanized of any Broadway non-musical.*

well without the rapid shifting and organic evolution of one scene into the next that he provided. His settings controlled not only the crucial pacing but, in the case of *Annie*, the whole style of the show.

To understand the evolution of *Annie*, it is necessary to know how Mitchell builds set models. While constructing the basic set structure Mitchell photocopies appropriate items to put on the set, ranging from images for a backdrop to furniture and cars. The photocopies are then glued onto cardboard cutouts that can be moved around within the model. The finished design, of course, is in Mitchell's style, but this is an easy method for working out ideas while also doing necessary research.

The concept for *Annie* unintentionally evolved from this way of working. Mitchell began collecting everything he could find on New York City in the 1930s, whether it applied to the script or not. As he explains:

Before we got into designing specific scenes, I felt we should finally get all the material together so we could montage it. We scaled everything up or down by photostating so it was all roughly in accurate scale—½ inch to a foot. We had this table top full of all these cutouts and Mike Nichols and Marty Charnin came in and saw them. They didn't quite know

*Miguel Piñero's* Short Eyes *(New York Shakespeare Festival, 1974). Mitchell's prison set was an intricate grid of squares and rectangles.*

what to make of them, but they liked them. We put the cutouts in the model and tried them in various combinations. I had an idea that I'd like to see a kind of moving background of New York so we made a montage out of the cutouts—it created a kind of playful atmosphere and loosened things up a bit. They weren't just looking at things that I had drawn and deciding whether they worked or not—there was a sense of participation for the people involved. Everybody had ideas and they could go in and play with things in the model.

The photocopy cutouts became the look of the show—which ultimately featured a great number of photo blowups. Mitchell felt that this style suggested the comic strips that inspired the show, but that the realism inherent in the photographs helped to undercut the inevitable sentimentality of the script. "The photographic cutouts," he explains, "were a nice combination of drawings and reality—a two-dimensional reality without being heavy; a witty reality."

The show's two treadmills evolved out of an attempt to solve specific problems. Mitchell felt that the first song he should tackle was "NYC," a big production number. In the original script, Daddy Warbucks, Grace Farrell and Sandy had to walk from Warbuck's mansion on 85th Street—"I imagined it to be opposite the Metropolitan Museum"—to the Roxy. "So what do you do?" asks Mitchell, "The dog can't mime walking in place." The treadmill seemed an obvious solution. But once there was a treadmill to carry people down the street, a second one was needed to create traffic flowing the opposite direction. "The treadmills provided us with ways to shape the production, and from that idea, a lot of visual solutions began to evolve." From the research came the idea of using cars and trucks for transitions—characters "rode" on or off the stage in cars on the treadmill. "The Dusenberg was not written in the script," Mitchell remembers, "it just happened. We found one in our research and

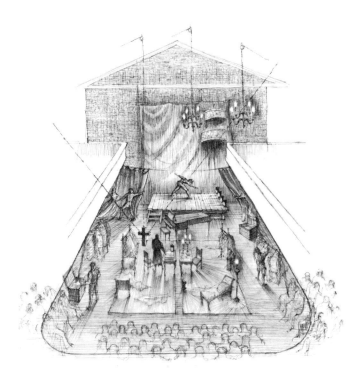

put it on the model and I said, 'Wouldn't it look good to have these people around that car?' Then the transitions were worked in and Marty Charnin suggested the idea of the laundry truck. It became a method of moving the scene shifts along. I felt instinctively that we had to have open and interesting scene shifts."

Mitchell, like most other designers of mobile scenery, sees the transitions as the most essential aspect of the design. "The scenes became less important than the way you got in and out of them," says Mitchell. "Once I allocated a certain look to a scene I began to make whatever changes were necessary to get into the scene."

The treadmills, of course, created a side-to-side movement resembling a cinematic pan shot. A whole style evolved out of that and, according to Mitchell, when choreographer Peter Gennaro first saw it he exclaimed, "That's it, that's our style!" The lateral movement became a sort of signature for the show.

*Pencil sketch for Bulgakov's* Cabal of Hypocrites *(Actors Studio, 1984). The space and budget of the Studio are not conducive to elaborate scenery, so Mitchell substituted moving bodies for moving scenery. The sketches included in this chapter attest to Mitchell's talents as one of the most evocative artists in stage design.*

In *La Cage aux Folles*, although Mitchell was not consciously trying to recreate the feel of the movie, the movement was cinematic. The opening sequence and first two musical numbers, for instance, were the equivalent of a tracking shot that moved from the St. Tropez harbor, through the club, the dressing room, backstage and to Georges and Albin's apartment. The curtain rose on a painted backdrop of the harbor with a free-standing building in the foreground. The building tracked downstage and opened to form the buildings along a street and to reveal the facade of the nightclub. The street units then moved offstage, the nightclub unit moved downstage and a white curtain dropped in behind as Georges entered. After the opening number, the nightclub stage moved partially offstage left as the offstage area glided on from stage right. Subsequent scenes moved smoothly from the apartment to the dressing room to the stage again. As Mitchell explains:

It seemed important that if you were going to show the two worlds of the club and the surrounding locale you had to somehow show the nightclub and communicate that it was set in St. Tropez. You could do that simply by having Gene Barry say, "Welcome to La Cage aux Folles of St. Tropez," but that seemed weak in comparison to some kind of visual indication of it. It's very important to get a forceful image at the top of the show to draw the audience in. So I had the idea of a street and a club outside and people going into the club. We didn't use that—it was very similar to the film—but it could, I thought, have a slightly surreal tone to it in the tradition of French painters, particularly the Surrealists. A vista down the street with this club at the end could be very intriguing. It could be strange and exotic with characters and so on. Later, the idea of having the town in perspective—presented once again in a slightly surreal way—opening up, developed from that idea. Arthur Laurents liked that im-

mediately as a way of balancing things out and preparing you for the street scenes later on instead of just opening in the club. It also provided a visual accompaniment to the overture.

Mitchell's influence on a production becomes even more apparent when his relationship with the director is understood. Although it is increasingly common for plays to develop in workshops or resident professional theatres—which tend to provide a relatively long, collaborative gestation—much of Mitchell's Broadway work is straightforward commercial theatre, in which a production company is put together with only a few months—or in extreme cases, a few weeks—to prepare before rehearsals begin. For Neil Simon's *Biloxi Blues*, for instance, Mitchell built models, completed the drafting and obtained shop bids well before the shows were in production. While the style of the design, certain details and a sense of the rhythm and overall feeling came from discussions with the directors and playwrights, of course, it is arguable that the look and pacing of the shows result from Mitchell's solutions to the problems. *Biloxi Blues* makes 15 transitions through 11 locations, and the use of a painted scrim and the winch and track system were Mitchell's. Because the transitions are so integral to the success of the production, Mitchell's design cannot help but significantly affect the tone, rhythm and impact of the play.

Mitchell's interest in mobile scenery was first evident in *The Incomparable Max*, a play about English critic Sir Max Beerbohm that appeared briefly on Broadway in 1972. The movement of scenery through 13 scenes—including a train wreck and an Edwardian vision of the future—was accomplished primarily through the use of winches and hangers (scenic elements flown in). But Mitchell also relied heavily on rear-screen projections, a device that he has continued to use with great subtlety in subsequent productions.

Mitchell next experimented with kinetic scenery in the 1975 New York Shakespeare Festival Production of Arthur Wing Pinero's *Trelawney of the Wells*.

He had done a production of *Trelawney* at the Shakespeare Festival in 1970, in which sets were changed by stagehands between each scene. But the new production was on the thrust stage of the Beaumont which created different demands. Moreover, director A.J. Antoon felt that the action must be continuous so some form of mechanized scenery became necessary.

Mitchell worked out a system of moving platforms operated by a hand-cranked winch. He constructed a false proscenium at the rear of the thrust—"a collage of stage boxes to give a sense of an old-fashioned theatre"—and an act curtain and dimensional wall units at the back painted like a series of stored flats and props, creating the illusion that the audience was looking into a bare stage. The walls, flats and hanging battens moved aside, and from way upstage an interior scene on a platform appeared and rolled downstage—with performers in action as it moved—"a moving thrust stage," as Mitchell describes it. The upstage walls closed as the unit moved to its downstage position. "It utilized the depth of the Beaumont in a way that had never been attempted before. The changes were first visible from 60 feet away. The set came down through the proscenium and right onto the thrust so if you were sitting in the first row it was really an amazing sight because you were looking 60 feet away at this set that was eventually going to be two feet away. I began to see the possibilities of a moving set."

While Mitchell is known for his kinetic scenery and detailed realism, he is one of the contemporary theatre's most painterly designers and probably its foremost proponent of projected scenery. Because his projections are rarely spectacular and "high tech," but are used instead to reinforce the painterly quality, this is often overlooked. Mitchell frequently uses multiple layers of scrim or combinations of scrim, opaque translucencies and other materials to create his backgrounds and then projects images on top of that. One technique is to paint images onto a scrim drop and then rear-project a picture of the image onto the drop, thereby doubling the richness

and texture. "No matter how many winches, no matter how many technical devices he uses," notes Abramson, "there is still an overlay of rich, painterly quality in David's sets."

Mitchell's process generally involves immersing himself in research—whether it's travel to locations like Georgia, St. Tropez or Brighton Beach, or collecting pictures from books and archives. The next step may be a rough sketch or a model depending on the demands of the show. Models are preferred, and as mentioned, these are sometimes pasteups. A white model is often the first view of Mitchell's set that a producer or director sees. Once it is approved, he moves on to the finished model. "It's a matter of making sure you understand all the problems before getting to the model," he says. "But there's only so far you can go with a model because the element of the stage is another step. A model is unsatisfac-

*Model for* Henry V *(Delacorte Theater, 1976). The tower on stage left could turn and move, thus creating various spatial configurations while suggesting a number of locales. The tower and the upstage poles provided a sharp vertical thrust in the open space of the stage. Mitchell carefully researched the weaponry of the time and the cannons could actually fire.*

tory as a representation of a show—it lacks the atmosphere and presence of the theatre." The drafting is done by Mitchell's assistants from his sketches. Sometimes a show is redrafted a few times as the concept takes shape.

Most of the renderings Mitchell does are for the backdrops. These are usually highly textured, almost Impressionistic paintings. Abramson notes that Mitchell used to texture the whole panel before he began painting in order to get the rich textured quality he desired.

"Of course," Mitchell notes, "a musical is another thing. You use many of the same techniques with individual scenes, but it develops with several people working on individual set pieces while another person is continuously updating the ground-plan in sections. That way, when new ideas are introduced, the movement of the show and the fluidity of everything is being constantly perfected and worked out."

After *Annie*, Mitchell was able to renovate a brownstone on Manhattan's upper West Side, and the main floor serves as his studio. He also uses a room on the third floor as a private space in which to paint. His basement is overflowing with models, renderings and plans. The elegance of his studio stands out in sharp contrast to the makeshift, cramped and chaotic quality of many other designers' studios. In keeping with Mitchell's sense of theatre-as-business, his residence-cum-studio has the air of a professional office. Several assistants go about their work drafting, model-building, answering phones and doing correspondence. Drafting tables are covered with work while sketches, model pieces and odd objects lie scattered about, yet the finished models mounted on pedestals and lighted by baby spots and the posters on the wood-panelled walls give everything a sense of order. At around 6:00 p.m. the assistants leave and the studio becomes part of a home again.

Mitchell developed his interest in theatre relatively late—it was not until he was a graduate student at Boston University in the 1950s that he made the decision to pursue it—but he had an early interest in art. He remembers drawing on the slate sidewalks with colored stones in Honesdale as a small boy. In high school he began painting with watercolors and oils. "I basically taught myself to draw. I learned perspective from Classical examples, copying painters. I thought Hans Holbein was the pinnacle because he was so realistic." Mitchell saw no theatre until he was in college, although he was fascinated by movies. He went to Kutztown State Teachers College (now Pennsylvania State College) with the idea that he would teach. Art education courses there introduced him to all the great modern artists. "I also discovered the Russian Constructivists," he notes. "In terms of theatre, I read and instantly liked Gordon Craig." He also took a general theatre course and his ability to solve stage design problems led a teacher to suggest that he consider the field. Primarily though, his undergraduate days were an introduction to art history and technique. While at Kutztown, Mitchell also produced a musical—someone else designed it—"but I liked the whole idea and mechanics of putting a show together."

After the Army in 1957, with vague ideas of working in the theatre, he went to Boston University, eventually studying design with Horace Armistead, although he never completed the graduate degree.

His earliest jobs were at public television station WGBH in Boston, local dinner theatres and the Charles Playhouse. He came to New York in 1961 and began designing at the Meadowbrook Dinner Theatre in New Jersey—it was run by the same people who ran the theatre in Boston at which he had worked. Robin Wagner was working at Meadowbrook at the same time. "He and I worked on shows back-to-back," recalls Mitchell. "Robin would design the sets on envelopes on the bus on the way out there." Mitchell also designed at dinner theatres in Westchester. Although he felt that the work was not very fulfilling, it brought in money which he badly needed since his first child was on the way. But the conditions did not allow the quality

*Facing page*, Naked Hamlet *(New York Shakespeare Festival, 1967). This was Joseph Papp's "modernized" production of Shakespeare's play.*

of design Mitchell wanted and he quit in frustration. "I just gave it up and did temporary work and began taking odd jobs."

While working at these "odd jobs," Mitchell put together a portfolio and began designing Off-Off Broadway. He got a job in the summer of 1964 at the Atlanta Theatre Under the Stars—"the most money I'd ever made up till then." Just before leaving for Atlanta, Juilliard called him to help paint a drop for Ming Cho Lee. He stayed on to become Lee's principal assistant on the production, and Lee asked him to work in his studio when he returned from Atlanta. Mitchell went to Lee's studio in the fall of 1964 and remained there through 1967. Douglas Schmidt was working at the studio at the same time.

"Ming and I got along instantly. He became a mentor. Through the years we have remained very friendly. As designers, we were compatible. We both had an admiration for Brechtian stagecraft at the time, and we shared some of the same viewpoints on the use of space, color and props." Mitchell painted sets for Lee as well as the usual drafting, model-building and plans. "You learned exactly where the pencil should go to get Ming's approval," recalls Mitchell. "His style was imprinted strongly—it was hard to break away from that." To this day Mitchell feels the influence of Lee, but he is perfectly comfortable with that. "I wouldn't have remained at the studio so long," he explains, "unless there had been a certain agreement about things."

It was through Lee, of course, that Mitchell began working for the New York Shakespeare Festival in 1965. His second production there was the school tour of *Henry V* directed by Joseph Papp. Mitchell quickly established a good working rapport with Papp and designed several of the shows he directed through the mid–1970s. Also through Lee, he met opera director Tito Capobianco and began to design operas for him, first in South America and later at the New York City Opera. Mitchell knew nothing of opera at the time but feels that his naivete may have contributed to his new solutions for old problems.

He also feels that opera helped him develop his skills with color. "The painting style in opera can be rich. It doesn't have to be garish, it just requires a good subtle use of color on a big scale—you can't fill it with detail. The evolution of acrylic paints in the 1960s was a great help because I had always been intimidated by watercolor. I wanted to experiment and acrylics allowed me to make mistakes, paint over, do unorthodox combinations."

Mitchell has also worked on ballet and film. His ballet work began when Georges Dayde, whom he had met at the Paris Opera, asked him to supervise the sets and costumes for *Gaspar de la Nuit* for the Ravel Festival at the New York City Ballet in 1974. Mitchell ended up supervising most of the presentations at the Festival. George Balanchine then asked him to design *The Steadfast Tin Soldier* and he subsequently designed for Peter Martins. Mitchell's experiments with projections fascinated Balanchine. Balanchine was developing a ballet for the Bicentennial depicting a trip across America and ending with fireworks over San Francisco. John James Audubon was to be the central figure. "Balanchine really wanted to move beyond scenery," explains Mitchell, "to be able to conjure up images so that the scenery wasn't standing between his own idea of what the space should look like and those images he had in his mind. He wanted the images

*Backdrop for* Annie *(Neil Simon Theatre, 1977). Mitchell was using paste-ups of photocopies for the rough model and this became the inspiration for photo-blowups in the final design. The technique captured a sense of both realism and newspaper cartoons.*

to vanish like cinema—appear and go away. It was fascinating to him at that point because it meant that he then might, in a much purer form, be able to come back to story ballet in a new way, without having to rely on all those sets. He began talking about the possibility of doing *Sleeping Beauty* this way." Ultimately, an adequate projection system was too expensive and impractical for the repertory and the Bicentennial ballet was never done. Mitchell was working on a new production of *Don Quixote* in 1983 when Balanchine died.

Normally Mitchell designs only sets. "Under the pressures of a musical you'd have to be crazy these days to do both sets and costumes," he says. "But the ballet is different. Sets and costumes have to be an entity. Elements can be picked up and echoed from one to the other—it's a very delicate balance."

Mitchell's film work began almost accidentally as a result of his theatre work. His first project was a film of *Short Eyes*. Some of the producers of that film were subsequently involved in *Rich Kids* and brought Mitchell in at the last minute. Despite being thrust into a project already in progress, in an unfamiliar medium, he was not intimidated. "I could see what had to be done, what had to be changed," he explained. "I always felt that film was something I could do." For Mitchell, the most interesting aspect of his work in film is not the design of the settings themselves but the working out of the storyboards, setups and shooting concepts with the director. "I think you feel closest to things that way—where the camera moves is the whole thing, that's where the challenge is."

Mitchell's best known film to date has been Louis Malle's *My Dinner with Andre*. He explains the evolution of the set:

We decided that it should take place in a French or Middle European restaurant and visited several in New York, but we had to go somewhere out of town because we couldn't afford the union situation. Basically, we con-structed a set inside the ballroom of the Jefferson Hotel in Richmond, Virginia—suggested by costume designer Jeffrey Ullman—because it was deserted for renovations. It was all open space. Louis had an idea that we needed mirrors—certainly the ballroom had mirrors—and we needed a comfortable sitting area. I constructed a model in New York and put the pieces in. The molding and detail on the set was an exact copy of everything on the walls of the ballroom so we had a built-in cover shot whenever we shot off the mirror in the set—it all matched because it was reflecting the ballroom. We built the bar and the back of the bar on casters so that anywhere they had to shoot, the bar could be used as an automatic cover in that one area. We built three columns and had one fake wall section with a translight out a

*Barnum (St. James Theatre, 1980). Mitchell created a one-ring circus for this musical about P. T. Barnum. Aside from the rigging, which was anchored into the structure of the theatre itself, Mitchell provided a host of special effects to suggest caged animals, Jumbo the elephant and Tom Thumb. Devices popped up from the floor, flew in from above, and moved across the stage. A hot-air balloon was supposed to carry performers over the audience but the scene was cut because of high insurance costs.*

window that you glimpsed briefly. Every mirror was faceted and adjustable for the lights. They were all mirrex panels that could be pushed in and out so that they could be adjusted for every camera angle.

In addition to film, Mitchell spent one year developing and working on the visual concept for the now-defunct CBS Cable channel. This included not only the physical environment but even a style of camera movement. "I was consciously trying to evoke the early days of television, like *Omnibus*," notes Mitchell.

While working Off-Off Broadway in those early years, Mitchell, like many of his colleagues, was filled with idealism and believed that it was possible to work in all levels of theatre—"to have it all, the experimental and the Broadway successes" as he says. His inspiration was Jo Mielziner, whom he met through Lee. "I'd go and look at those drawings and sketches that Mielziner did for Tennessee Williams, for Arthur Miller's *Death of a Salesman*, and it's part of theatre history. It's what attracted all of us to stage design—it inspired a lot of people. I think I was initially attracted to those renderings of light and characters in space, particularly in *Glass Menagerie*, *Salesman* and *Streetcar*. Those were groundbreaking designs, yet Mielziner also had a successful commercial career."

Aside from Mielziner, Mitchell claims to have been influenced by pictures of the Berliner Ensemble, notably the work of designers Teo Otto, Caspar Neher and Karl von Appen. (He finally visited the Ensemble in 1972 and was not disappointed.) "Ot-

*David Rabe's* The Basic Training of Pavlo Hummel *(New York Shakespeare Festival, 1971). The Vietnam War drama, despite a sense of gritty realism, is actually a dream or memory play.*

to's work in particular seemed innovative, fresh and daring. I hadn't seen the equivalent here. Everything in the 1950s and early 1960s became very predictable—very much of a storybook style—except for Boris Aronson. His design for *The Firstborn* [1958] really opened my eyes. It was a wonderful set the way it all worked together—like a big sculpture." Mitchell also admires the work of Norman Bel Geddes who did theatrical and industrial design in the 1920s through 1940s.

Mitchell struggled long and hard to achieve his current position. In the process, he has evolved a style that combines a flair for bigness with an attention to minute details and textures. "I like to do big sets," he acknowledges, "but the challenge is placing people in an artfully designed space. That can be very satisfying." It follows that his favorite set is not one of the musicals, but *The Gin Game*, a two-person play that featured Hume Cronyn and Jessica Tandy. The locale of the play was the porch of an old age home, but Mitchell, with Mike Nichols' encouragement, designed a large, deep space. What pleases him is that the space, rather than overwhelming the actors "added a peculiar kind of intimacy."

"To be successful in theatre," Mitchell concludes, "you have to be overqualified. As a designer you have to think like an actor or director. They, in turn, have to be conscious of the division and articulation of space." Some designers talk constantly about the collaborative process—Mitchell seldom does, although when talking about design in general he describes "the magic combination when you no longer know who suggested what." It seems to reflect his craftsman-like approach. he has developed no long-standing working relationship with a director—although he has worked several times with Joe Layton and Gene Saks—or with other designers except perhaps costume designer Theoni Aldredge. He works well and easily, however, with almost

everyone he has been teamed with. His ideas come from directorial concepts, he welcomes input from others and freely acknowledges contributions. Yet finally the work is his and his alone. He almost prefers the rush and pressure of tight schedules to the "leisurely" collaborative approach that designers such as Robin Wagner and Eugene Lee have established. Some of his best designs, he notes, have been last-minute jobs. "Designers," he says, "are really the first ones in the trenches."

The Steadfast Tin Soldier (*New York City Ballet, 1976*). *For ballet, Mitchell designs costumes as well as sets.*

# DOUGLAS SCHMIDT

Douglas Schmidt, virtually alone among designers, has revived the spirit of 19th-century spectacle. His hallmark is the ability to work on a large, even monumental, scale whether designing realistic interiors or grand opera. There is a larger-than-life quality to his settings, and along with Robin Wagner and David Mitchell, he is one of the masters of multi-scene designs and moving scenery. Tom Moore, who directed the Schmidt-designed Broadway productions of *Grease* (1972), *Over Here!* (1974) and *Frankenstein* (1981), among others is excited when working with Schmidt because "he is outrageously bold. He can give something size and scale—which is very hard to do with grace in the theatre."

Although Schmidt, like most designers, firmly believes that the setting must serve the overall production—he calls the decor the "physical binder" that holds the ideas together—his scenery has, on several occasions, drawn attention to itself directly. He may be the only designer ever mentioned above Luciano Pavarotti or Placido Domingo in reviews. Martin Bernheimer, music critic of *The Los Angeles Times*, spent the first six paragraphs of his review of the San Francisco Opera's *Samson et Dalila* (1980) which starred Domingo, praising the sets and costumes (by Carrie Robbins), calling it "a smash-bang, razzle-dazzle, sock-it-to-'em spectacular, no-holds-barred doozy of a production. Douglas Schmidt is the hero." The critique in the *Saturday Review* of San Francisco's *Aïda* (1981) was titled "Pavarotti Outdone" and began with a discussion of the set.

Schmidt, by his own admission, is eclectic. He seems equally at home with Verdi or Sam Shepard and has created settings for spaces ranging in size from Radio City Music Hall to the Off Broadway Chelsea Upstairs. His early work with sculptural settings, open stages and material such as wood planks, clearly shows the influence of Ming Cho Lee whom he assisted in the mid–1960s. But his later work, aside from the scale, shows a multiplicity of styles.

I've always felt that one should be eclectic and open emotionally to whatever the situation calls for, and be able to switch gears. Frankly, that's what keeps me interested. At one time, looking back on the body of my work, it didn't seem to hang together real well—it could have been five different designers. I became somewhat concerned about that. But at this point, since I don't really have a strong graphic style that imprints itself on every production, I'm left with what I've got. I just do what I do.

But there is, after all, something that distinguishes Schmidt's kinetic scenery from that of Wagner or Mitchell. Rarely does he opt for the high-tech look (although he proved capable of it in the 1979 Broadway production, *They're Playing Our Song*) and rarely does he create a spare, minimalist decor. Schmidt's stages are usually full, richly detailed, occasionally overwhelming. He exhibits an almost child-like fascination with tricks, gimmicks and wonder-filled images. There is also a painterly quality to his work that does not exist in the designs of most others, and a theatricality associated with 19th-century production styles. It is a quality best summed up by Tom Moore: "In *Frankenstein* we

*Facing page, model for* Over Here! *(Shubert Theatre, 1974). This musical with the Andrews Sisters was Schmidt's first production to use kinetic scenery on a large scale. It incorporated three treadmills, an upstage elevator for the band and seven rear projection screens.*

tried to throw out one marvel after another so that the audience could have the sort of experience you have as a kid of wanting to see something that will constantly surprise and delight."

Related to the imagery is the use of movement and moving parts. The garden set for Maxim Gorky's *Enemies* (Vivian Beaumont Theatre, 1972) revolved to show the set from different angles; *Macbeth* at the American Shakespeare Festival (1973) had a back wall of silver-colored, moving, interlocking sections (and as a result became known as the "stainless-steel *Macbeth*"). For *Agamemnon* (Beaumont, 1977) part of the audience was seated onstage on two bleacher-like structures that glided about the stage from time to time on air casters—devices originally created by NASA to move heavy loads on a cushion of air. The back wall of Brecht and Weill's *Threepenny Opera* set (Beaumont, 1976) moved menacingly toward the audience; the walls of *Stages* by Stuart Ostrow shifted and turned; the set for Neil Simon's *They're Playing Our Song* was described by critic Clive Barnes as "handsomely driving in and out of the stage as if it had a life of its own." The list goes on to include treadmills, flying and crashing airplanes, crashing trains, exploding laboratories, collapsing temples, revolving and winch-driven scenery of all kinds and for *Truckload* (Broadway, 1975)—a play that closed in previews—a real truck that was driven onto the stage directly toward the audience from an alley in back of the theatre. The cab of the truck was redesigned as a huge red piano and as the truck drove on, performer Louis St. Louis was playing the overture on that piano.

Schmidt believes that the scenery in such shows is not only as important as the actors, but, in its own way, the scenery becomes a performer. It is not merely background or an efficient way to denote a scene change, but an integral part of the audience's experience of the play. "Especially in a multi-scene show," he notes, "you have a responsibility to the playwright to help keep the audience involved." The important thing, Schmidt feels, is to design the

transitions, to "design in between the pictures—then the pictures will take care of themselves. I put great effort into devising a scheme that will permit us to get from place to place in as efficient and attractive a manner as possible." Schmidt is, in essence, designing the rhythm and pacing of the show as well as the space.

For Schmidt, the process of working on a show is often more important than the final product. He loves the collaborative experience and his favorite designs are determined largely by the success of the collaboration rather than by any critical judgment. He feels his most successful collaboration was the otherwise ill-fated *Frankenstein*. "I think I came closest to realizing an idea completely on the stage and to feeling the most communication among the creative parts," he explains. Director Tom Moore concurs that the sense of community in that production was the greatest he had ever experienced. "When that family kind of thing happens," Schmidt continues, "when that chemistry happens, everyone is working not only for him or herself but for the production. It becomes a very special thing which may not have so much to do with what ends up onstage. The product comes secondary to the process." That final statement, more than anything else, sums up Schmidt's approach to theatre. Along with the productions directed by Moore, he cherishes his work with director-playwright Des McAnuff on such plays as *The Crazy Locomotive* (Chelsea Upstairs, 1977) and *The Death of von Richtofen as Witnessed from Earth* (New York Shakespeare Festival, 1982), and the work with director Jack O'Brien at the Old Globe in San Diego.

Since the early 1970s he has designed more than two dozen productions with costume designer Carrie Robbins, including all those directed by Tom Moore, and shared his small studio with her for about three years. Robbins attributes their successful collaboration to complementary personalities—she claims to be very disorganized while he is almost compulsively organized (he is the only working designer with a complete record of his designs).

They also seem to share a similar sensibility regarding color and texture and inevitably arrive at compatible designs with a minimal amount of discussion.

Like most designers, Schmidt is vague about the concrete process of design. When offered a project he says he asks himself such questions as, "How do I feel about the piece? What is the production situation? Do I have a shot at achieving what I and the director want to achieve? Is it worth doing emotionally? Financially?" He is not above designing for financial reward alone and offers the Milliken Breakfast Show (1980)—an annual, elaborate, industrial sales show—as proof. As to what constitutes an emotionally appealing play, it is "as simple as, 'do I have a *take* on it?'"

Having agreed to design a production, he has no set working pattern. Sometimes a gut feeling about a play will form in his mind. When this is the case he finds it very difficult to change later. Often he will draw upon ideas he has stored in his memory for possible future use. He notes, for example, that he was impressed with artist Stanley Landsman's infinity boxes—mirror-lined constructions that created infinite reflections of images—and thought, "What if these were built 40 feet wide on a stage?" The idea remained with him for years until he used it for a a disco scene in a production of *Alice* (1978), a musical version of *Alice in Wonderland* produced by Mike Nichols. He built a 40-foot by 30-foot infinity box on the stage by lining the back wall with mirrors and placing two-way mirrors in six foot sections along the front of the stage. As the audience looked through the front mirrors they saw a chorus that had become a "cast of thousands." The show closed in Philadelphia and the mirrors were bought by Studio 54, a then-popular New York disco.

His working process, he says, "is just like everyone else's—sketches, rough drafts, rough model, etc." John Lee Beatty, who worked as Schmidt's assistant, claims that he never saw the creative process: "I would come in the next day and clean up from what he had done the night before and there would be the design." Nor was there much discussion about it, Beatty says. "Designers don't talk about design. It just doesn't come up naturally in

*Long Island Expressway projection for Neil Simon's* They're Playing Our Song *(Imperial Theatre, 1978). Schmidt used 18 projectors in this show. The projections, together with sliding panels, kept it moving at a rapid pace despite its many locales.*

conversation—that's an idealized view. We gossip, or talk about sex."

Beatty does shed some light, however, on Schmidt's day-to-day working process. Schmidt is excellent at drafting, having learned under Ming Cho Lee, and does most of it himself, but he capitalized on Beatty's drawing abilities. As Beatty explains:

A lot of times I would just paint and he would hang over my shoulder and say, 'Make that blue, or make that green, or put an arch there.' Sometimes he would do a pencil rough of a set and then he'd open a book and show me the color scheme, or say 'this drapery should go on this arch,' and I would put it together. He was

always doing a little white model himself which he could do incredibly fast and beautifully. And he did almost all the drafting himself because that's what ends up being built. He was interested in getting the general thing right and then going back and designing the details, unlike Ming who uses a very deliberate process of refinement.

Schmidt claims with a grin that his interest in theatre was sparked at the age of eight when he saw the magician Harry Blackstone, Sr. at the Taft Theatre in Cincinnati. In high school, Schmidt did some acting and directing and designed several plays. "Every designer starts out to be an actor," says Schmidt. "It's the most immediate manifestation of

*Left, preliminary sketch for the laboratory in* Frankenstein *(Palace Theatre, 1981); right, the set as it appeared onstage. The production was a tour de force of scenic and special effects (by Bran Ferren) that thrilled preview audiences but did not appease critics—it became one of the most spectacular flops in Broadway history. In the penultimate scene, Dr. Frankenstein's lab collapsed in a conflagration of lightning, flames, smoke and rubble. The curtain descended in the midst of the chaos, only to rise a mere five seconds later on a totally bare stage.*

this racket." In high school he also saw a touring production of the Folies Bergère and remembers that while it was "the most threadbare and cheaply done production you can imagine . . . there was a sense of wonder to it." He contrasts this to many lavish Las Vegas revues that have not "a single moment of magic."

He entered Boston University in 1961 as a directing major, but at a departmental meeting in which students were divided according to their discipline, he noted the great number of actors and directors and the few designers. He decided that design would provide a better, more personal edu-

cation and studied with Raymond Sovey and Horace Armistead, his first contacts with professional design.

In the summer of 1963, Schmidt returned to his home town of Cincinnati and happened to be in the right place at the right time when a scene designer was needed at the Playhouse in the Park. He designed there that summer, returning in 1965 as principal designer and later consulted on the construction of its new theatre built in 1966.

Boston University was in the process of shifting from a professionally oriented program to an academic one and Schmidt dropped out in 1964, the

spring of his third year. He sent out some 40 letters seeking employment in summer stock and his application to the New York Shakespeare Festival was received by Martin Aronstein who passed it on to Ming Cho Lee, who hired him as an assistant.

It was in Ming's studio that my point of view began to develop and my appreciation for the craft evolved. I learned all of my technique in that studio. It would be hard to find a better teacher of craft than Ming. He, more than anyone I can think of, has an eye for proportion and division of space, and that is what I came away with more than anything else. His style is so impressive and strong—he has such a sure hand—that it is hard for a young designer not to come away from him imprinted to some degree. Many of us who were working there at that time felt Ming over our shoulder for years

after. With the passage of time, I've become much more objective and can really use what I learned rather than simply reacting to it. I owe him a lot.

When Schmidt first came to New York, he also took courses with designer and scene painter Lester Polakov. At that time, Polakov's studio was the only place in New York that specifically prepared people for the Union exams. Schmidt now teaches there himself and is on the board of directors.

Schmidt spent four years working with Lee in the mid–1960s while continuing to design productions at Cincinnati, other resident professional theatres including the New York Shakespeare Festival, and Off Broadway. In 1969 he became resident designer for the Repertory Theatre of Lincoln Center at the Vivian Beaumont Theatre and designed 18 productions in their two theatres over the next four years—

*Collage-rendering for the "Stainless Steel" Macbeth (American Shakespeare Festival, 1973). The background consisted of interlocking parts painted to look like steel, that opened and closed to create different configurations.*

until the demise of the company. He also continued to design other productions including two unmemorable ones on Broadway.

These early productions, although showing a variety of influences, were clearly influenced by Ming Cho Lee, and in their use of materials, images and space were definitely products of their time. A common element in many of them was the use of raw-wood planking for the stage floor. Because so many were done on thrust stages, the settings tended to be sculptural with large, open spaces defined by fragmentary scenery in vertical contrast to the horizontal floor. Productions such as *Camino Real* (Cincinnati Playhouse in the Park, 1968) and *The Goodwoman of Setzuan* (Repertory Theatre of Lincoln Center, 1970) used pipe frame and wood beam scaffolding—a trademark of Lee's New York Shakespeare Festival productions. There was also a moody, almost ethereal quality about many of these early works that was lacking or different in later designs.

Schmidt's first Broadway hit—and to date, most financially successful show—was *Grease*. The final design was a sort of junk collage of 1950s images enclosed by a false proscenium lined with the actors' high school yearbook pictures. But that was a design that evolved throughout the production period. Director Tom Moore said that as the play went into previews it was as if there were something missing, and he credits Schmidt with analyzing the problem and solving it scenically. Originally there had been a pictorial collage but it was inadequate. As Moore describes it, "It was a rather formal-looking set with several large photographs of the '50s on it." They felt that the solution was to create a greater sense of chaos. For his part, Moore transformed the carefully controlled scene changes into chaotic activity. Schmidt added pictures everywhere. "There were pictures on everything," said Moore. "When a flat rolled on, there was a picture of the burger palace behind it." Schmidt also realized that the size of the stage was making focus difficult. Although it was a musical, it was basically a small show. In order to tighten it up, "to pull it in," as Moore says, Schmidt added the picture-collage proscenium.

Subsequent productions included Tennessee Williams' *A Streetcar Named Desire* (1973) in which the house became a fragmented structure, sitting like an island in the center of the vast, unmasked Beaumont stage, surrounded by ramped sidewalks and exposed light booms; *Veronica's Room* (Broadway, 1973) which consisted of an interior painted in deep, rich colors and created a sense of monumentality and intimacy at the same time; and *Over Here!* (Broadway, 1974), for which he received a Drama Desk Award.

The stage for *Over Here!* was framed by three arched portals reminiscent of the old Paramount Theatre, on which were painted images, faces and logos evocative of the 1940s—FDR, Benny Good-

*Rendering for* Chaplin *(Dorothy Chandler Pavilion, 1983). Schmidt created 42 scenes for the musical about Charlie Chaplin, with a simple but effective use of drops and projections on scrims. The sets were praised as some of Schmidt's finest, but the show was a failure and never made it to New York.*

man, Dumbo, Superman, Betty Grable—a sort of toned down version of the *Grease* framework, painted in a poster style and airbrush technique typical of the period. The portals were made of translucent muslin and framed with aluminum. The stage had four levels and three main playing areas with three treadmills. There was also an upstage elevator for the band. The scenery was augmented by seven rear-projection screens to create the image of a coast-to-coast train trip. Because the train journey was meant to evoke the mobilized state of the country at the time, Schmidt thought of the show as "one giant segue." The treadmill idea seemed to be a logical technique for moving from one scene to the next. "The audience, in a sense," Schmidt explains, "was riding along parallel to it. The treadmill became a participant in the choreography of the show. I suppose that goes back to my wanting to be an actor. I don't much like going to the theatre and not having it draw me in."

*The Threepenny Opera* (New York Shakespeare Festival at Lincoln Center, 1976) was staged by avant-garde director Richard Foreman and provoked strong feelings among spectators. They either loved it or hated it; few came away unopinionated. Foreman incorporated many of his own visual trademarks: objects with no apparent relation to the play such as strings, Victorian lamps, and frames—all familiar to Foreman's Off-Off Broadway audiences. Two scenic elements dominated the stage: lamps with large brown shades (like oversized pool hall lights) that were flown in and out over the front of the stage, sometimes obstructing the view from the balcony seats; and a large wall with clerestory windows at the rear of the stage that was vaguely suggestive of a Victorian warehouse or train station. The wall moved downstage toward the audience at times—an effect Schmidt recreated more playfully and spectacularly in *Frankenstein*. Although the Beaumont has a deep thrust stage, the set was symmetrical and very definitely proscenium-like in its frontality. Schmidt explained the apparently contradictory arrangement of space:

It's very hard to do an essentially asymmetrical, therefore Romantic, design for a play that wants to confront the audience—really keep them at arm's length. There was no attempt at illusion in the production at all, and it became obvious early on that this would have to be quite formal and quite symmetrical. The only way to do that is to make it proscenium style, and once you've done that, it means that the actors are acting "out there" and the wall is back here. It was not the ideal house for that show. There were compromises we had to make.

John Lee Beatty says that he admires Schmidt for his "bravery in things like *The Threepenny Opera* where he would make a set that was not going to be pretty. That's quite a commitment for a designer."

Clearly, much of the design was Foreman's idea. Schmidt saw it as his job to "get that aesthetic on the stage." Although his work with Foreman is not collaborative the way it is with Moore or O'Brien (he also designed *Stages*, 1978, for Foreman), he trusts Foreman's judgment implicitly. He feels that he is not only a good director, but "one of the best *designers* working in the American theatre"—a view essentially echoed by designer Santo Loquasto.

One of Schmidt's favorite productions was *The Crazy Locomotive* which featured a train wreck and marked his first collaboration with Des McAnuff. The play, written in 1923 by Polish playwright Stanislaw Witkiewicz, involves several bizarre characters and an anarchistic attempt to hijack a train. The result is a high-speed collision of two locomotives—difficult to achieve on a small Off Broadway stage! The train as described by Schmidt was a "kind of Russian Constructivist idea of a locomotive—rather abstract with moving wheels, streamlined pipe construction and dials that whirled." The scenic structure was built on a turntable which was not apparent to the audience. For the climax, a scrim was pulled across the front of the stage and a five- or

*Facing page, Gorky's* Enemies *(Vivian Beaumont Theatre, 1972). Schmidt turned a realistic interior into a surrealistic vision with the oversized upstage window and the collage of faces peering in.*

six-second film of a real collision was projected on that. During that sequence the turntable revolved, removing the center section of the train while leaving the two sides and bringing around a whole locomotive on end with buckled tracks, smashed parts and people lying all about. As the film sequence ended the lighting allowed the image of the wreck to bleed through the scrim. The surprise of seeing the debris of the collision brought applause at every performance.

*Agamemnon*, directed by Andrei Serban, brought Schmidt a Joseph Maharam Foundation award. Interestingly, this was one of his most minimal designs. Except for a few props and hanging scenic pieces to create a primitive, ritualistic mood, the set was a bare stage on which two seating tiers were located. The onstage audience faced the regular seats of the Beaumont Theatre, allowing the spectators a performer's-eye-view of the auditorium and backstage. Periodically, air casters were turned on and stagehands moved the two seating banks to different positions. "What we were really doing," explains Schmidt, "was exploring new configurations for that space. We wanted to see what would happen if we played with the audience and what would happen to the dynamics of the space." For the onstage spectators the result was probably little more than a gimmick, and the formal qualities of the theatre still dominated, but it was a daring experiment for an essentially commercial production.

*They're Playing Our Song* is jokingly referred to by Schmidt as the first "high tech" musical. Eighteen projectors were used to create images of "realistic stuff like windows and hospital corridors . . . but all rendered in a slick, contemporary, graphic style." The projections, in keeping with Schmidt's concern for scenery as a rhythmic element, were intended to abet the rapid flow of the show as it moved from a disco to a recording studio to the Long Island Expressway to a *trompe l'oeil* Manhattan apartment. The projections, aided by sliding panels, kept the set in almost constant motion.

Bernard Slade's *Romantic Comedy* (Broadway,

1979) is of interest because of its contrast to some of Schmidt's earlier work. As the title suggests, it was an old-fashioned sentimental tribute to a bygone form of theatre. Schmidt created a simple box set that he saw as "an affectionate salute to that style of theatre." For inspiration he looked to his first teacher, Raymond Sovey, "a master of the form," who had done such classics as *Arsenic and Old Lace.* Schmidt's watchword was, "Don't do anything that Ray Sovey wouldn't do."

The production of Saint-Saëns' *Samson et Dalila* at the San Francisco Opera was, in effect, a prelude to the epic *Frankenstein.* Schmidt enjoys opera and feels that it differs from legitimate theatre primarily in its mechanics. "It tends to be far less agonized over than legitimate theatre and has far more to do with stage pictures—space for crowds to mass." *Samson et Dalila* "started from a pictorial point of

view" and was an attempt to emulate the style of 19th-century grand opera but with "enough tongue-in-cheek to keep us in 1980—without lapsing into camp." The basic look of the show was derived from 19th-century artist Alma Tedema. The spirit of the production was captured in *The Los Angeles Times* review which noted, "It fuses Art Nouveau opulence with Art Deco vulgarity with Victorian trivia with Cecil B. DeMille extravagance with operatic hoopty-doo."

The climax of the opera—indeed, about the only thing that happens—is the destruction of the Temple in the final moments. Schmidt created an illusion of great havoc, when in actuality there was little scenic movement. The Temple columns were constructed of Styrofoam blocks stacked on top of each other. They were held in position by a cable through the center of each column. When the ten-

*Witkiewicz' The Crazy Locomotive (Chelsea Theater Center, 1977). Schmidt describes this as a "Russian Constructivist idea of a locomotive." The climax of the play was a high-speed collision between two locomotives. The set was built on a turntable; as the moment approached, a scrim dropped down, a five-second film of a collision was projected, and the set revolved to reveal tangled wreckage as the scrim rose.*

sion on the cable was released, the columns collapsed—a device used in children's toys. In the fly space above the stage were two black mesh nets to which were attached what appeared to be architectural debris—chunks of plaster, sections of statues, and the like. These were lit in silhouette and lowered at different speeds to create an illusion of depth—those falling slower appeared to be farther away. The stage was filled with smoke from insect foggers and there was a flash of fire, all of which created diversions and obscured the mechanics of the effect. As the debris was falling the curtain was descending so that there was no time for the audience to think about, or study the effect. On opening night someone in the audience screamed as the Temple crumbled. That moment remains one of Schmidt's favorites in the theatre.

*Samson et Dalila* was followed a few months later by *Frankenstein*. When the show closed after one performance at a loss of over $2 million, it was the most colossal failure in Broadway history. Schmidt, Tom Moore and the others involved in the production were utterly astonished and baffled by the virulent critical response. They had all spent more than two years evolving the show and believed strongly in it. Furthermore, preview audiences had been wildly enthusiastic. So confident were they in this production that Schmidt suggested that his friends wait to see it until after opening night.

*Frankenstein* encompassed virtually every technique and gimmick that Schmidt had previously used. "The intention," says Schmidt, "was to render a 19th-century gothic pictorial treatment of the play, not that far removed from the movie—a slightly different sensibility—extremely Victorian, while maintaining the fluidity of a musical comedy." Eight sets had to move on and off the stage through 13 scenes that included the North Pole, a graveyard, a sitting room, a bedroom, a cottage exterior and interior, a forest and the laboratory. The Palace Theatre has a relatively shallow stage and little wing space so simply getting from one scene to another was a major design problem. Schmidt

devised a half-turntable wagon that could revolve or move on and off the stage. Twenty-five electric winches were used.

The design incorporated a false proscenium and isolated scenic pieces "floating" in stage space. Bran Ferren, well known for his work in both film and theatre, created the special effects for the show. The smoke and other effects were used not only within scenes but to aid in transitions. Certain sets, for instance, were revealed by revolving the turntable while hidden in a cloud of fog. The cottage was built on a revolve, with the exterior on one side and the interior on the other (an idea Schmidt would repeat in *Porgy and Bess*). The laboratory rolled all the way downstage from the back. Moore says, "It was such a massive piece that it provided an excitement all its own." The whole show, continues Moore, "had this colossal scale and perspective so that you were overwhelmed by it rather than being comfortable with it."

As with *Samson et Dalila*, the climax was a scene of destruction—this time of Frankenstein's laboratory—enhanced by Ferren's effects. The principle

*Collage-rendering for Schmidt's first hit,* Grease *(Eden Theatre, 1972). The picture collage proscenium was a late addition to the design which helped tighten the focus on what was essentially a small show.*

was essentially the same as for the opera, but Schmidt did not want to simply repeat himself. So in this case, within five seconds of the curtain falling, it rose again on a completely bare stage! The back wall of the laboratory set was hinged and controlled by a counterweight system. As the explosion occurred, the wall fell backwards. Meanwhile, two 40-foot high backdrops, textured and appliqued with foam to suggest rubble, blocks and girders, began to descend. They started simultaneously but descended at different speeds, and they were timed with the house curtain. Chunks of black foam rubber resembling debris were wired together and blown about the stage with air mortars. Smoke and pyrotechnic effects filled the stage and an effects projector threw images on the swirling smoke and scenery. As the front curtain reached the stage floor, the back wall of the set returned to its upright position and the platform holding the laboratory set rolled offstage. The debris drops were raised back up and the foam debris—all wired together—was easily hauled offstage by a single stage hand. Thus the front curtain could rise within seconds on a bare stage.

*New York Times* drama critic Frank Rich, like most of his colleagues, could only see the show as a failed piece of literature, and in an article a month after the play closed said that "this show's magic tricks were actually pointless from both an artistic and commercial standpoint. If the script had been fun, no one would have demanded electronic effects as well." Only Michael Feingold of the *Village Voice* grasped the sensibility of the production. Referring to the scenery Feingold stated:

With the exception of the projected snowstorm and the electric flashes, [the sets] generally belong to the days when Dion Boucicault was barnstorming. . . . The wittiest [effects]—the horse-drawn carriage that comes on and off without showing us the horses, and the trompe l'oeil french windows that turn out to be practical—belong . . . to the set designer Douglas

Schmidt, whose scenes all allude cleverly to Victorian magazine illustrations. (*Village Voice*, January 7–13, 1981.)

Despite the apparent historical references, Schmidt claims to have done little period research, either into style or production methods, but relied instead on a knowledge of the original film and a general gothic feeling that was desired. "The scale wanted to be in keeping with the mythological nature of it," he explains. He acknowledges, however, that "we were going for every gag in the book, reaching as far back as *Uncle Tom's Cabin* for illusionistic effects." The overall visual quality, however, evolved from studying autochromes—an early version of color photography—an image first suggested by Carrie Robbins. Both Schmidt and Robbins incorporated the sepia tones into the *Frankenstein* palette.

In general, Schmidt does little detailed research,

*Facing page, Des McAnuff's* **The Death of von Richtofen as Witnessed from Earth** *(New York Shakespeare Festival, 1982). On the small stage of the Newman Theatre, Schmidt succeeded in creating several acting areas as well as von Richtofen's plane flying on and off, floating bodies, explosions and scenes of war, a floating piano, a levitating saddle, a bathtub and doors that closed automatically. Above, Thornton Wilder's* The Skin of Our Teeth *at the Cincinnati Playhouse in the Park (1966).*

but he does have a knowledge of art history and period style which is most essential for the kinds of shows he does. His small studio overlooking Times Square contains a good collection of books on art, furniture, clothing and accessories. Research, for Schmidt, is usually a process of absorbing a particular sensibility. For *Grease*, anyone who had gone to high school in the 1950s was asked to bring in their yearbooks and the style and imagery of these sources helped shape the look of the show.

Following *Frankenstein*, Schmidt designed *Aïda* at the San Francisco Opera and, like *Samson et Dalila*, it was sheer 19th-century spectacle. Schmidt's next major production was *The Death of von Richtofen as Witnessed from Earth* (New York Shakespeare Festival, 1982). The play, written and directed by Des McAnuff, uses Baron von Richtofen as a focal point for exploring the political tides of Germany at the end of World War I. The production was originally scheduled for the outdoor Delacorte Theater and McAnuff envisioned a spectacular recreation of the atmosphere of a flying circus. But scheduling problems and technical complexities caused it to be shifted to the Public Theater where it was done in much more intimate surroundings. "I don't think I've ever had a production that's had so many specific difficulties and physical requirements, not even *Frankenstein*," exclaims Schmidt.

The production, designed to show several locales simultaneously, included an airplane flying on and off the stage and ultimately crashing, bodies being blown up and rising into the sky (and others floating down), a "floating" piano, onstage explosions in fox-holes, a hot-air balloon, a levitating saddle, doors that opened and closed automatically and a host of other effects. The Newman Theater has no fly space, so all the flying had to be dealt with horizontally, creating more technical problems. There was no budget for an effects person so Schmidt worked out the problems in conjunction with the Festival's technical directors Mervyn Haines and Andrew Mihok, rigging expert Peter Feller, Jr. and lighting designer Richard Nelson. The result, as

with McAnuff's production of *The Crazy Locomotive*, was a technical *tour de force* created within extreme financial and physical limitations. As much as Schmidt loves the possibilities of opera with its huge budgets and technical facilities, he seems to relish the challenge of a production like *von Richtofen* whose fee, he notes, did not even cover the rent on his studio during the time he spent on it.

*Porgy and Bess* (Arie Crown Theatre, Chicago and Radio City Music Hall, 1983) was another large-scale show with scenic problems. The first difficulty was that it was a recreation of the Houston Opera's 1976 production, and though most of the people involved in the production had also been in Houston, Schmidt was a newcomer. The second problem was the scale of Radio City Music Hall. Schmidt notes that it is impossible for performers not to be dwarfed on that stage—they are literally a block-and-a-half away from some spectators. The solution is to build the scenery in human scale—to make everything life-size or just a bit smaller. Thus, Schmidt had to build a small town on the stage, as well as a mangrove swamp.

Finally, the production was going to tour after its run at Radio City, so the scenery had to be transportable and capable of fitting into theatres one third the size. As a result, Schmidt could not use the wonderful machinery of the Music Hall, and had to work out scene changes without the use of a deck or understage machinery. It also meant that the scenery had to be shallow—Serena's house was only six feet deep—which seemed strange on that stage.

Unlike some of Schmidt's other productions, there was no stylization. Given the size of the setting, he went for detailed realism right down to stains and cracks on the buildings.

Schmidt once said that despite the pleasures of working in regional theatre and television, Broadway was his favorite. "Broadway is where you get the chance to do it for real. There's no way I would have had the chance to do *Frankenstein* full out anywhere in the world but Broadway. That's why I like it. I enjoy the energy. We're all there for one reason—the production. We're not part of a season, we're not part of a company. We don't have responsibilities beyond this production. You can hand-pick the people you are working with, or they pick you and I really like that. There's more freedom in it for me." Nonetheless, given the diminished activity on Broadway in the 1980s and the recent trend to develop plays outside New York, much of Schmidt' work in the post-*Frankenstein* period has been on the West Coast.

The rapidly escalating costs of theatre production are also placing constraints on the types of shows that Schmidt does best. Despite a seeming trend in the late 1970s and early 1980s toward a revival of spectacle, minimalism and simplicity are economically more feasible and attractive. And with the example of *Frankenstein* still fresh in their memories,

producers are reluctant to take chances on productions that, whatever their appeal, do not cater to the literary tastes of the New York critics. Schmidt finished the 1983 season with a production called *Chaplin* that closed after its tryout at the Dorothy Chandler Pavilion in Los Angeles. The play consisted of 42 scenes created by drops, projections on scrims and elaborate lighting by Ken Billington. Schmidt's designs got rave reviews, but not the show. There was a time when the spectacle alone might have made the show successful on Broadway, but no money could be raised to bring it to New York.

Schmidt remains optimistic, however. Even before the *Chaplin* plans and sketches were filed away, he began work on a new Broadway musical, a large-scale revival and a play in London. And they all had Schmidt's favorite ingredient: "Lots of scenery."

King John *(Delacorte Theater, 1967). Although the design shows the influence of Ming Cho Lee, it is unusual in its open background revealing the lake.*

# ROBIN WAGNER

By almost any standard, Robin Wagner is the most successful stage designer of the contemporary American theatre. To review his credits since the late 1960s is to read a list of Broadway's greatest musical hits, including *Hair* (1968), *A Chorus Line* (1976), *On the 20th Century* (1979), *42nd Street* (1980) and *Dreamgirls* (1983). This list also gives some sense of his financial success. While other designers frantically churn out show after show at theatres all across the country—at least in part for their own survival—Wagner has designed an average of no more than two or three plays per season since the mid–1970s, while taking time off to travel, write and explore new avenues of creativity such as designing theatres, houses and restaurants.

Wagner is a warm, friendly, generous man with a quiet sense of humor. Despite the fact that he has a distinctive way of using space, movement, mechanics and materials, and despite his association with scenographic spectacle and style-setting decor, he rejects the concept of designer-dominated productions, praising instead thorough collaboration. "Theatre is a collaborative art form," he said in an article in *Theatre Design & Technology*. "It's the process of merging visions into some kind of oneness. It's like fibre optic strands that eventually throw a great beam of light—but only because they are made of a series of minute little channels of energy focused in the same direction." At various times in his career, Wagner has successfully collaborated with directors Edwin Sherin, Tom O'Horgan, Gower Champion and, most recently, Michael Bennett. And on the Bennett productions, a whole collaborative team—a creative ensemble—has developed that includes lighting designer Tharon Musser, costume designer Theoni Aldredge and Bennett's co-producer and co-choreographer Bob Avian.

These successful productions have allowed Michael Bennett to purchase a building on lower Broadway that now houses studios for Wagner and Aldredge, as well as rehearsal spaces, dance studios, a costume construction shop, the offices of American Ballet Theatre and, eventually, two theatre spaces. Wagner's corner loft studio with two walls of windows may be the most spacious design studio in New York—it could contain the studios of every other designer in this book with room to spare.

Wagner accidentally stumbled into theatre design and has had no formal training. As a result, he has never formulated an approach or sense of a "right way to do it." He is willing to take risks and try almost anything. When a director or producer asks for something complicated or outrageous, Wagner's response is generally to say, "Sure, we can do that," and then figure out how—frequently with the help of theatre technicians Peter Feller and, more recently, Peter Feller, Jr., whose shops constructed the mechanical apparatus for *Jesus Christ Superstar*, *42nd Street*, *Dreamgirls* and others.

Wagner recalls that as a child, what interested him in theatre were the "magical moments." As a result, he approaches his work by asking: "How do you do something that makes you hold your breath for a second? How do you make the hair rise on the backs of people's necks? By what alchemy are these things possible?" (*Theatre Crafts*, Nov/Dec 1973.) It

*Facing page*, Dreamgirls *(Imperial Theatre, 1981). In order to achieve the "high-tech" look appropriate for the world of the recording studio, and to facilitate smooth changes in rapidly shifting scenes, Wagner resorted to light towers and bridges. Because of the seemingly constant movement of the towers, which seemed to dance, audiences had an impression of lots of scenery, but the set was really very minimal.*

is partly for this reason that Wagner dislikes, and seldom designs, classics and revivals. "I'd rather do a new show that expresses our age and our problems and in some way holds up a 20th-century mirror," he says. While agreeing that there should be an historical or "museum" theatre to preserve the past, he would rather see than do that sort of theatre.

There are three basic elements to Wagner's style. The first is his use of space: Wagner's scenery is sculptural. "I hate painted scenery. It's trying to pretend that it's something real but no matter how beautiful it is, it's always lifeless to me." But when trying to evoke a certain style, as in *42nd Street*, he is capable of creating striking painted backdrops. He views the stage space as a cubic volume in which all the space is to be used. As a result, many of his sets are vertical and multi-leveled, including towers, structures and bridges. As he describes it, the whole theatre is a volume of space in which the audience is looking down one end—"somewhat like looking into a tunnel." Describing the use of space in *Dreamgirls*, in which space and locale were altered primarily through the almost constant movement of five light towers and a light bridge, Wagner noted that the "cube" of the stage space and the relationship of the stage to the audience was constantly altered. "By changing the size and shape of the cube," he explained, "you feel like you're in a different place. In reality, we have changed the relation of the cube to the audience so their perception of it is changed. It's like having a cinematic long shot. By dropping the bridges and tapering the towers, we made a 'tunnel' that appears much longer to the eye than it really is. Reverse that and it turns around—the stage opens in the other direction. So we're playing with the perspective of the audience but in a sculptural sense; we're changing spatial relationships."

The second element in Wagner's style is movement, which, as the *Dreamgirls* example indicates, is closely tied to spatial perception. He has said that he designs dynamics, not places. "A play or a musical," he explains, "is not a series of places. It is a matter of how you perceive the event moving in its sequence, or rather, an event that is a number of events. A scene is an event, a meeting is an event, a phone call is an event. How these events are sequenced is more important than telling the audience where they are. The bridging of scenes or events can help tell the story. How something moves in these 'in-between' moments can tell you as much as the place at which the movement arrives. Certainly we know that from dance."

The movement of Wagner's sets has been described as "dancing scenery" and this is a more apt analogy than the more frequent "cinematic." Wagner's scenery is cinematic only insofar as it moves and segues smoothly from moment to moment. But it is different from, say, David Mitchell's scenery, which takes the spectator from specific locale to specific locale and often duplicates particular types of moving camera shots. Wagner's kinetic scenery tends toward abstract or pure movement. While his scenery may "track," it is usually for an almost formal alteration of spectator perceptions, not simply to create an alternative visual point of view.

Because so much of the effect of a Wagner set is in the movement, it is sometimes startling when looking at photographs of his productions to see how little scenery is there, or how it blends into the background. "You see the scenery when you don't see the actors," explains Michael Bennett, "and when you see the actors, in an interesting way, you don't see the scenery. When you look at *Chorus Line* and *Dreamgirls*, that becomes clear. You go, 'Wow!' about the scenery when it is changing for eight seconds—not a minute-and-a-half, mind you—and you know where you are. And yet, there is nothing more out there than you need to see."

The final ingredient is his use of materials. Although Wagner did not invent the use of mylar for mirrors in *A Chorus Line* and *Ballroom*, he certainly popularized it. Other materials he has used to great effect have ranged from chrome and formica in *On the 20th Century* to bathroom tiles and bagels in the

1972 *Lenny*. Although Wagner has never created a design around a particular material he has discovered—nor has he purposely sought out unusual materials—he does not rely on standard theatrical materials to create images. "When I have a show in my head, I'm always looking for something that reflects the play—the basic nature of the show. Certain textures and substances are very expressive. I think that if I were a sculptor or an artist really interested in the nature of materials, I might create a work based on a material. But I'm not. I'm interested in the plays, in being excited, in having something revealed."

Wagner was born in San Francisco in 1933 and, because his father was connected with the Coast Guard, grew up in light houses. He saw little theatre as a child because, as he wryly notes, "there's not much theatre in light houses." But his father was an engineer, so he learned about drafting and building, and his mother had been a concert pianist in New Zealand "so there was always music and a sensibility of the arts around." After high school in San Francisco, he went to the California School of Fine Arts (1952–54) with dreams of working for Walt Disney. While there, someone asked him to run lights for a production at the Theatre Arts Colony. When it was discovered that he was an art student, he was asked to design sets for the Golden Gate

*42nd Street (Winter Garden Theatre, 1980), the musical based on the Busby Berkeley movie. The set employed five turntables, five tracks and four revolving stage towers as well as elegant painted drops—an unusual element for Wagner. This scene used a revolving unit reflected in mirrors at the sides of the stage.*

Opera Workshop and a group called Contemporary Dancers. (In various interviews, Wagner has given slightly different versions of his beginnings in theatre. In Lynn Pecktal's *Designing and Painting for the Theatre* he claims to have begun by answering an ad for a set designer for the Opera Workshop on a lark.) This led to designing sets for the young and innovative Actors' Workshop headed by Jules Irving and Herbert Blau (the group that ultimately became the Repertory Theatre of Lincoln Center in 1965).

In those early days, he just did pretty much what the directors wanted because he had little idea of

what stage design should be. He was supporting himself designing window displays. "Theatre design was so different from sculpture or painting," he says, "that it was very revealing to me. I was learning something that I really knew nothing about." Also, since much of his early work was for dance—he also designed for the San Francisco Ballet—his designs tended to be minimal and semi-abstract. Designing for these companies also entailed building everything himself or with minimal help so he learned a lot through trial and error. When road companies came through San Francisco he would

*Berlioz's* The Trojans *at the Vienna State Opera (1976), directed by Tom O'Horgan. The horse rolled toward the audience from some 80 feet upstage, and then "exploded" as all the armor plates turned out to be shields held by Greek warriors. The spectacular production was not well received by the more traditional Viennese spectators.*

often go backstage to see how things were constructed.

When he began to work with the Actors' Workshop, Herbert Blau "brainwashed him," as Wagner puts it, giving him vast quantities of reading material for each production—not on design, but background material on the play itself. This began Wagner's involvement in the concept of the production, an involvement he maintains to this day. Wagner notes that for their 1957 production of Samuel Beckett's *Waiting for Godot*, for instance, Blau "made me read everything that Beckett had ever written: all the novels, every script, every line, everything. Then we'd sit and talk about it for hours. So the design became a kind of evolutionary thing—trying to understand what really had to be on the stage to make the play work." Bennett approaches collaboration the same way. "Robin is in on any project I work on from day one," he says. "I discuss it with him the same way I would with actors—not only the plot and the sequence of scenes, but the subtext of the play, what I want to achieve, what we've done before and don't want to do, and where it is we want to go."

The production of *Godot* was eventually taken to New York and the Brussels World's Fair. After that, Wagner remained in New York "beating on doors" because he had virtually no professional connections. He supported himself painting in scenic studios. Over the next few years he designed at dinner and winter stock theatres in New Jersey and did more than 20 Off Broadway shows while assisting designers Ben Edwards and Oliver Smith.

"Ben was doing highly precise interiors," explains Wagner. "He would dress the sets to within an inch of their lives; he cared about every detail including scratches on the wall around the light plates. The realism was extraordinary—it was almost like photorealism. I learned from him that no wall is ever flat and no door is ever straight." Wagner also learned his theatre drafting from a long-time Edwards assistant.

The work with Smith was very different. Wagner describes his approach as "a modular system—everything was either on an axis, or modular or it was 30–60–90 degrees. His system allowed him to do musicals that could basically fit into any theatre. It had to do with how they looked as opposed to the problems of theatre solving, so his shows always had an 'Oliver Smith look.' I probably learned more about musicals from Oliver than anybody," states Wagner. He also worked with Smith on designing restaurants.

While working at a winter stock theatre in Totowa, New Jersey in 1960, Wagner met Ed Sherin, who was acting in a play there. Sherin was going to Milwaukee to direct Shaw's *Major Barbara* at the Fred Miller Theatre and began to talk with Wagner about production ideas. "I was discussing it with Robin," remembers Sherin, "and I said, 'I want a set where everything can be walked on or sat on.' He liked that idea. Out of that came a spontaneous and exciting working relationship. The result was really an extraordinarily simple but brilliant design that was conceived, I think, by both of us." There were

*Rendering for* And the Wind Blows *(1959). This was Wagner's first Off Broadway production. The romantic, poetic qualities, warm colors and painterly style contrast sharply with the work for which he is best known today.*

no funds to bring Wagner out to Milwaukee so he designed the play in New York and mailed the plans to Sherin, who supervised construction. These were still pioneer days in resident professional theatre, and large production budgets and technical staffs just didn't exist. Wagner points out that Sherin's ability to supervise the design is typical of all the good directors he has worked with. "They know what the design will do and what it won't. They're not at all foggy about the stage; they're technically as good as most designers."

When Sherin went to Arena Stage as associate director in 1964, Wagner joined him and remained as principal designer for three years. Sherin believes that it was Wagner's experiences there that shaped his style of kinetic scenery and three-dimensional design in later years. Their first collaboration there was *Dark of the Moon* by Howard Richardson and William Berney, and it had a significant impact on the Arena's production style for years to come. Prior to this production, designs for the Arena tended to be simple and spare. Artistic director Zelda Fichandler explains that, "We always designed space. We treated it as a cube with the floors, the backdrops and the kinetic sense of forces coming towards the center and moving out from the center. But we didn't use that much scenery." Wagner filled the space with scenery—platforms, ramps, Constructivist creations, bridges. Suddenly, the possibilities exploded. Wagner's work at the Arena established a style that future designers and directors followed or reacted to. "Robin had a major influence," says Fichandler.

Sherin says that the impetus for the *Dark of the Moon* set was a desire to explore the full three-dimensionality of the space. They removed part of the stage floor to create another 10 feet of vertical space (an approach which has since become fairly common in the Arena). In order to use the height, a bridge was built across the vomitory that spanned, in Sherin's estimation, 90 feet across a 35-foot vertical height. "One person talking to another across that space was something extraordinary," he claims.

For Wagner, this and subsequent plays forced him to deal with space and surfaces in a new way because the demands of that theatre space (the "cube" as Fichandler calls it) were so different from what he had worked with. "The floor became a very important element," he notes. "It almost became like a cyclorama. Here we had another dimension that we could carve into." Fichandler remembers that he frequently "extended the space by taking that neutral cube and filling it up in various ways—torturing the space and elongating it by using the vomitories and building platforms in and over."

During his three years there, Wagner continually explored the possibilities of the Arena space. "The Arena wasn't very old at the time," remembers Wagner, "and I think every show I did there was a major learning experience because we weren't doing anything that anyone had any experience with—including us." The second play he did there was Brecht's *Galileo* (1964). Sherin was strongly influenced by the work of the Berliner Ensemble that he had seen in London in 1956, and the Brecht model figured strongly in the *Galileo* design. Between his work with Blau and his work with Sherin, Wagner's formative period was heavily influenced by Brechtian aesthetics.

His next major influence was director Tom O'Horgan. "Tom had a freeing impact on my view of the theatre because he was not the least bit interested in any convention. When we did *Hair*, he was interested in making the moments come to life. It was not about creating the illusion of some other place."

Ming Cho Lee had designed the original version of *Hair* at the New York Shakespeare Festival's Public Theater as a collage of contemporary images, but this was apparently too "designed" for O'Horgan's image of the play. There were also changes in producers which led to a different creative staff when the play was done on Broadway. O'Horgan says that all he wanted was a "deck and a rake." "Tom was looking to do the most *undesigned* show that he could do," remembers Wagner.

I'd just come out of the Arena at that time and we met and started talking about the show. It turned into a really silly conversation about all the things we could do that were unconventional or anti-conventional and about how to make the whole theatre into a playing space. He never did say, 'You have the job.' I just started building it—I built a lot of it in a garage. It just started by talking and being a little insane. We were all hippies then.

The result was an essentially bare stage with some pipe-scaffold towers—including a "totem pole" scaffold covered with icons of American popular culture ranging from a Coke bottle to a Santa Claus face. Ironically, it used Ming Cho Lee's design vocabulary of scaffolding and collage, but without Lee's sensibility. Proportion and symmetry were seemingly abandoned in favor of the freewheeling, chaotic, almost vulgar style that typified Wagner's work at the time. Just as the play was a radical break with the narrative musicals of the past, Wagner's design was a break with the pictorial and prettified scenery associated with Broadway musicals. It was probably Broadway's first "functional" design.

*Sketch for* Dark of the Moon *(1965), Wagner's first Arena Stage production. This design fundamentally changed the approach to design at the Arena. Wagner removed part of the stage floor and built under it—something Ming Cho Lee would do more than 10 years later; he explored the vertical space of the theatre, and filled the theatre with ramps, bridges and constructions not only to provide a variety of acting areas but to create a rhythmic and dynamic space.*

Their next project together was Julian Barry's *Lenny* (Broadway, 1971) about comedian Lenny Bruce. Again, the concept evolved out of "silly" conversations. "That's the way Tom loved to work," explains Wagner. "It was always like the circus." For a number about the Pope, Wagner created a stained-glass window out of bagels. The climax of the play was a scene in Bruce's bathroom where he dies from an overdose of drugs given to him by FBI agents. A huge shroud which had provided the backdrop for most of the show fell away to reveal a travesty of Mount Rushmore featuring the heads of Eisenhower, Nixon, Kennedy and Johnson, all made of bathroom tiles. The actual bathroom was contained in Nixon's mouth. The idea for Rushmore

apparently evolved from Lenny's line, "It's like granite out there," while the bathroom tiles, according to O'Horgan, were an attempt to give the play a "urinal look" to complement the bathroom humor.

*Jesus Christ Superstar*, produced later the same year on Broadway, used hydraulic lifts to create a stage floor that could tilt up to seal off the proscenium. The general look of the production came from a decision to look at the story as if it were being retold 10,000 years in the future. From that vantage point, the distinction among art styles separated by only a thousand years would be easily confused. "If I asked you what sculpture or architecture looked like 5,000 years ago," explains Wagner, "you would get it confused with art of 2,000 years ago. So we

*Above, model for* Kicks, *another backstage musical collaboration with Michael Bennett, scheduled for 1985. Facing page, sketch for the "totem pole" in* Hair *(Biltmore Theatre, 1967). Wagner used a simple scaffold structure, not, he claims, under the influence of Ming Cho Lee, but because of its flexibility, simplicity and cost. The totem pole was covered with icons of pop culture.*

started dealing with protozoas and dinosaur bones and blowing them up into objects for a Palm Sunday parade." O'Horgan claims that he was going after a Blake-like look.

The play began with the wall in the "up" position; slowly it fell back as the performers scrambled over the top. At the end of the first act the wall rose again, locking Judas out of the stage space. The idea for the wall arose when O'Horgan and Wagner were sitting in the second balcony of the Mark Hellinger Theatre—one of the largest theatres on Broadway—looking down at the stage. Someone was sweeping the floor and O'Horgan mused that it would be nice to have the same view of the stage floor from the orchestra seats. As Wagner jokingly recalls, he said, "Sure, piece of cake," then immediately called Pete Feller. What Feller came up with was telescoping pistons normally used to lift machinery. There were none large enough to lift a whole stage floor, so it was constructed in three sections. A similar piston was used to create a chrysalis that rose 16 feet above the floor and opened to reveal Jesus.

Ming Cho Lee has said that certain designs succeed—even gain excitement—despite poor proportion and line, because they make strong statements. He includes *Superstar* in this category. "I think Robin Wagner's *Jesus Christ Superstar* is kind of a bad design, but the idea is so vulgar that it gets across. It makes a statement about the show."

*Hair* was the first commercial production that moved beyond the proscenium and into the audience space. Andre Gregory, with designer John Conklin, had broken through the proscenium earlier at the Theatre of the Living Arts in Philadelphia, and Adrian Hall and designer Eugene Lee were beginning to do so at Trinity Square in Providence. Richard Schechner had explored what he called "environmental theatre" in New Orleans and was about to open his Performance Group production of *Dionysus in 69*. And there were the Happenings of the early 1960s. But *Hair*, because of its popularity, seemed to challenge the traditional theatre,

suggesting that the death of the proscenium might be at hand. Ironically, with *Lenny* and *Superstar* O'Horgan and Wagner retreated to the picture-frame stage. After *Hair*, according to Wagner, O'Horgan became interested again in pictorial images, especially for *Superstar*. "If you think of old religious subjects," notes Wagner, "they're very pictorial; they're not these big, surround sculptural things." Ultimately, however, Wagner feels that the decision whether or not to move beyond the proscenium had little to do with theory. It was simply part of a cycle of trying different approaches—"breathe in, breathe out," he shrugs.

O'Horgan and Wagner did several more projects together including *Sgt. Pepper's Lonely Hearts Club Band On the Road*—a pastiche of Beatles music that they created together. Their last, and probably most elaborate collaboration was for Hector Berlioz's opera, *The Trojans* at the Vienna State Opera (1976). The stage was dominated in the opening scene by a huge horse's head that moved 80 feet downstage. As it reached the front it "exploded," as O'Horgan describes it, and the horse's armor was revealed to be a chorus of soldiers carrying shields. The effect was stunning.

Wagner first worked with Michael Bennett on the Broadway musical *Promises, Promises* (1968), and next in 1973 when Bennett replaced Ed Sherin as director of *Seesaw* (Broadway, 1973). Bennett took what had been a fairly static set and, says Wagner, "suddenly it was dancing."

Bennett began to work on *A Chorus Line* in 1974 and called Wagner, saying, "I'm going to do this thing—maybe you'd like to do it. It's just going to be a little Off Broadway show." It was his experience at the Arena combined with his early experience at various music tents with their arena-style stages that Wagner brought to *A Chorus Line* and later productions. For all his association with spectacle, he is one of the finest minimalist designers in the theatre. There is never anything superfluous or gratuitous in his work, and his deceptively simple set for *A Chorus Line*—a white line on the floor and a

mirrored back wall—is highly praised by fellow designers as one of the best designs of the contemporary theatre.

"Because of the circumstance of arena staging in the tents," explains Wagner, "what little was allowed onstage always had to make a statement. It had to be there for a purpose. There was no such thing as gratuitous decor. If a scene called for a table there was a table—and that table had to make a statement for the whole room. Economy of staging became very, very important and that experience—together with the use of systems and axes I got from Oliver Smith, and finding the right details which I got from Ben Edwards—has shaped my designing."

Much of Wagner's design is a process of stripping away. *A Chorus Line*, which developed in workshops under the aegis of the New York Shakespeare Festival over a two-year period, began with a lot of scenery, including a staircase for the grand finale and even toboggans as part of a sort of Ziegfeld Follies number. But, as Wagner explains, all that was really necessary were black velours, a stage and a back wall of mirrors "because it was about ballet classes, the studio space and the finale. Over the two years we culled and culled, and distilled and distilled until we finally got down to the basics. I think it's as close as I've ever gotten to the real essence of what a play needs in order to survive. Maybe 'live' is a better word, because it certainly does more than survive."

*Dreamgirls* went through essentially the same process. The setting consists primarily of five moving chrome light towers plus light bridges, a step unit and a sliding palette with tables and chairs for the nightclub scenes. This setting encompasses the 28 locations through which the play moves (there were originally 40). The process through which this evolved is typical of the way Wagner works with Bennett and the others on his team.

We knew we were doing a show about a lot of people in show business—in this instance a show about recording studios, sound stages, hotel clubs, restaurant theatres, television. It had to be about high technology, about people entrapped by that technology. We had to confront the audience with it so that they could sense the entrapment. I suggested what I thought was a basic solution: take light towers from rock-and-roll and move them on and off. Michael called up from Fire Island one night at 4:00 a.m. and said, 'Can the towers turn?' The bridges came in mainly because we wanted to be able to have intimate scenes or big, open spacious scenes. It was clear that we couldn't just drop borders in and out because this was a show about technology. And we needed the bridges for the lights to come in and out. The next question was: Can we put people on the bridges and towers? Of course we could put people on them. The design had to be what it was—there was no two ways about it.

"Robin has a fabulous attitude as a scenic designer," says Bennett. "He hates scenery. I think he is the most gifted scenic artist alive today."

Discussing Wagner's process of designing can be problematic since so much of his work—from the earliest days—has been collaborative, and his work methods are determined in large part by the style of the director. The two-year workshops typical of recent Michael Bennett musicals have little to do with the process of a musical like *Merlin* (Broadway, 1983) or *Il Barbiere di Siviglia* (Metropolitan Opera, 1982). The basic process involves reading the script, talking to the director, doing research, then examining the theatre space. For musicals, of course, he needs to listen to the music. "The music helps things become very clear visually," he said in the *Theatre Design & Technology* article.

Is it a dark show or a light show? Is it colorful or somber? All these things are clear in the music. . . . You also need to find out who the major characters are, how important each scene is, which are the obligatory scenes and

*Julian Barry's* Lenny *(Brooks Atkinson Theatre, 1971). Wagner and director Tom O'Horgan set the characters in a sometimes comic, sometimes nightmare landscape of American images including bathroom tiles, a stained-glass window made of bagels, a Mount Rushmore with the faces of Eisenhower, Nixon, Kennedy and LBJ, and the 15-foot marionettes seen here.*

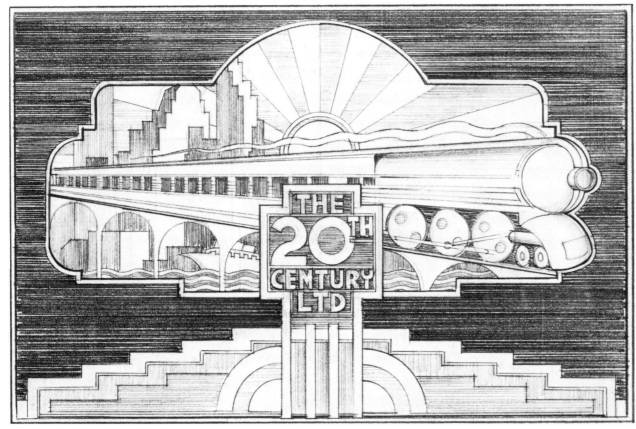

which ones are going to need production. You need that kind of organization before you can even draw. And then, of course, you must pick the director's mind clean—every feeling, every nuance, every vision, every idea, everything that comes out.

Wagner describes research as "sort of like washing yourself in all the material." For the Bennett musicals—which have all been about show business—the traditional research was minimal. For *Galileo*, on the other hand, Wagner did extensive research into the science and machinery of the period, and recreated Galileo's telescope and scientific instruments in great detail.

"I try not to draw anything until I have all the factors," he explains. "I look at it as feeding the computer: If I have all the right and necessary information then I find that the design is inevitable." The factors include not only the research but input from the director, writers and producers (the realities of budget and space), and "what's going on in your life at the moment and what's going on around you." When possible, Wagner likes to take this input and "sleep on it." The more time he has to read the play over and over, to discuss ideas, to "verbalize ideas as opposed to drawing them" the better.

Sherin says that he and Wagner would always look for the "irreversible moment," which he describes as "that moment which is usually most complex—where the play goes way out and gets most intricate—the point from which it cannot retreat. It

*Left, sketch for a backdrop in* On the 20th Century *(St. James Theatre, 1978). Right, a scene aboard the train. Wagner's design is credited with helping the revival of interest in Art Deco.*

is the most complex point at which you can define the play scenically. The effort is to resolve that moment physically and make everything else integrate around that moment so it's very logical. Once that's defined there are usually dozens of thumbnail groundplans—and I mean *thumbnail*." Although it has become something of a joke among his friends, much of Wagner's rough sketching is done on napkins.

Wagner claims not to draw well and never sketches. He used to have his assistants create drawings but, especially if the drawings were beautiful in themselves, he felt they were deceptive because they were not what a representation of what the set looked like in his head. After "scribbled" sketches and ground plans, Wagner builds a ¼-inch scale white model "just to get a sense of balance and a cube." This is followed by highly detailed ½-inch models that eventually become the paint elevations. In this way he can avoid doing any paintings for the shop. Since so many of his settings use nontraditional materials, he incorporates them into the models. The towers in the *Dreamgirls* model are made of brass painted silver; the step units are made

of plexiglass. Even so, Wagner is a bit uncomfortable with the idea that models represent a set. "There's a certain lie in it, because you can't get ½-inch scale people walking around in it, and you can't light it without them. I think a set that lives on its own has got to be a lousy set." As a result of this attitude, he has rarely allowed his work to be displayed in exhibitions.

Wagner usually employs two assistants, but in a busy period may hire up to six. He also has the luxury of a receptionist. The assistants build the pieces that go into the original model, then rebuild the model after Wagner and the director have worked on it. One assistant then drafts plans from the model. Wagner allows and encourages input from his assistants and insists that the directors hold design meetings at his studio so the assistants can be in on the sessions. He also tries to involve people from the scene shops. Wagner refers to this as a synthesizing period—"letting them [director, assistants, technicians] go at each other, because the input is enormous and I'm very dependent on that input. If somebody comes up with a great idea, I'll throw everything out the window." It is for this rea-

son, in fact, that he has not particularly enjoyed his experiences with opera. Despite the incredible facilities, staffs and budgets, each member of the creative team tends to be isolated.

Given the nature of the directors with whom he has worked, Wagner tends to be a "contingency designer"—designing in such a way that scenery can be discarded or redone at the last moment as new production ideas evolve. He sounds a bit nostalgic when talking of the days when "you'd arrive in Washington or Boston with five trucks full of scenery and then you'd get to throw away two and have a better design because of it. It's unfortunate that you can't do that now. I try to do that work before it's built now so that it doesn't cost an arm and a leg." One of the reasons Wagner used to be so dependent on scaffolding and modular scenery was its flexibility. "I believe that often the best work in design is done on the stage. If you're using pieces that are modular or flexible you have a chance to discover and explore." This process of elimination has even carried over into his few dance experiences. When he was working on *I'm Old Fashioned* for Jerome Robbins and the New York City Ballet (1983), he kept bringing in new ideas and changing the design. Finally, at dress rehearsal, Robbins turned to Wagner and said, "Something's wrong." Wagner replied, "There's too much scenery. You don't need any scenery." Robbins agreed and it was all thrown out. Wagner admits that he does not have the right temperament for ballet. "In ballet you do surrounds, but that's not what I'm about, really, in terms of my vision of helping something come to life. I think ballet is where the artist really lives— where the artist can do extraordinary, beautiful things—I'm not that kind of craftsman."

Although a chronology of his productions gives the impression that he is not very busy, the high percentage of box office successes translates into a great number of road companies for which new designs and adaptations must be developed. "These are new companies," sighs Wagner. "You go to the shop, you build the scenery, you have to supervise the painting and the technicals. You have to be there every second to make it work. Because Bennett, like Tom O'Horgan, gets bored simply recreating what has already been done, the road companies are often substantially different from the Broadway production: *Dreamgirls* in Los Angeles was more elaborate than in New York.

Aside from theatre, opera and ballet, Wagner has designed several rock concerts including the 1973 Bette Midler tour and the 1975 Rolling Stones Tour of America. The Stones set included an 80-foot lotus with folding petals made of chromium and devices that extended into the auditorium. The petals were operated by hydraulic tailgate lifts. Wagner was hired by Mick Jagger in much the same way that he was first hired by O'Horgan—"silly" conversations filled with outrageous ideas.

If you're working with Mick Jagger you don't arrive at a design. He's got a lot of ideas and it's all one-upsmanship. He gives you an idea but he wants something better. He said [Wagner assumes his best Liverpool accent], 'What can we do that's really different?' And I said, 'Well, we could have you all shot into space and you could give the first live concert from space.' And he said, 'Oh, we don't want to go so far from home, you know.' 'Well,' I said, 'why don't you restore the Coliseum and do an around the world satellite concert from there? For the finale, you play the violin and I'll burn the city.' And he said, 'Oh, that's not very nice.' This went on for about six hours and the next thing I knew, I had a job.

Wagner is designing two theatre spaces in Bennett's building—a 600-seat public theatre and an 80-seat workshop. Despite all his years of designing, however, he has no ideal theatre. At least one of the new spaces will be an endstage because it provides good sightlines and fits the space available. "The perfect theatre for me," he says, "is a place where the show works. I don't think a theatre space can really alter a good play."

Wagner is constantly seeking new areas that will challenge his imagination. He designed the house he lives in, and has also begun designing restaurants, just as Oliver Smith had done. He finds it not unlike designing for the stage. He has also written several plays in order, he says, to discover more about the writer's process and to see how this might help his own designing. "None of the plays I wrote had any scenery in them and I would say, 'How do you create an ambience out of nothing?'" He has also done a bit of directing, mostly staged readings, but dislikes it—largely because it entails being in rehearsal constantly.

Despite his forays into other areas of design, and despite his sabbaticals from the theatre to travel to Africa, South America, the Himalayas, Katmandu and other exotic places, and despite joking about wanting to open a taco stand in Baja California, theatre is his passion. "I could never get out of theatre. I wouldn't know what else to do. It's still very exciting to me. It's exciting to hear good material for the first time. I still get chills when I see something really great onstage—I get physically excited and I don't know any other place where that can happen. I never wanted to be a solitary artist and I just think the theatre is a wonderful place to live and work."

*Act I, Scene 2 from* Il Barbiere di Siviglia *(Metropolitan Opera, 1982). "The first thing they told me at the Met was, 'We don't have enough turntable sets, why don't you try to use the turntable?' " He used the turntable to its fullest in the second act orchestral passage, in which the hero walked through a rainstorm past several neighborhood buildings that revolved by. He then climbed a ladder into Rosina's apartment and the set revolved to show him climbing through the window from the other side.*

# CHRONOLOGIES

The following are year-by-year listings of the work of each designer discussed in this book, through June 1984. Unless otherwise indicated, the designer was responsible for settings only. "S & L" indicates the individual designed both sets and lights; "S & C" signifies sets and costumes. Road companies and foreign productions of Broadway shows are generally not included. Not all the designers keep complete records of their work. These listings are as complete and accurate as possible.

## JOHN LEE BEATTY

**1969**
College Light Opera, Falmouth, MA (9 shows)

**1970**
Weston Playhouse, VT (8 shows)

**1972**
Wayside Theatre, Middletown, VA (6 shows)

**1973**
Wayside Theatre (6 shows)
*Marouf* (S & C), Manhattan Theatre Club, NYC

**1974**
*The Amorous Flea* (S & C), Queens Playhouse, NY
*Some People, Some Other People, and What They Finally Do*, Stage 73, NYC
*Room Service*, Queens Playhouse
*Come Back, Little Sheba*, Queens Playhouse
*An Evening with Cole Porter* (S & C), Manhattan Theatre Club

*The Wager*, Manhattan Theatre Club
*The Diary of a Scoundrel*, Gene Frankel Workshop, NYC
*Two Offenbach Operettas*, Theatre at Noon, NYC
*Battle of Angels*, Circle Repertory Company, NYC

**1975**
*The Mound Builders*, Circle Repertory Company
*Down by the River Where Waterlilies Are Disfigured Every Day*, Circle Repertory Company
*Philadelphia, Here I Come!*, Queensboro Community College, NY
*The Caucasian Chalk Circle*, Queensboro Community College
*Harry Outside*, Circle Repertory Company
*Not to Worry*, Circle Repertory Company
*Arms and the Man*, The Acting Company, Saratoga Springs, NY
*The Mound Builders* (Art Director), Theatre in America (PBS Television)
*Golden Boy*, Manhattan Theatre Club
*The Elephant in the House*, Circle Repertory Company
*Jumpers*, Seattle Repertory Company, WA
*Long Day's Journey Into Night*, Indiana Repertory Company, Indianapolis

**1976**
*Knock, Knock*, Circle Repertory Company
*The Tot Family*, Arena Stage (Kreeger Theater), Washington, DC
*Knock Knock*, Biltmore Theatre, NYC
*La Perichole* (S & C), San Francisco Opera (Spring Opera Theatre)
*The Contrast*, Cincinnati Playhouse in the Park, OH
*Serenading Louie*, Circle Repertory Company

*Rebel Women*, New York Shakespeare Festival (Public Theater)
*Mrs. Murray's Farm*, Circle Repertory Company
*Duck Variations* and *Rosemary*, The Acting Company
*The Farm*, Circle Repertory Company
*The Innocents*, Morosco Theatre, NYC
*The Bed Before Yesterday*, Wilmington Playhouse, DE
*A Tribute to Lily Lamont*, Circle Repertory Company
*Ashes*, Manhattan Theatre Club

**1977**
*A Month in the Country*, Cincinnati Playhouse in the Park
*Ashes*, New York Shakespeare Festival (Public Theater)
*Heartbreak House*, Cincinnati Playhouse in the Park
*Irma La Douce*, Los Angeles Civic Light Opera
*Hit the Deck*, Goodspeed Opera House, East Haddam, CT
*Sherlock Holmes*, Williamstown Theatre Festival, MA
*Tobacco Road*, Academy Festival Theatre, Lake Forest, IL
*Red-Bluegrass Western Flyer Show*, Goodspeed Opera House
*Old Times*, Academy Festival Theatre
*A Life in the Theatre*, Theatre de Lys, NYC
*Out of Our Father's House*, Theatre of Riverside Church, NYC
*Ulysses in Traction*, Circle Repertory Company
*The Water Engine*, New York Shakespeare Festival (Public Theater)

**1978**
*The Middle Ages*, Hartman Theatre Company, Stamford, CT
*A Streetcar Named Desire*, Arena Stage

*Lulu*, Circle Repertory Company
*The Water Engine*, Plymouth Theatre, NYC
*The House of Bernarda Alba*, Cincinnati Playhouse in the Park
*Catsplay*, Manhattan Theatre Club
*Tip Toes*, Goodspeed Opera House
*Duck Variations*, The Acting Company
*The Fifth of July*, Circle Repertory Company
*Ain't Misbehavin'*, Longacre Theatre, NYC
*Out of Our Father's House*, The White House, Washington, DC
*Catsplay*, Promenade Theatre, NYC
*Whoopee!*, Goodspeed Opera House
*After the Season*, Academy Festival Theatre
*Out of Our Father's House*, Great Performances (WNET Television)
*No Time for Comedy* (S & C), McCarter Theatre Company, Princeton, NJ
*The Rear Column*, Manhattan Theatre Club
*She Loves Me*, Goodspeed Opera House
*Serenading Louie*, Academy Festival Theatre

**1979**
*Broadway*, The Acting Company
*Storeyville*, Ford's Theatre, Washington, DC
*Whoopee!*, ANTA Theatre, NYC
*Merton of the Movies*, Milwaukee Repertory Theater, WI
*Tip Toes*, Brooklyn Academy of Music, NY
*The Faith Healer*, Longacre Theatre
*The Woods*, New York Shakespeare Festival (Public Theatre)
*Talley's Folly*, Circle Repertory Company
*Poet and the Rent*, Circle Repertory Company
*The Curse of An Aching Heart*, St. Nicholas Theatre, Chicago, IL

*Lone Canoe*, Goodman Theatre, Chicago, IL
*The Five O'Clock Girl*, Goodspeed Opera House
*The Rose Tattoo*, Berkshire Theatre Festival, Lenox, MA
*Talley's Folly*, Mark Taper Forum, Los Angeles, CA
*It's a Long Way to Boston*, Goodspeed Opera House
*Dark Pony* and *Reunion*, Circle Repertory Company
*Jail Diary of Albie Sachs*, Manhattan Theatre Club
*Something Wonderful*, Westchester Regional Theatre, NY

### 1980

*Talley's Folly*, Brooks Atkinson Theatre, NYC
*Johnny On A Spot*, Brooklyn Academy of Music
*Biography*, Manhattan Theatre Club
*The Happy Time*, Goodspeed Opera House
*Talley's Folly*, Goodman Theatre
*Hide and Seek*, Belasco Theatre, NYC
*Cyrano de Bergerac*, Goodman Theatre
*Reverberation Fire Curtain*, Opera Lab of the University of Texas, Austin
*Little Johnny Jones*, Goodspeed Opera House
*The Lady and the Clarinet*, Mark Taper Forum
*Holiday*, Center Theatre Group (Ahmanson Theatre), Los Angeles, CA
*The Diviners*, Circle Repertory Company
*The Fifth of July*, New Apollo Theatre, NYC
*Crimes of the Heart*, Manhattan Theatre Club

### 1981

*The Five O'Clock Girl*, Helen Hayes Theatre, NYC
*Close of Play*, Manhattan Theatre Club
*The Wild Duck*, Brooklyn Academy of Music
*Jitters*, Walnut Street Theatre, Philadelphia, PA
*The Curse of Kulyenchikov* (later *Fools*), Eugene O'Neill Theatre, NYC
*Kaufman At Large*, Perry Street Theatre, NYC
*Is There Life After High School?*, Hartford Stage Company, CT

*A Tale Told*, Circle Repertory Company
*The Diviners* (co-designed with David Potts), Saratoga Performing Arts Center, NY
*Foxfire*, Guthrie Theater, Minneapolis, MN
*A Tale Told*, Mark Taper Forum
*Crimes of the Heart*, John Golden Theatre, NYC
*Medusa*, The First All Children's Theatre, NYC
*Monday After the Miracle*, Actors' Studio, NYC
*Duet for One*, Royale Theatre, NYC

### 1982

*The Curse of An Aching Heart*, Little Theatre, NYC
*Livin' Dolls*, Manhattan Theatre Club
*Is There Life After High School?*, Ethel Barrymore Theatre, NYC
*Young Playwright's Festival*, Circle Repertory Company
*Monday After the Miracle*, Spoleto Festival, Charleston, SC
*Angels Fall*, Miami Festival (Coconut Grove Playhouse), Miami, FL
*The Holdup*, Saratoga Performing Arts Center
*Angels Fall*, Saratoga Performing Arts Center
*Angels Fall*, Circle Repertory Company
*Monday After the Miracle*, Kennedy Center (Eisenhower Theatre), Washington, DC
*Monday After the Miracle*, Eugene O'Neill Theatre
*Alice in Wonderland*, Virginia Theatre, NYC

### 1983

*Cat On a Hot Tin Roof*, Mark Taper Forum
*Passion*, Longacre Theatre
*Alice In Wonderland*, PBS Television
*Angels Fall*, Longacre Theatre
*What I Did Last Summer*, Circle Repertory Company
*The Middle Ages*, St. Peter's Church, NYC
*Crimes of the Heart*, Ahmanson Theatre
*The Seagull*, Saratoga Performing Arts Center
*Baby*, Ethel Barrymore Theatre
*The Seagull*, Circle Repertory Company

### 1984

*Park Your Car in Harvard Yard*, Manhattan Theatre Club
*Other Places*, Manhattan Theatre Club
*The Abduction of Figaro*, Minnesota Opera, Minneapolis
*The Miss Firecracker Contest*, Manhattan Theatre Club


## JOHN CONKLIN

### 1956

*The Lady's Not for Burning* (S & C), Yale Dramatic Association, New Haven, CT

### 1957

*The Crucible*, Yale Dramatic Association
*A View from the Bridge*, Yale Dramatic Association

### 1958

*Cyrano de Bergerac*, Yale Dramatic Association
*The Skin of Our Teeth*, Yale Dramatic Association
*Time Remembered*, Williamstown Theatre Festival, MA
*Danton's Death*, Yale Dramatic Association

### 1959

*The Brothers Karamazov* (S & L), Williamstown Theatre Festival
*Charley's Aunt*, Williamstown Theatre Festival
*The Inspector General*, Yale Dramatic Association
*Volpone*, Yale School of Drama, New Haven, CT
*Grand Tour*, Yale Dramatic Association

### 1960

*The Way of the World* (co-designed with Richard Casler), Institute for Advanced Studies in the Theatre Arts, NYC
*Camino Real*, Yale Dramatic Association

### 1961

*Becket*, Williamstown Theatre Festival
*The Sap of Life*, Williamstown Theatre Festival
*Toys in the Attic*, Williamstown Theatre Festival

*Once in a Lifetime* (S & C), Williamstown Theatre Festival
*The Five Finger Exercise*, Williamstown Theatre Festival
*Othello*, Williamstown Theatre Festival
*The Sap of Life* (S & C), One Sheridan Square, NYC
*Thieves' Carnival*, Yale Dramatic Association
*Booth is Back in Town*, Yale Dramatic Association
*The Decameron*, East 74th Street Theatre, NYC

### 1963

*Peer Gynt*, Yale School of Drama
*Mr. Booth*, Williamstown Theatre Festival
*A Birthday Party for Shakespeare*, Williamstown Theatre Festival
*The Cherry Orchard*, Williamstown Theatre Festival
*Tambourines to Glory* (S & C), The Little Theatre, NYC

### 1964

*Othello* (S & C), Hartford Stage Company, CT
*The Rivals*, McCarter Theatre Company, Princeton, NJ
*As You Desire Me*, McCarter Theatre Company
*The Birds*, McCarter Theatre Company

### 1965

*Uncle Vanya*, Hartford Stage Company
*She Stoops to Conquer* (S & C), Hartford Stage Company
*Waiting for Godot* (S & C), Hartford Stage Company
*The Tempest* (S & C), Hartford Stage Company
*The Night Chanter*, Hunter College, NYC

### 1966

*The Play of Daniel*, New York Pro Musica, NYC
*The Play of Herod*, New York Pro Musica
*The Importance of Being Earnest* (S & C), Hartford Stage Company
*Twelfth Night* (S & C), Hartford Stage Company
*The Beggar's Opera* (Costumes only), Yale School of Drama
*Ondine*, Williamstown Theatre Festival

*Marat/Sade*, Williamstown Theatre Festival

*Dialogues of the Carmelites*, New York State Theatre, NYC

*Annie Get Your Gun*, Williamstown Theatre Festival

*The Balcony* (S & C), Hartford Stage Company

*USA* (S & C), Theatre of the Living Arts, Philadelphia, PA

**1967**

*Enrico IV* (S & C), Hartford Stage Company

*The Servant of Two Masters*, Hartford Stage Company

*The Fantasticks*, Hartford Stage Company

*Who's Afraid of Virginia Woolf?*, Hartford Stage Company

*Beclch*, Theatre of the Living Arts

*The Old Maid, Thief* and *The Medium*, Western Opera Theatre, San Francisco, CA

*Saint Joan* (S & C), Williamstown Theatre Festival

*Peer Gynt* (S & C), Williamstown Theatre Festival

*Skinflint Out West* (S & C), Hartford Stage Company

*A View from the Bridge*, Hartford Stage Company

*The Playboy of the Western World*, Long Wharf Theatre, New Haven, CT

*The Rivals*, Seattle Repertory Theatre, WA

**1968**

*Bagatelles*, Pennsylvania Ballet, Philadelphia

*Antigone* (S & C), Hartford Stage Company

*The Firebugs*, Hartford Stage Company

*The Threepenny Opera* (S & C), Hartford Stage Company

*Galileo*, Williamstown Theatre Festival

*Iphigenia at Aulis* (S & C), Williamstown Theatre Festival

*Camino Real*, Williamstown Theatre Festival

*Six Characters in Search of an Author*, Arena Stage, Washington, DC

*The Duchess of Malfi*, Long Wharf Theatre

*The Threepenny Opera*, Arena Stage

*Marat/Sade*, Arena Stage

*Salome*, Baltimore Civic Light Opera, MD

**1969**

*Cosi fan tutte*, Santa Fe Opera, NM

*The Threepenny Opera* (S & C), Williamstown Theatre Festival

**1970**

*Macbeth*, McCarter Theatre Company

*The Skin of Our Teeth*, Long Wharf Theatre

*A Place Without Doors*, Long Wharf Theatre

**1971**

*Mother Courage*, Williamstown Theatre Festival

*Scratch*, St. James Theatre, NYC

*Beatrix Cenci*, Opera Society of Washington, DC

*What the Butler Saw*, Arena Stage (Kreeger Theater)

*Cyrano de Bergerac* (S & C), Williamstown Theatre Festival

*Hamlet* (S & C), Long Wharf Theatre

*The Marriage of Figaro* (S & C), Minnesota Opera, St. Paul

*Overture, The Grand Tour*, and *O.W.* (S & C), Royal Ballet, London

**1972**

*Once in a Lifetime*, Williamstown Theatre Festival

*The Resistible Rise of Arturo Ui*, Williamstown Theatre Festival

*The Hostage*, Arena Stage (Kreeger Theater)

*The Nutcracker* (S & C), Pennsylvania Ballet

*Agamemnon*, McCarter Theatre Company

*The Misanthrope*, Hartford Stage Company

*Loot*, Hartford Stage Company

*Swan Lake, Act II*, Pennsylvania Ballet

*Orfeo* (S & C), San Francisco Opera, CA

*Mary Stuart* (S & C), Williamstown Theatre Festival

*Twelfth Night*, Arena Stage

*What Price Glory?*, Long Wharf Theatre

*The Barber of Seville* (S & C), Minnesota Opera

**1973**

*The Master Builder*, Long Wharf Theatre

*Nobody's Earnest*, Williamstown Theatre Festival

*The Good Woman of Setzuan* (S & C), Williamstown Theatre Festival

*Beatrix Cenci*, New York City Opera

*Indians* (S & C), Temple University (Tomlinson Theatre), Philadelphia, PA

*The Au Pair Man*, New York Shakespeare Festival (Vivian Beaumont Theatre)

*Cosi fan tutte* (S & C), John F. Kennedy Center, Washington, DC

*Saint Joan* (S & C), Ahmanson Theatre, Los Angeles, CA

*Other Voices, Other Rooms*, Studio Arena Theatre, Buffalo, NY

*Saint Joan* (S & C), Williamstown Theatre Festival

*Ubu Roi* (S & C), Hartford Stage Company

*The Resistible Rise of Arturo Ui*, Long Wharf Theatre

*The Marriage of Figaro* (S & C), Houston Grand Opera, Houston, TX

*The Barber of Seville* (S & C), Opera Society of Washington

**1974**

*Lorelei*, The Palace Theatre, NYC

*Cat on a Hot Tin Roof*, American Shakespeare Festival, Stratford, CT

*Romeo and Juliet*, American Shakespeare Festival

*Twelfth Night*, American Shakespeare Festival

*Pericles* (Costumes only), New York Shakespeare Festival (Delacorte Theater)

*Richard III* (S & C), New York Shakespeare Festival (Vivian Beaumont Theatre)

*Juno and the Paycock*, Mark Taper Forum, Los Angeles, CA

*Richard III* (S & C), Long Wharf Theatre

*The Threepenny Opera* (S & C), Williamstown Theatre Festival

**1975**

*Room Service*, Hartford Stage Company

*Savages*, Williamstown Theatre Festival

*A Death in Venice*, San Francisco Opera

*The Winter's Tale*, American Shakespeare Festival

*Our Town*, American Shakespeare Festival

*Kismet* (S & C), Wolf Trap Theatre, Reston, VA

*The Scarecrow*, Kennedy Center (Eisenhower Theatre)

*The Leaf People*, Booth Theatre, NYC

**1976**

*Merton of the Movies*, Ahmanson Theatre

*Rex* (S & C), Lunt-Fontanne Theatre, NYC

*Cat on a Hot Tin Roof*, Guthrie Theater, Minneapolis, MN

*Rosencrantz and Guildenstern Are Dead* (S & C), Guthrie Theater

*The Rose Tattoo*, Long Wharf Theatre

*A History of the American Film*, Mark Taper Forum

*As You Like It*, American Shakespeare Festival

*A Midsummer Night's Dream* [opera] (S & C), Wolf Trap Theatre, VA

*Waltz of the Toreadors*, Hartford Stage Company

**1977**

*A Moon for the Misbegotten*, Guthrie Theater

*Un ballo in maschera* (S & C), San Francisco Opera

*Fedora*, Santa Fe Opera

*Angel City*, Mark Taper Forum

*Chez Nous*, Manhattan Theatre Club, NYC

*Romeo and Juliet* (Costumes only), Circle in the Square, NYC

*Julius Caesar* (Costumes only), American Conservatory Theatre, San Francisco

*The Recruiting Officer* (S & C), Long Wharf Theatre

*Bully!* (S & C), 46th Street Theatre, NYC

*All the Way Home*, Hartford Stage Company

**1978**

*Rain*, Hartford Stage Company

*A Month in the Country*, Williamstown Theatre Festival

*Eugene Onegin*, Santa Fe Opera

*The Duchess of Malfi*, Santa Fe Opera

*Julius Caesar* [opera] (S & C), San Francisco Opera

*La Traviata* (S & C), Minnesota Opera

*The Turk in Italy* (S & C), New York City Opera

**1979**

*Medea*, New York City Opera
*Galileo* (S & C), Hartford Stage Company
*Miss Havisham's Fire* (S & C), New York City Opera
*Lulu* (S & C), Santa Fe Opera
*Cyrano de Bergerac* (S & C), Long Wharf Theatre
*Journey's End*, Long Wharf Theatre
*Romeo and Juliet* (S & C), California Shakespeare Festival, Visalia, CA
*The Resistible Rise of Arturo Ui*, Williamstown Theatre Festival
*Werther* (S & C), Houston Opera
*The Merry Widow*, Central City Opera, Denver, CO
*A Lovely Sunday for Creve Coeur*, Hudson Guild Theatre, NYC
*Camino Real*, Williamstown Theatre Festival
*La Traviata*, St. Louis Opera, MO

**1980**

*Ardèle*, Hartford Stage Company
*Chekhov in Yalta* (Costumes only), Mark Taper Forum
*Twelfth Night* (Costumes only), Mark Taper Forum
*Romeo and Juliet* (S & C) Hartford Ballet
*The Bacchae* (S & C), Circle in the Square
*The Magic Flute* (S & C), St. Louis Opera
*Hamlet* (S & C), California Shakespeare Festival
*A Midsummer Night's Dream* (S & C), California Shakespeare Festival
*The Philadelphia Story*, Vivian Beaumont Theatre, NYC
*Don Pasquale*, San Francisco Opera

**1981**

*Cymbeline* (S & C), Hartford Stage Company
*Don Quichotte* (S & C), Netherlands Opera, Amsterdam
*Daphne*, Santa Fe Opera
*Antony and Cleopatra* (S & C), Hartford Stage Company
*Kean* (S & C), Hartford Stage Company

**1982**

*Colette*, Fifth Avenue Theatre, Seattle, WA
*The Greeks* (S & C), Hartford Stage Company

*The Portage to San Cristobal of A.H.*, Hartford Stage Company

**1983**

*Die Walküre*, San Francisco Opera
*Das Rheingold*, San Francisco Opera
*Pollichino* (S & C), Cabrillo Festival, Aptos, CA
*Arabella*, Santa Fe Opera
*Terra Nova*, Portland Stage Company, Portland, ME
*La Grande-Duchesse de Gérolstein* New York City Opera

**1984**

*The Three Sisters*, Hartford Stage Company
*Awake and Sing!*, Circle in the Square
*Siegfried*, San Francisco Opera
*Cosi fan tutte*, Netherlands Opera
*We Come to the River*, Santa Fe Opera
*Marriage of Figaro*, Netherlands Opera
*Battle of Legnano*, Pittsburgh Opera, PA

## KARL EIGSTI

**1959**

*Speaking of Murder*, White Cloud Playhouse, MI
*Picnic*, White Cloud Playhouse

**1965**

*Billy Budd*, Arena Stage, Washington, DC
*Heartbreak House*, Arena Stage
*Long Day's Journey into Night*, Arena Stage
*The Critic* (S & L), Theatre of the Living Arts, Philadelphia, PA
*They* (S & L), Theatre of the Living Arts

**1966**

*The Man in the Moon* (Director only), Long Wharf Theatre, New Haven, CT
*Thumby*, Long Wharf Theatre
*The Three Sisters*, Arena Stage
*Mr. Welk and Jersey Jim*, Arena Stage
*The Lesson*, Arena Stage
*The Collection*, Arena Stage

**1967**

*Marat/Sade*, Studio Arena Theatre, Buffalo, NY

*Fisher* (Director only), La Mama, E.T.C., NYC
*Inner City Macbeth* (Director only), Cherry County Playhouse, Traverse City, MI
*The Dumbwaiter*, Actors Theatre of Louisville, KY
*The Private Ear*, Actors Theatre of Louisville
*The Miracle Worker*, Actors Theatre of Louisville

**1968**

*Bananas*, Repertory Theatre of Lincoln Center (Forum Theater), NYC
Director of New Plays, Repertory Theatre of Lincoln Center
*Serjeant Musgrave's Dance* (S & C), Guthrie Theater, Minneapolis, MN

**1969**

*Henry V*, American Shakespeare Festival, Stratford, CT
*Hamlet*, American Shakespeare Festival
*Mourning Becomes Electra* (S & C), Guthrie Theater
*Henry V*, ANTA Theatre, NYC

**1970**

*Inquest*, Music Box Theatre, NYC
*Boesman and Lena*, Circle in the Square, NYC
*Othello*, American Shakespeare Festival
*Othello*, ANTA Theatre

**1971**

*The House of Blue Leaves*, Truck and Warehouse Theatre, NYC
*Buying Out*, Studio Arena Theatre
*The Passion of Antigona Perez*, Puerto Rican Traveling Theatre, NYC
Industrial for Armstrong Cork Company
TV commercials

**1972**

*Grease* (Lights only), Eden Theatre, NYC
*Sitting* and *The Saving Grace*, Studio Arena Theatre

**1973**

*The Karl Marx Play*, American Place Theatre, NYC
*Baba Goya*, American Place Theatre

*Nourish the Beast* (retitled version of *Baba Goya*), Cherry Lane Playhouse, NYC

**1974**

*The Resistible Rise of Arturo Ui*, Arena Stage
*Horatio*, Arena Stage
*Death of a Salesman*, Arena Stage
*Who's Afraid of Virginia Woolf?*, Arena Stage
*The Front Page*, Arena Stage
*Yentl the Yeshiva Boy*, Chelsea Theater Center, NYC

**1975**

*The Secret Place*, La Mama E.T.C.
*Wings*, Eastside Playhouse, NYC
*The Last Meeting of the Knights of the White Magnolia*, Arena Stage (Kreeger Theater)
*The Dybbuk*, Arena Stage
*Long Day's Journey into Night*, Arena Stage (Kreeger Theater)
*Yentl*, Eugene O'Neill Theatre, NYC
*Once in a Lifetime*, Arena Stage
*Sweet Bird of Youth*, Academy Festival Theatre, Lake Forest, IL; Kennedy Center, Washington, DC; Harkness Theatre, NYC

**1976**

*Dandelion Wine*, Arena Stage (Kreeger Theater)
*Monty Python Live!*, City Center, NYC
*The House of Blue Leaves*, Westport Country Playhouse, CT
*When You Comin' Back, Red Ryder?*, Cincinnati Playhouse in the Park, OH
*Saint Joan*, Arena Stage
*Saturday, Sunday, Monday*, Arena Stage

**1977**

*Catsplay*, Arena Stage (Kreeger Theater)
*Guerramore, Diary of One Who Vanished, Aventures et Nouvelles Aventures*, Brooklyn Academy of Music, NY
*On the Lock In*, New York Shakespeare Festival (Public Theater)
*Sizwe Bansi Is Dead*, Pittsburgh Public Theater, PA and Studio Arena Theatre
*JoAnne!*, Theatre of Riverside Church, NYC
*The Imaginary Invalid*, Cincinnati Playhouse in the Park

*Daddy*, New Federal Theatre, NYC
*Cold Storage* (S & C), Lyceum Theatre, NYC

**1978**
*Slow Dance on the Killing Ground*, Pittsburgh Public Theater
*Medal of Honor Rag*, Pittsburgh Public Theater
*The National Health*, Arena Stage
*Duck Hunting*, Arena Stage
*Once in a Lifetime*, Circle in the Square
*Albee Directs Albee*, Tour
*Eubie!*, Ambassador Theatre, NYC
*Annie Get Your Gun*, Jones Beach Marine Theatre, NY
*The Diary of Anne Frank*, Theatre Four, NYC

**1979**
*Room Service*, Cincinnati Playhouse in the Park
*Curse of the Starving Class*, Arena Stage (Kreeger Theater)
*The Buddy System*, Cincinnati Playhouse in the Park
*Knockout*, Helen Hayes Theatre, NYC
*Murder at the Howard Johnson's*, John Golden Theatre, NYC
Industrial for Avon
*A Hundred Percent Alive*, Westwood Playhouse, Los Angeles, CA
*Losing Time*, Manhattan Theatre Club, NYC
*You Can't Take It with You*, Arena Stage (Kreeger Theater and Hong Kong Arts Festival, 1980)
*Twelfth Night*, Cincinnati Playhouse in the Park

**1980**
*The Caretaker*, Long Wharf Theatre
*After the Fall*, Arena Stage (and Hong Kong Arts Festival)
*Julius Caesar*, Milwaukee Repertory Theater, WI
*The Downstairs Boys*, Cincinnati Playhouse in the Park
*The Baker's Wife*, Cincinnati Playhouse in the Park
*The Guests of the Nation*, PBS Television
*The Woolgatherer*, Circle Repertory Company, NYC
*One Mo' Time*, Arena Stage (Kreeger Theater)

*Frimbo*, Grand Central Terminal, Tracks 39–42, NYC
*The American Clock*, Biltmore Theatre, NYC

**1981**
*Disability: A Comedy*, Arena Stage (Kreeger Theater)
*The Child*, Arena Stage (Kreeger Theater)
*Cold Storage*, Arena Stage (Kreeger Theater)
*Bodies*, Long Wharf Theatre
*Julius Caesar*, Milwaukee Repertory Theater
*The Red Snake*, New York Shakespeare Festival (Public Theater)
*Pantomime*, Arena Stage (Kreeger Theater)
*Joseph and the Amazing Technicolor Dreamcoat*, Entermedia Theatre, NYC
*Our Town*, Guthrie Theater
*Shady Hill Kidnapping*, American Playhouse (PBS Television)

**1982**
*A Delicate Balance*, Arena Stage
*Joseph and the Amazing Technicolor Dreamcoat*, Royale Theatre, NYC
*Macbeth*, Cincinnati Playhouse in the Park
*The World of Sholom Aleichem*, Rialto Theatre, NYC
Industrial for IBM
*Richard II*, Circle Repertory Company (Entermedia Theatre)
*The Great Grandson of Jedediah Kohler*, Circle Repertory Company (Entermedia Theatre)
*The File on Jill Hatch*, PBS/BBC Television
*May I Have This Dance?*, Tel Aviv, Israel
*Almost an Eagle*, Longacre Theatre, NYC

**1983**
*Screenplay*, Arena Stage
*Free and Clear*, Long Wharf Theatre
*Amen Corner*, Nederlander Theatre, NYC
*Solomon Northrup's Odyssey*, PBS Television
Industrial for IBM

**1984**
*Julius Caesar*, Cincinnati Playhouse in the Park
*Accidental Death of an Anarchist*, Arena Stage (Kreeger Theater)
Industrial for IBM
Industrial for Equitable Life Assurance
*Winston Churchill Speaks*, David Susskind Productions (Television)

## RALPH FUNICELLO

**1969**
*A Wonderfull Yeare*, New York Shakespeare Festival (Public Theater)
*The Figures of Chartres*, New York Shakespeare Festival (Public Theater)

**1971**
*A Gun Play* (Co-designed with Marjorie Kellogg), Cherry Lane Theatre, NYC
*Rodalinda*, The Curtis Institute of Music, Philadelphia, PA

**1972**
*The Rape of Lucretia*, The Curtis Institute of Music
*The Hunter*, New York Shakespeare Festival (Public Theater)
*The House of Blue Leaves*, American Conservatory Theatre, San Francisco, CA
*A Doll's House*, American Conservatory Theatre

**1973**
*Dear Antoine*, Loeb Drama Center, Boston, MA
*That Championship Season*, American Conservatory Theatre
*The Taming of the Shrew*, American Conservatory Theatre
*The Miser*, American Conservatory Theatre
*The House of Bernarda Alba*, American Conservatory Theatre

**1974**
*Broadway*, American Conservatory Theatre
*Pillars of the Community*, American Conservatory Theatre
*Horatio*, American Conservatory Theatre

*Brigadoon*, Pacific Conservatory of the Performing Arts, Santa Maria, CA
*The Taming of the Shrew*, Pacific Conservatory of the Performing Arts
*The Visit*, Pacific Conservatory of the Performing Arts
*Oklahoma!*, Pacific Conservatory of the Performing Arts

**1975**
*General Gorgeous*, American Conservatory Theatre
*He Who Gets Slapped*, Pacific Conservatory of the Performing Arts
*Guys and Dolls*, Pacific Conservatory of the Performing Arts
*Peer Gynt*, Pacific Conservatory of the Performing Arts
*Dracula*, Pacific Conservatory of the Performing Arts
*The House of Blue Leaves*, Pacific Conservatory of the Performing Arts

**1976**
*Peer Gynt*, American Conservatory Theatre
*The Ballad of the Sad Cafe*, Pacific Conservatory of the Performing Arts
*Romeo and Juliet*, Pacific Conservatory of the Performing Arts
*Doctor Faustus*, Guthrie Theater, Minneapolis, MN
*The Importance of Being Earnest*, Mark Taper Forum, Los Angeles, CA
*The Taming of the Shrew*, PBS Television (American Conservatory Theatre production)
*Don Pasquale*, San Francisco Opera, Western Opera Theatre

**1977**
*She Stoops to Conquer*, Guthrie Theater
*La Ronde*, Guthrie Theater
*The Utter Glory of Morrissey Hall*, Pacific Conservatory of the Performing Arts
*The Alcestiad*, Pacific Conservatory of the Performing Arts
*The Master Builder*, American Conservatory Theatre
*Travesties*, Mark Taper Forum

**1978**
*Absurd Person Singular*, American Conservatory Theatre
*The Winter Dancers*, Mark Taper Forum
*All the Way Home*, American Conservatory Theatre

*Ring Round the Moon*, Pacific Conservatory of the Performing Arts
*Hamlet*, Pacific Conservatory of the Performing Arts
*Dusa, Fish, Stas and Vi*, Mark Taper Forum
*Ah, Wilderness!*, American Conservatory Theatre
Toyota Industrial

**1979**
*Heartbreak House*, American Conservatory Theatre
*The Play's the Thing*, California Actors Theatre, Los Gatos
*Hay Fever*, American Conservatory Theatre
*The Winter's Tale*, Pacific Conservatory of the Performing Arts
*Romeo and Juliet*, American Conservatory Theatre
*Hay Fever*, McCarter Theatre Company, Princeton, NJ
Toyota Industrial

**1980**
*Pantagleize*, American Conservatory Theatre
*Division Street*, Mark Taper Forum
*The Learned Ladies*, Denver Center Theatre Company, CO
*The Caucasian Chalk Circle*, Denver Center Theatre Company
*Ghosts*, American Conservatory Theatre

**1981**
*Pygmalion*, Berkeley Repertory Theatre, CA
*Another Part of the Forest*, American Conservatory Theatre
*The Dance of Death*, Seattle Repertory Theatre, WA
*Da*, South Coast Repertory, Costa Mesa, CA
*Macbeth*, Sherwood Shakespeare Festival, Oxnard, CA
*A Midsummer Night's Dream*, Sherwood Shakespeare Festival
*Division Street*, Ambassador Theatre, NYC

**1982**
*Number Our Days*, Mark Taper Forum
*A Flea in Her Ear*, Mark Taper Forum
*The Misanthrope*, Mark Taper Forum
*I Remember Mama*, American Conservatory Theatre

*Black Comedy* and *The Browning Version*, American Conservatory Theatre
*Mourning Becomes Electra*, American Conservatory Theatre
*Savages*, Seattle Repertory Theatre
*The Front Page*, Seattle Repertory Theatre
Ralph Lauren Fashion Show for Wilks-Bashford, San Francisco, CA

**1983**
*Uncle Vanya*, American Conservatory Theatre
*Mornings At Seven*, American Conservatory Theatre
*Richard III*, Mark Taper Forum
*American Buffalo*, Berkeley Repertory Theatre and Milwaukee Repertory Theater

**1984**
*Good*, South Coast Repertory
*Master Harold . . . and the boys*, Seattle Repertory Theatre
*Savages*, Seattle Repertory Theatre
*La Rondine*, New York City Opera
*John Gabriel Borkman*, American Conservatory Theatre
*Angels Fall*, American Conservatory Theatre
*The Dolly*, American Conservatory Theatre
*The American Clock*, Mark Taper Forum
*Wild Oats*, Mark Taper Forum
*Moby Dick—Rehearsed*, Mark Taper Forum
*A Streetcar Named Desire*, Stratford Festival, Ontario

## MARJORIE BRADLEY KELLOGG

**1969**
*Sambo* (co-designed with Ming Cho Lee), New York Shakespeare Festival (Public Theater)

**1970**
*The Happiness Cage*, New York Shakespeare Festival (Public Theater)

**1971**
*A Gun Play* (co-designed with Ralph Funicello), Cherry Lane Theatre, NYC

*The Black Terror*, New York Shakespeare Festival (Public Theater)

**1972**
*A Swansong*, Long Wharf Theatre, New Haven, CT
*Death of a Salesman*, Center Stage, Baltimore, MD
*Old Times*, Goodman Theatre, Chicago, IL
*The Lady's Not for Burning*, Long Wharf Theatre
*The Country Girl*, Williamstown Theatre Festival, MA

**1973**
*Juno and the Paycock*, Long Wharf Theatre
*Getting Married*, Hartford Stage Company, CT
*Three Men on a Horse*, Arena Stage, Washington, DC
*Candida*, PAF Playhouse, Huntington Station, NY
*Twelfth Night*, PAF Playhouse
*The Country Girl*, Williamstown Theatre Festival

**1974**
*The Killdeer*, New York Shakespeare Festival (Public Theater)
*Private Lives*, Williamstown Theatre Festival
*A Touch of the Poet*, Hartford Stage Company
*The Hot L Baltimore*, Hartford Stage Company
*Sweet Talk*, New York Shakespeare Festival (Public Theater)
*Where's Charley?*, Circle in the Square, NYC
*Studs Edsel*, Ensemble Studio Theatre, NYC
*La Cambiale di Matrimonio*, Opera Buffa of New York, NYC
*The Merry Wives of Windsor*, Augusta Repertory Theatre, ME
*Private Lives*, Williamstown Theatre Festival
*Bits and Pieces*, Manhattan Theatre Club, NYC

**1975**
*Pygmalion*, Long Wharf Theatre
*Afternoon Tea*, Hartford Stage Company
*The Beggar's Opera*, Williams College, Williamstown, MA

*Death of a Salesman*, Circle in the Square
*Life Class*, Manhattan Theate Club
*Sea Marks*, Manhattan Theatre Club
*The Sea*, Manhattan Theatre Club
*All Over*, Hartford Stage Company
*The Front* (Assistant Art Director), Columbia Pictures (Film)
*The Poison Tree*, Ambassador Theatre, NYC
*All God's Chillun Got Wings*, Circle in the Square

**1976**
*The Estate*, Hartford Stage Company
*Awake and Sing!*, McCarter Theatre Company, Princeton, NJ
*The House of Mirth*, Long Wharf Theatre
*Seven Keys to Baldpate*, American Stage Festival, Milford, NH
*Twelfth Night*, American Stage Festival
*Major Barbara*, McCarter Theatre Company
*Children*, Manhattan Theatre Club
*Alphabetical Order*, Long Wharf Theatre
*The Show-Off*, Goodman Theatre
*Green Pond* (S & C), Stage South, Columbia, SC
*All Over*, Theatre in America (PBS Television)

**1977**
*Sleuth*, Syracuse Stage, NY
*Saint Joan*, Long Wharf Theatre
*Paul Bunyan*, Manhattan School of Music
*Molly* (S & C), Spoleto Festival, Charleston, SC
*Green Pond*, Chelsea Theater Center, NYC
*Arms and the Man*, American Stage Festival
*A Flea in Her Ear*, American Stage Festival
*The Confirmation*, McCarter Theatre Company

**1978**
*The Seagull*, Indiana Repertory Theatre, Indianapolis
*A Flea in Her Ear*, Hartford Stage Company
*The Trial of the Moke*, Great Performances (PBS Television)
*Spokesong*, Long Wharf Theatre
*Da*, Hudson Guild Theatre, NYC

*The Best Little Whorehouse in Texas,*
Entermedia Theatre, NYC
*The Best Little Whorehouse in Texas,* 46th
Street Theatre, NYC
*Bonjour, La Bonjour,* Guthrie Theater,
Minneapolis, MN
*Fathers and Sons,* New York Shakespeare
Festival (Public Theater)
*Under This Sky,* Red Cloud Productions
(Film)
*The Taming of the Shrew,* Milwaukee
Repertory Theater, WI

### 1979
*Hedda Gabler,* Cincinnati Playhouse in
the Park, OH
*Spokesong,* Circle in the Square
*Summerfolk,* Long Wharf Theatre
*Right of Way,* Guthrie Theater
*Wine Untouched,* Harold Clurman The-
atre, NYC
*Oldsmobile Industrial*
*O'Neill Theater Center* (resident de-
signer), Waterford, CT
*Open Window,* Park Lane Productions
(Film)

### 1980
*Salt Lake City Skyline,* New York Shake-
speare Festival (Public Theater)
*A Midsummer Night's Dream,* Denver
Theatre Center, CO
*Mary Barnes,* Long Wharf Theatre
*Second Avenue Rag,* Phoenix Theatre
(Marymount Manhattan Theatre),
NYC
*American Buffalo,* Long Wharf Theatre
*After the Season,* Wilmington Playhouse,
DE and Colonial Theatre, Boston
*Solomon's Child,* Long Wharf Theatre
*Bonjour, Là Bonjour,* Phoenix Theatre
(Marymount Manhattan Theatre)

### 1981
*Children's Crusade,* The First All Chil-
dren's Theatre, NYC
*The Medal of Honor Rag,* American
Playhouse (PBS Television)
*Showdown at the Adobe Motel,* Hartman
Theatre, Stamford, CT
*Plenty,* Goodman Theatre
*Kean,* Arena Stage
*The Father,* Circle in the Square
*Isn't It Romantic?,* Phoenix Theatre
(Marymount Manhattan Theatre)
*American Buffalo,* Circle in the Square
Downtown

*Hedda Gabler,* Boston University
*A Day in the Death of Joe Egg,*
Long Wharf Theatre
*Kaufman at Large,* Phoenix Theatre
(Marymount Manhattan Theatre)

### 1982
*Solomon's Child,* Little Theatre, NYC
*Ethan Frome,* Long Wharf Theatre
*The Woods,* The Second Stage, NYC
*Corpse!,* American Stage Festival
*Present Laughter,* Circle in the Square
*Steaming,* Brooks Atkinson Theatre,
NYC
*Open Admissions,* Long Wharf Theatre
*Extremities,* Cheryl Crawford Theatre,
NYC

### 1983
*Another Country,* Long Wharf Theatre
*The Misanthrope,* Circle in the Square
*Moose Murders,* Eugene O'Neill Theatre
*A Lesson from Aloes,* La Jolla Playhouse,
CA
*Wild Life,* Vandam Street Theatre, NYC
*Under the Ilex,* The Repertory Theatre of
St. Louis, MO
*Hot Lunch Apostles,* La Mama E.T.C.,
NYC
*American Buffalo,* Booth Theatre, NYC
*Extremities,* Los Angeles Public Theatre
*Lunching,* New Broadway Theatre, Chi-
cago, IL
*A Mad World, My Masters,* La Jolla Play-
house
*Heartbreak House,* Circle in the Square
*Old Times,* Roundabout Theatre, NYC
*A Private View,* New York Shakespeare
Festival (Public Theater)

### 1984
*The Value of Names,* Hartford Stage
Company
*Cantorial,* Hartman Theatre
*Requiem for a Heavyweight,* Long Wharf
Theatre
*The Bathers,* Long Wharf Theatre
*Under the Ilex,* Long Wharf Theatre

## EUGENE LEE

### 1965
*Endgame,* Theatre of the Living Arts,
Philadelphia, PA

### 1966
*Poor Bitos,* Theatre of the Living Arts
*Fitz and Biscuit,* Circle in the Square,
NYC
*A Dream of Love,* Theatre of the Living
Arts
*Beclch* (Costumes only), Theatre of the
Living Arts
*Endgame,* Yale Repertory Theatre, New
Haven, CT

### 1967
*The Threepenny Opera,* Studio Arena
Theatre, Buffalo, NY
*The Threepenny Opera,* Trinity Square
Repertory Company, Providence, RI
*The Imaginary Invalid,* Studio Arena
Theatre
*H.M.S. Pinafore,* Studio Arena Theatre
*The Importance of Being Earnest,* Trinity
Square

### 1968
*Enrico IV,* Studio Arena Theatre
*A Delicate Balance,* Studio Arena The-
atre
*Years of the Locust,* Trinity Square
*An Enemy of the People,* Trinity Square
*Phaedra,* Trinity Square
*Brother to Dragons* (S & L), Trinity
Square

### 1969
*Macbeth,* Trinity Square
*The Homecoming,* Trinity Square
*Billy Budd,* Trinity Square
*World War 2½,* Martinique Theatre,
NYC
*Exiles,* Trinity Square
*The Old Glory (Endecott and the Red
Cross; My Kinsman Major Molineux;
Benito Cereno)* (S & L), Trinity
Square
*The Recruiting Officer,* Theatre of the
Living Arts
*House of Breath* and *Black/White,* Trinity
Square
*Slave Ship,* Chelsea Theater Center
(Brooklyn Academy of Music), NY
*Harry, Noon and Night,* Theatre of the
Living Arts
*Gargoyle Cartoons,* Theatre of the Living
Arts
*Wilson in the Promise Land,* Trinity
Square

### 1970
*Wilson in the Promise Land,* Rhode Is-
land School of Design Theatre
*Slave Ship,* Theatre-in-the-Church,
NYC
*The Skin of Our Teeth,* Trinity Square
*Lovecraft's Follies,* Trinity Square
*The Universal Nigger,* Brooklyn Academy
of Music
*Wilson in the Promise Land,* ANTA The-
atre, NYC
*Alice in Wonderland* (S & L), Manhattan
Project (The Extension Theatre),
NYC
*You Can't Take It with You,* Trinity Square
*Saved,* Chelsea Theater Center
*Son of Man and the Family,* Trinity
Square
*Mother Courage and Her Children,* Arena
Stage, Washington, D.C.
*The Taming of the Shrew,* Trinity Square

### 1971
*The Good and Bad Times of Cady Francis
McCullum and Friends,* Trinity
Square
*The Threepenny Opera,* Trinity Square
*Orghast,* Shiraz Festival, Iran
*Troilus and Cressida,* Trinity Square
*Down by the River Where Waterlilies Are
Disfigured Every Day,* Trinity Square

### 1972
*Alice in Wonderland,* Manhattan Project
(The Performing Garage), NYC
*Old Times,* Trinity Square
*Endgame,* Manhattan Project
*Dude,* Broadway Theatre, NYC

### 1973
*The Royal Hunt of the Sun,* Trinity
Square
*Feasting with Panthers,* Trinity Square
*Ghost Dance,* Trinity Square
*Aimee,* Trinity Square
*Brother to Dragons,* Trinity Square
*Candide,* Chelsea Theater Center

### 1974
*A Man for All Seasons,* Trinity Square
*Candide,* Broadway Theatre
*Saturday Night Live* (through 1980),
NBC Television
*Well Hung* (S & L), Trinity Square
*Gabrielle,* Studio Arena Theatre

*Feasting with Panthers*, Theatre in America (PBS Television)

**1975**
*Peer Gynt* (S & L), Trinity Square
*Tom Jones* (S & L), Trinity Square
*Seven Keys to Baldpate* (S & L), Trinity Square
*The Skin of Our Teeth*, Mark Hellinger Theatre, NYC
*Cathedral of Ice*, Trinity Square
*Two Gentlemen of Verona*, Trinity Square
*Brother to Dragons*, Theatre in America (PBS Television)

**1976**
*Dream on Monkey Mountain*, Center Stage, Baltimore, MD
*Bastard Son*, Trinity Square
*Eustace Chisholm and the Works*, Trinity Square
*Of Mice and Men* (S & L), Trinity Square
*Life Among the Lowly*, Visions (PBS Television)

**1977**
*King Lear* (S & L), Trinity Square
*Some of My Best Friends*, Longacre Theatre, NYC
*Ethan Frome* (S & L), Trinity Square
*Rosmersholm*, Trinity Square
*Seduced* (S & L), Trinity Square

**1978**
*Uncle Tom's Cabin: A History* (Lights only), Trinity Square
*La Fanciulla del West*, Lyric Opera of Chicago, IL

**1979**
*Sweeney Todd, the Demon Barber of Fleet Street*, Uris Theatre, NYC
*Gilda Radner, Live from New York*, Winter Garden Theatre, NYC
*The Scarlet Letter*, PBS Television
*Sweeney Todd*, London

**1980**
*Kaspar* (S & L), International Center for Theatre Research, Paris

**1981**
*It's Me, Sylvia*, Playhouse Theatre, NYC
*Willie Stark*, Kennedy Center Opera House, Washington, DC
*Inherit the Wind*, Trinity Square

*Simon and Garfunkel Concert*, Central Park, NYC
*Faust*, Opera Company of Boston, MA
*Of Mice and Men* (S & L), Trinity Square (tour)
*Buried Child*, Trinity Square (tour)
*Steve Martin Special*, NBC Television
*Merrily We Roll Along*, Alvin Theatre, NYC
*House of Mirth*, PBS Television

**1982**
*The Little Prince and the Aviator*, Alvin Theatre
*The Hothouse* (S & L), Trinity Square
*Agnes of God*, Music Box Theatre, NYC
*Simon and Garfunkel*, Tokyo
*The Hothouse* (S & L), Playhouse Theatre, NYC
*Hammett*, Zoetrope Studios (Film)
*The Web*, Trinity Square
*Bone Songs*, Twyla Tharp Dance Foundation (Cubiculo Theatre), NYC
*Easy Money*, Orion Films

**1983**
*The Tempest* (S & L), Trinity Square
*Letters from Prison: In the Belly of the Beast* (S & L), Trinity Square
*Newsweek 50th Anniversary*, New York State Theatre, NYC
*Galileo* (S & L), Trinity Square
*The Wild Duck*, Trinity Square
*The Ballad of Soapy Smith*, Seattle Repertory Company, WA
*Billy Bishop Goes to War*, Bradford Theatre, Boston, MA
*Randy Newman Live at the Odeon*, Showtime (Television)

**1984**
*The New Show*, NBC Television
*The Wild Duck*, Dallas Theater Center (Arts District Theater), TX
*Jonestown Express*, Trinity Square
*Tom Jones* (S & L), Dallas Theater Center (Arts District Theater)
*Seven Keys to Baldpate* (S & L), Dallas Theater Center (Arts District Theater)
*Galileo*, Dallas Theater Center (Kalita Humphreys Theater)
*Fool for Love*, Dallas Theater Center (Humphreys Theater)
*Misalliance*, Dallas Theater Center (Humphreys Theater)

*The Ballad of Soapy Smith*, New York Shakespeare Festival (Public Theater)

## MING CHO LEE

**1955**
*Guys and Dolls*, Grist Mill Playhouse, Andover, NJ

**1958**
*The Infernal Machine*, Phoenix Theatre, NYC
*Missa Brevis*, Juilliard Opera Theatre, NYC
*The Crucible*, Martinique Theatre, NYC
*Triad*, Theater Marquee, NYC

**1959**
*Three Short Dances*, Connecticut College, New London, CT
*The Turk in Italy* (S & L), Peabody Arts Theatre, Baltimore, MD

**1960**
*The Old Maid and the Thief* (S & L), Peabody Arts Theatre
*The Fall of the City* (S & L), Peabody Arts Theatre
*La Bohème* (S & L), Peabody Arts Theatre
*Kata Kabanova*, Empire State Music Festival, Bear Mountain, NY
*Peter Ibbetson*, Empire State Music Festival

**1961**
*Amahl and the Night Visitors* (S & L), Peabody Arts Theatre
*Three by Offenbach* (S & L), Peabody Arts Theatre
*Don Giovanni* (S & L), Peabody Arts Theatre
*The Pearl Fishers*, Empire State Music Festival
Resident designer, San Francisco Opera

**1962**
*Tristan and Isolde* (S & L), Baltimore Civic Opera, Baltimore, MD
*Werther* (S & L), Peabody Arts Theatre
*The Merchant of Venice*, New York Shakespeare Festival (Delacorte Theater)

*The Tempest*, New York Shakespeare Festival (Delacorte Theater)
*King Lear*, New York Shakespeare Festival (Delacorte Theater)
*Macbeth*, New York Shakespeare Festival (Delacorte Theater)
*A Look at Lightning*, Martha Graham Dance Company, NYC
*The Moon Beseiged*, Lyceum Theatre, NYC
*Hamlet* (S & L), Peabody Arts Theatre
*Madama Butterfly* (S & L), Opera Company of Boston (school tour), MA

**1963**
*Antony and Cleopatra*, New York Shakespeare Festival (Delacorte Theater)
*As You Like It*, New York Shakespeare Festival (Delacorte Theater)
*A Winter's Tale*, New York Shakespeare Festival (Delacorte Theater)
*Twelfth Night*, New York Shakespeare Festival (Delacorte Theater)
*Mother Courage and Her Children*, Martin Beck Theatre, NYC
*Conversations in the Dark*, (Pre-Broadway)
*Walk in Darkness*, Greenwich Mews Theatre, NYC
*Sea Shadow*, Joffrey Ballet, NYC
*Sideshow*, (Pre-Broadway)

**1964**
*Hamlet*, New York Shakespeare Festival (Delacorte Theater)
*Othello*, New York Shakespeare Festival (Delacorte Theater)
*Electra*, New York Shakespeare Festival (Delacorte Theater)
*A Midsummer Night's Dream*, New York Shakespeare Festival (Delacorte Theater)
*Il Tabarro*, Juilliard Opera Theatre
*Gianni Schicchi*, Juilliard Opera Theatre
*Kata Kabanova*, Juilliard Opera Theatre

**1965**
*Love's Labour's Lost*, New York Shakespeare Festival (Delacorte Theater)
*Coriolanus*, New York Shakespeare Festival (Delacorte Theater)
*Troilus and Cressida*, New York Shakespeare Festival (Delacorte Theater)
*The Taming of the Shrew*, New York Shakespeare Festival (Delacorte Theater)

*Henry V*, New York Shakespeare Festival (Delacorte Theater)
*Ariadne*, Alvin Ailey Dance Company, NYC
*The Witch of Endor*, Martha Graham Dance Company
*Madama Butterfly*, Metropolitan Opera National Company
*Fidelio*, Juilliard Opera Theatre
*The Magic Flute*, Juilliard Opera Theatre

**1966**
*All's Well That Ends Well*, New York Shakespeare Festival (Delacorte Theater)
*Measure for Measure*, New York Shakespeare Festival (Delacorte Theater)
*Richard III*, New York Shakespeare Festival (Delacorte Theater)
*Slapstick Tragedy*, Longacre Theatre, NYC
*A Time for Singing*, Broadway Theatre, NYC
*Olympics*, Joffrey Ballet
*Night Wings*, Joffrey Ballet
*Don Rodrigo*, New York City Opera
*Julius Caesar*, New York City Opera
*The Marriage of Figaro*, Metropolitan Opera National Company
*The Trial of Lucullus*, Juilliard Opera Theatre

**1967**
*A Comedy of Errors*, New York Shakespeare Festival (Delacorte Theater)
*Titus Andronicus*, New York Shakespeare Festival (Delacorte Theater)
*Hair*, New York Shakespeare Festival (Public Theater)
*Little Murders*, Broadhurst Theatre, NYC
*The Crucible*, Arena Stage, Washington, DC
*Elegy*, Joffrey Ballet
*The Rape of Lucretia*, Juilliard Opera Theatre
*Bomarzo*, Opera Society of Washington, DC
*Le Coq d'or*, New York City Opera
*Boris Godunov*, Associated Opera Companies of America

**1968**
*Henry IV, Parts 1 and 2*, New York Shakespeare Festival (Delacorte Theater)

*Romeo and Juliet*, New York Shakespeare Festival (Delacorte Theater)
*Ergo*, New York Shakespeare Festival (Public Theater)
*Here's Where I Belong*, Billy Rose Theatre, NYC
*The Tenth Man*, Arena Stage
*Room Service*, Arena Stage
*The Iceman Cometh*, Arena Stage
*King Lear*, Repertory Theatre of Lincoln Center, NYC
*A Light Fantastic*, Joffrey Ballet
*The Lady of the House of Sleep*, Martha Graham Dance Company
*Secret Places*, Joffrey Ballet
*Bomarzo*, New York City Opera
*L'Ormindo*, Juilliard Opera Theatre
*Faust*, New York City Opera

**1969**
*Peer Gynt*, New York Shakespeare Festival (Delacorte Theater)
*Cities in Bezique*, New York Shakespeare Festival (Public Theater)
*Invitation to a Beheading* New York Shakespeare Festival (Public Theater)
*Electra*, New York Shakespeare Festival (Mobile Unit)
*Sambo* (co-designed with Marjorie Kellogg), New York Shakespeare Festival (Public Theater)
*Billy*, Billy Rose Theatre,
*La Strada*, Lunt-Fontanne Theatre, NYC
*Animus*, Joffrey Ballet
*The Poppet*, Joffrey Ballet
*Julius Caesar*, Hamburg State Opera, Hamburg, Germany
*The Barber of Seville*, American Opera Center, NYC
*Help! Help! The Globolinks*, New York City Center

**1970**
*The Wars of the Roses*, New York Shakespeare Festival (Delacorte Theater)
*Jack MacGowran in the Works of Samuel Beckett*, New York Shakespeare Festival (Public Theater)
*Gandhi*, Playhouse Theatre, NYC
*The Night Thoreau Spent in Jail*, Arena Stage
*Roberto Devereux*, New York City Opera
*The Rake's Progress*, Juilliard Opera Theatre

*Il Giuramento*, American Opera Center
*Othello* (unproduced project)

**1971**
*Timon of Athens*, New York Shakespeare Festival (Delacorte Theater)
*Two Gentlemen of Verona*, New York Shakespeare Festival (Delacorte Theater)
*Lolita, My Love*, Shubert Theatre, Philadelphia
*Remote Asylum*, Ahmanson Theatre, Los Angeles
*Ariodante*, Kennedy Center, Washington, DC
*Susannah*, New York City Opera
*Two Gentlemen of Verona*, St. James Theatre, NYC

**1972**
*Hamlet*, New York Shakespeare Festival (Delacorte Theater)
*Much Ado About Nothing*, New York Shakespeare Festival (Delacorte Theater)
*Much Ado About Nothing*, Winter Garden Theatre, NYC
*Older People*, New York Shakespeare Festival (Public Theater)
*Wedding Band*, New York Shakespeare Festival (Public Theater)
*Volpone*, Mark Taper Forum, Los Angeles
*Henry IV*, Mark Taper Forum
*Our Town*, Arena Stage
*Maria Stuarda*, New York City Opera
*Tales of Hoffman*, New York City Opera
*La Bohème*, American Opera Center
*Lucia de Lammermoor*, Teatro Colon, Buenos Aires
*Bomarzo*, Teatro Colon

**1973**
*Inherit the Wind*, Arena Stage
*Lear*, Yale Repertory Theatre, New Haven, CT
*Don Juan*, San Francisco Ballet
*Myth of a Voyage*, Martha Graham Dance Company
*Four Saints in Three Acts*, Metropolitan Opera at the Forum
*Syllabaire Pour Phedre*, Metropolitan Opera at the Forum
*Dido and Aeneas*, Metropolitan Opera at the Forum
*Anna Bolena*, New York City Opera

*St. Matthew's Passion*, San Francisco Opera
*La Favorita*, San Francisco Opera
*Le Coq d'or*, Dallas Civic Center, TX

**1974**
*The Seagull*, New York Shakespeare Festival (Public Theater)
*Whispers of Darkness*, National Ballet of Canada
*Boris Godunov*, Metropolitan Opera
*Idomeneo*, Kennedy Center

**1975**
*All God's Chillun Got Wings*, Circle in the Square, NYC
*The Glass Menagerie*, Circle in the Square
*Julius Caesar*, Arena Stage
*The Ascent of Mt. Fuji*, Arena Stage (Kreeger Theater)
*In Quest of the Sun*, Royal Winnipeg Ballet, Canada
*The Leaves Are Fading*, American Ballet Theatre, NYC
*Idomeneo*, New York City Opera

**1976**
*For Colored Girls who have Considered Suicide/When the Rainbow is Enuf*, New York Shakespeare Festival (Public Theater)
*Waiting for Godot*, Arena Stage
*I Puritani*, Metropolitan Opera
*Lohengrin*, Metropolitan Opera
*Bilby's Doll*, Houston Grand Opera, TX

**1977**
*Caesar and Cleopatra*, Palace Theatre, NYC
*Romeo and Juliet*, Circle in the Square
*The Shadow Box*, Long Wharf Theatre, New Haven, CT
*The Shadow Box*, Morosco Theatre, NYC
*Mother Courage*, The Acting Company, NYC
*For Colored Girls . . . .*, Mark Taper Forum
*Unproduced project for Martha Graham*

**1978**
*Angel*, Minskoff Theatre, NYC
*The Grand Tour*, Palace Theatre
*King Lear*, The Acting Company
*Hamlet*, Arena Stage

*Twelfth Night*, American Shakespeare Festival, Stratford, CT
*The Tiller in the Fields*, American Ballet Theatre
*Madama Butterfly*, Lyric Opera of Chicago
*Astor Court Garden*, Chinese Wing of Metropolitan Museum of Art

**1979**

*Don Juan*, Arena Stage
*The Tempest*, Mark Taper Forum
*The Glass Menagerie*, Guthrie Theater, Minneapolis, MN
*Saint Joan*, Seattle Repertory Theatre, WA
*The Tempest*, American Shakespeare Festival

**1980**

*Plenty*, Arena Stage
*Boris Godunov*, Lyric Opera of Chicago
*Attila*, Lyric Opera of Chicago

**1981**

*Oedipus*, Brooklyn Academy of Music, NY
*Attila*, New York City Opera
*La Donna del Lago*, Houston Grand Opera
*Madama Butterfly*, Chilean Opera Society

**1982**

*K2*, Arena Stage (Kreeger Theater)
*Mary Stuart*, Stratford Festival, Ontario
*Alceste*, New York City Opera
*Montezuma*, American Opera Center

**1983**

*K2*, Brooks Atkinson Theatre, NYC
*Death of a Salesman*, Stratford Festival
*Desire Under the Elms*, Indiana Repertory Theatre, Indianapolis
*I Capuleti e I Montecchi*, American Opera Center
*The Glass Menagerie*, Eugene O'Neill Theatre, NYC
*Turandot*, Opera Company of Boston

**1984**

*The Cuban Swimmer* and *Dog Lady*, Intar Theatre, NYC

# SANTO LOQUASTO

**1965**

*Cat on a Hot Tin Roof*, Williamstown Theatre Festival, MA

**1966**

*The Subject Was Roses*, Williamstown Theatre Festival

**1967**

*Luv*, Williamstown Theatre Festival
*The Little Foxes*, Williamstown Theatre Festival
*Little Malcolm and His Struggle Against the Eunuchs* Yale School of Drama, New Haven, CT

**1968**

*The Hostage*, Hartford Stage Company, CT
*Tiny Alice*, Long Wharf Theatre, New Haven, CT
*Black Comedy/White Lies*, Williamstown Theatre Festival
*Camino Real*, Williamstown Theatre Festival
*Wait Until Dark*, Williamstown Theatre Festival
*Galileo* (Costumes only), Williamstown Theatre Festival
*How to Succeed in Business Without Really Trying*, Williamstown Theatre Festival
*The Rose Tattoo*, Hartford Stage Company

**1969**

*The Waltz Invention*, Hartford Stage Company
*The Homecoming*, Hartford Stage Company
*The Bacchae* (S & C), Yale Repertory Theatre, New Haven, CT
*Ring Round the Moon* (Costumes only), Williamstown Theatre Festival
*Tartuffe* (S & C), Williamstown Theatre Festival
*The Cherry Orchard* (S & C), Williamstown Theatre Festival
*The Unseen Hand* and *Forensic and the Navigators*, Astor Place Theatre, NYC
*A Delicate Balance* (S & C), Hartford Stage Company

*Narrow Road to the Deep North* (S & C), Charles Playhouse, Boston, MA
*The Farce of Scapin* (S & C), Hartford Stage Company

**1970**

*A Day in the Death of Joe Egg*, Hartford Stage Company
*Misalliance* (S & C), Hartford Stage Company
*The Trial of A. Lincoln*, Hartford Stage Company
*Anything Goes* (S & C), Hartford Stage Company
*Rosencrantz and Guildenstern Are Dead* (S & C), Williamstown Theatre Festival
*The Price* (S & C), Williamstown Theatre Festival
*Yale Repertory Season of Story Theatre* (S & C), John Drew Theatre, East Hampton, NY
*Rosencrantz and Guildenstern Are Dead* (S & C), Hartford Stage Company
*The Skin of Our Teeth* (Costumes only), Long Wharf Theatre
*The Revenger's Tragedy*, Yale Repertory Theatre

**1971**

*Ring Round the Moon*, Hartford Stage Company
*A Gun Play*, Hartford Stage Company
*Long Day's Journey into Night* (S & C), Hartford Stage Company
*The Seven Deadly Sins* (S & C), Yale Repertory Theatre
*Wipe-Out Games*, Arena Stage (Kreeger Theater), Washington, DC
*The Sign in Sidney Brustein's Window*, Arena Stage
*The Birthday Party* (S & C), Williamstown Theatre Festival
*Plaza Suite* (S & C), Williamstown Theatre Festival
*Mother Courage and Her Children* (Costumes only), Williamstown Theatre Festival
*Hedda Gabler* (S & C), Williamstown Theatre Festival
*Pantagleize*, Arena Stage (Kreeger Theater)
*The House of Blue Leaves*, Arena Stage (Kreeger Theater)
*Uptight*, Arena Stage (Kreeger Theater)
*Sticks and Bones*, New York Shakespeare Festival (Public Theater)

*The Barber of Seville* (S & C), San Francisco Spring Opera

**1972**

*That Championship Season* (S & C), New York Shakespeare Festival (Public Theater)
*Old Times*, Mark Taper Forum, Los Angeles
*Henry V* (S & C), Hartford Stage Company
*The Resistible Rise of Arturo Ui* (Costumes only), Williamstown Theatre Festival
*Uncle Vanya* (S & C), Williamstown Theatre Festival
*A Streetcar Named Desire*, Hartford Stage Company
*Sticks and Bones*, Golden Theatre, NYC
*The Secret Affairs of Mildred Wild*, Ambassador Theatre, NYC
*That Championship Season*, Booth Theatre, NYC
*The Rake's Progress*, Kennedy Center Opera House, Washington, DC
*Sunset*, Chelsea Theater, NYC
*A Public Prosecutor Is Sick of It All*, Arena Stage (Kreeger Theater)

**1973**

*The Orphan*, New York Shakespeare Festival (Public Theater)
*The Siamese Connection*, New York Shakespeare Festival (Public Theater)
*You Can't Take It with You*, Hartford Stage Company
*As You Like It*, New York Shakespeare Festival (Delacorte Theater)
*King Lear*, New York Shakespeare Festival (Delacorte Theater)
*La Dafne* (S & C), New York Pro Musica Antiqua, Spoleto, Italy
*In the Boom Boom Room* (S & C), New York Shakespeare Festival (Vivian Beaumont Theatre)
*The Tempest* (S & C), New York Shakespeare Festival (Mitzi E. Newhouse Theatre)
*What the Wine Sellers Buy*, New York Shakespeare Festival (Vivian Beaumont Theatre)

**1974**

*The Dance of Death*, New York Shakespeare Festival (Vivian Beaumont Theatre)

*Macbeth* (S & C), New York Shakespeare Festival (Mitzi E. Newhouse Theatre)

*Pericles*, New York Shakespeare Festival (Delacorte Theater)

*The Merry Wives of Windsor*, New York Shakespeare Festival (Delacorte Theater)

*Ah, Wilderness!* (S & C), Williamstown Theatre Festival

*Mert and Phil*, New York Shakespeare Festival (Vivian Beaumont Theatre)

*Richard III*, New York Shakespeare Festival (Mitzi E. Newhouse Theatre)

*A Midsummer Night's Dream* (S & C), New York Shakespeare Festival (Mitzi E. Newhouse Theatre)

### 1975

*A Doll's House*, New York Shakespeare Festival (Vivian Beaumont Theatre)

*The Cherry Orchard*, Hartford Stage Company

*Hamlet*, New York Shakespeare Festival (Delacorte Theater)

*The Comedy of Errors* (S & C), New York Shakespeare Festival (Delacorte Theater)

*Kennedy's Children* (S & C), Golden Theatre

*Rusalka* (S & C), San Diego Opera

*Murder Among Friends*, Biltmore Theatre, NYC

*Hamlet*, New York Shakespeare Festival (Vivian Beaumont Theatre)

*Sue's Leg* (Costumes only), Twyla Tharp Dance Foundation, NYC

*The Double Cross* (Costumes only), Twyla Tharp Dance Foundation

*Ocean's Motion* (Costumes only), Twyla Tharp Dance Foundation

*Awake and Sing!*, Hartford Stage Company

*Measure for Measure* (S & C), New York Shakespeare Festival (Delacorte Theater)

### 1976

*Legend* (S & C), Ethel Barrymore Theatre, NYC

*The Glass Menagerie* (S & C), Hartford Stage Company

*Other Dances* (Costumes only), American Ballet Theatre and New York City Ballet

*Push Comes to Shove* (Costumes only), American Ballet Theatre, NYC

*Heartbreak House*, Arena Stage

*Give and Take*, Twyla Tharp Dance Foundation

*Once More Frank*, American Ballet Theatre

*Country Dances*, Twyla Tharp Dance Foundation

*Happily Ever After*, Joffrey Ballet, NYC

*After All*, New York State Olympic Committee

*Washington Square* (S & C), Michigan Opera Company

### 1977

*The Cherry Orchard* (S & C), New York Shakespeare Festival (Vivian Beaumont Theatre)

*American Buffalo* (S & C), Ethel Barrymore Theatre

*Agamemnon* (Costumes only), New York Shakespeare Festival (Vivian Beaumont Theatre)

*The Lower Depths*, Arena Stage

*The Italian Straw Hat* (S & C), The Acting Company (Saratoga Spa Theatre, Saratoga, NY)

*Golda* (S & C), Morosco Theatre, NYC

*Miss Margarida's Way* (S & C), Ambassador Theatre

*Landscape of the Body* (S & C), New York Shakespeare Festival (Public Theater)

*The Caucasian Chalk Circle* (S & C), Arena Stage

*Mud Cacklin' Hen* (Costumes only), Twyla Tharp Dance Foundation

### 1978

*Don Quixote* (Costumes only), American Ballet Theatre

*The Mighty Gents*, Ambassador Theatre

*The Play's the Thing*, Brooklyn Academy of Music

*Curse of the Starving Class* (S & C), New York Shakespeare Festival (Public Theater)

*Heptagon* (Costumes only), Joffrey Ballet

*Stop the World, I Want to Get Off* (S & C), New York State Theatre and tour

*King of Hearts*, Minskoff Theatre, NYC

*Sarava* (S & C), Mark Hellinger Theatre, NYC

*Simon* (Costumes only), Martin Bregman Productions (Film)

### 1979

*The Four Seasons* (S & C), New York City Ballet

*1903 Baker's Dozen* (Costumes only), Twyla Tharp Dance Foundation

*The Goodbye People*, Belasco Theatre, NYC

*Daddy Goodness*, Pre-Broadway

*Sylvia Pas de Deux* (Costumes only), American Ballet Theatre

*Old World*, Hartford Stage Company

*Bent*, New Apollo Theatre, NYC

### 1980

*Stardust Memories* (Costumes only), Rollins and Joffe Productions, Inc. (Film)

*Chapters and Verses* (Costumes only), Twyla Tharp Dance Foundation

*Celebration* (Costumes only), Joffrey Ballet

*Le Corsaire Pas de Deux* (Costumes only), American Ballet Theatre

*The Fan* (Production Designer), Robert Stigwood Productions (Film)

*The Member of the Wedding*, Hartford Stage Company

*Emigres*, Arena Stage (Kreeger Theater)

*The Suicide* (S & C), ANTA Theatre, NYC

*Twyla Tharp and Dancers on Broadway* (Production Designer), Winter Garden Theatre, NYC

*Dances of Albion* (S & C), Royal Ballet, London

*Raymonda* (S & C), American Ballet Theatre

### 1981

*A Midsummer Night's Dream* (S & C), Brooklyn Academy of Music

*So Fine* (Production Designer), Warner Brothers (Film)

*The Floating Light Bulb* (S & C), Vivian Beaumont Theatre

*A Midsummer Night's Sex Comedy* (Costumes only), Rollins and Joffe Productions (Film)

*Concerto/Jardin Animé/Bournonville Pas de Trois/La Fille Mal Gardée Pas de Deux/Flower Festival Pas de Deux* (Costumes only), American Ballet Theatre

*Twyla Tharp and Dancers on Broadway/ The Catherine Wheel* (S & C), Winter Garden Theatre

*Crossing Niagara* (S & C), Manhattan Theatre Club, NYC

### 1982

*The Wake of Jamey Foster*, Hartford Stage Company

*Gershwin Concerto* (S & C), New York City Ballet

*As You Like It* (S & C), Guthrie Theater, Minneapolis, MN

*Gardenia*, Manhattan Theatre Club

*Harlequinade* (Costumes only), American Ballet Theatre

*Inconsequentials* (Costumes only), Ballet Théâtre Français

*The Catherine Wheel* (Production Designer), British Broadcasting Corporation (Television)

*The Wake of Jamey Foster*, Eugene O'Neill Theatre, NYC

*The Three Sisters*, Manhattan Theatre Club

### 1983

*Follow the Feet* and *Theme and Variations* (Costumes only), American Ballet Theatre

*Peer Gynt* (S & C), Guthrie Theater

*America Kicks Up Its Heels* (S & C), Playwrights Horizons, NYC

*Once Upon a Time* (Costumes only), American Ballet Theatre

*The Glass Menagerie* (S & C), Hartford Stage Company

*Richard III* (S & C), New York Shakespeare Festival (Delacorte Theater)

*Booth Is Back in Town*, Pepsico Summer Fare, Purchase, NY

*Orgasmo Adulto Escapes from the Zoo*, New York Shakespeare Festival (Public Theater)

*Uncle Vanya* (S & C), La Mama E.T.C., NYC

*The Photographer* (S & C), Next Wave Festival, Brooklyn Academy of Music

*Fait Accompli* (Costumes only), Twyla Tharp and Dancers

### 1984

*Cinderella* (S & C), American Ballet Theatre

*Falling in Love* (Production Designer), (Film)

*Desperately Seeking Susan* (Production Designer), (Film)

## DAVID MITCHELL

**1965**

*Henry V*, New York Shakespeare Festival (School tour)
*Medea*, Martinique Theatre, NYC

**1966**

*Macbeth*, New York Shakespeare Festival (Truck stage)
*Madama Butterfly*, Juilliard School of Music, NYC

**1967**

*Volpone*, New York Shakespeare Festival (Truck stage)
*Falstaff* [Opera], Teatro Municipale, Santiago, Chile
*La Bohème*, Augusta Opera Company, Augusta, GA
*Naked Hamlet*, New York Shakespeare Festival (Public Theater)

**1968**

*Aïda*, Teatro Municipale
*Naked Hamlet*, New York Shakespeare Festival (Truck stage)
*Take One Step*, New York Shakespeare Festival (Truck stage)
*A Cry of Players*, Berkshire Theatre Festival, Lenox, MA

**1969**

*Pelléas and Mélisande*, Loeb Drama Center, Boston, MA
*Mefistofele*, New York City Opera
*The Increased Difficulty of Concentration* (S & C), Repertory Theatre of Lincoln Center, NYC

**1970**

*Journeys*, Pennsylvania Ballet, Philadelphia, PA
*Grin and Bare It* and *Postcards*, Belasco Theatre, NYC
*Colette*, Ellen Stewart Theatre, NYC
*Steambath*, Truck and Warehouse Theatre, NYC
*Trelawney of the Wells*, New York Shakespeare Festival (Public Theater)

**1971**

*How the Other Half Loves*, Royale Theatre, NYC
*Fire in the Mindhouse*, Center Stage, Baltimore, MD

*The Basic Training of Pavlo Hummel*, New York Shakespeare Festival (Public Theater)
*Manon Lescaut*, San Francisco Opera
*The Incomparable Max*, Royale Theatre

**1972**

*Aïda*, Deutsche Oper, West Berlin
*Lord Byron*, Juilliard School of Music
*The Cherry Orchard*, New York Shakespeare Festival (Public Theater)

**1973**

*Il Trovatore*, Paris Opera
*Macbeth* [Opera], Washington, Houston, Philadelphia
*Così fan tutte*, Pennsylvania Music Academy
*Barbary Shore*, New York Shakespeare Festival (Public Theater)

**1974**

*Short Eyes*, New York Shakespeare Festival (Public Theater)
*Short Eyes*, New York Shakespeare Festival (Vivian Beaumont Theater)
*Boris Godunov*, Cincinnati Opera, OH
*The Cherry Orchard*, Goodman Theatre, Chicago, IL
*The Wager*, Eastside Playhouse, NYC
*In the Boom Boom Room*, New York Shakespeare Festival (Public Theater)
*Enter a Free Man*, Theatre of St. Clements Church, NYC

**1975**

*Little Black Sheep*, New York Shakespeare Festival (Vivian Beaumont Theater)
*The Ravel Festival* (Supervising Designer), New York City Ballet
*Shoe Shine Parlor*, New York Shakespeare Festival (Truck stage)
*Trelawney of the Wells*, New York Shakespeare Festival (Vivian Beaumont Theater)

**1976**

*Apple Pie*, New York Shakespeare Festival (Public Theater)
*Mrs. Warren's Profession*, New York Shakespeare Festival (Vivian Beaumont Theater)
*The Steadfast Tin Soldier* (S & C), New York City Ballet

*Henry V*, New York Shakespeare Festival (Delacorte Theater)

**1977**

*Mondongo*, New York Shakespeare Festival (Public Theater)
*I Love My Wife*, Ethel Barrymore Theatre, NYC
*Annie*, Alvin Theatre, NYC
*The Gin Game*, Long Wharf Theatre, New Haven, CT
*The Gin Game*, John Golden Theatre, NYC
*The Italian Straw Hat*, Santa Fe Opera, NM
*A Photograph*, New York Shakespeare Festival (Public Theater)
*Working*, Goodman Theatre

**1978**

*The Prince of Grand Street*, Forrest Theatre, Philadelphia, PA
*Working*, 46th Street Theatre, NYC
*End of the War*, Ensemble Studio Theatre, NYC
*Funny Face*, Studio Arena Theatre, Buffalo, NY
*The Steadfast Tin Soldier* (S & C), Dance in America (PBS Television)
*Rich Kids*, United Artists (Film)

**1979**

*I Remember Mama*, Imperial Theatre, NYC
*The Price*, Spoleto Festival, Charleston, SC; Harold Clurman Theatre, NYC; 46th Street Theatre
*One Trick Pony*, Warner Brothers (Film)

**1980**

*Barnum*, St. James Theatre, NYC

**1981**

*Bring Back Birdie*, Martin Beck Theatre, NYC
*Can Can*, Minskoff Theatre, NYC
*The Tempest*, New York Shakespeare Festival
*My Dinner With Andre* (Film)
CBS Cable Television (Concept design)
*Sizwe Bansi Is Dead*, CBS Cable Television
*Gertrude Stein*, CBS Cable Television

**1982**

*The Magic Flute*, New York City Ballet
*The Bournonville Dances*, Dance in America (PBS Television)
*Foxfire*, Ethel Barrymore Theatre
*Creation of the World* (S & C), New York City Ballet

**1983**

*Rossini Quartets*, *The Magic Flute*, *Stravinsky Pieces*, New York City Ballet
*Brighton Beach Memoirs*, Neil Simon Theatre, NYC
*Private Lives*, Lunt-Fontanne Theatre, NYC
*Dance a Little Closer*, Minskoff Theatre
*La Cage aux Folles*, Palace Theatre, NYC

**1984**

*The Old Flag*, George Street Playhouse, New Brunswick, NJ
*The Cabal of Hypocrites*, The Actors Studio, NYC

## DOUGLAS SCHMIDT

**1961**

*The Importance of Being Earnest*, Monmouth Repertory Company, ME
*The Devil's Disciple*, Monmouth Repertory Company
*Othello*, Monmouth Repertory Company
*Androcles and the Lion*, Monmouth Repertory Company

**1963**

*Blood Wedding*, Boston University Theatre, MA
*The Emperor*, Cincinnati Playhouse in the Park, OH
*The Caretaker*, Cincinnati Playhouse in the Park
*Twelfth Night*, Cincinnati Playhouse in the Park
*The Fantasticks*, Cincinnati Playhouse in the Park

**1964**

*Tiger At the Gates*, Boston University Theatre

**1965**

*Ghosts*, Cincinnati Playhouse in the Park
*The Collection* and *The Lover*, Cincinnati Playhouse in the Park

*Major Barbara*, Cincinnati Playhouse in the Park
*Summer of the Seventeenth Doll*, Cincinnati Playhouse in the Park
*She Stoops to Conquer*, Cincinnati Playhouse in the Park
*The Glass Menagerie*, Cincinnati Playhouse in the Park
*Caesar and Cleopatra*, Center Stage, Baltimore, MD
Festival Stage (Designer), Center Stage

**1966**

*La Bohème*, Juilliard Opera Theatre, NYC
*Man and Superman*, Cincinnati Playhouse in the Park
*Benito Cereno* and *The American Dream*, Cincinnati Playhouse in the Park
*Charley's Aunt*, Cincinnati Playhouse in the Park
*Eh?*, Cincinnati Playhouse in the Park
*The Skin of Our Teeth*, Cincinnati Playhouse in the Park
*The Ox Cart*, Greenwich Mews Theatre, NYC

**1967**

*The Marriage of Figaro*, Juilliard Opera Theatre
*A Clearing in the Woods*, The Theatre of Riverside Church, NYC
*The Mines of Sulphur*, Juilliard Opera Theatre
*The Importance of Being Earnest*, Cincinnati Playhouse in the Park
*To Bury a Cousin*, Bouwerie Lane Theatre, NYC
*The Cavern*, Cincinnati Playhouse in the Park
*King John*, New York Shakespeare Festival (Delacorte Theater)
*Anatol*, Cincinnati Playhouse in the Park
*Father Uxbridge Wants to Marry*, American Place Theatre, NYC
*The Entertainer*, The Theatre of the Living Arts, Philadelphia
*The Great White Hope*, Arena Stage, Washington, DC

**1968**

*Silent Night, Lonely Night*, The Theatre of Riverside Church
*Tonantzintla*, Juilliard Theatre
*Misalliance*, Cincinnati Playhouse in the Park

*The Memorandum*, New York Shakespeare Festival (Public Theater)
*Camino Real*, Cincinnati Playhouse in the Park
*The Madwoman of Chaillot*, Cincinnati Playhouse in the Park
*Huui, Huui*, New York Shakespeare Festival (St. Clement's Church)
*Trainer, Dean, Liepolt & Co.*, American Place Theatre
*Geese, Parents*, and *Children*, Players Theatre, NYC

**1969**

*La Pinata*, Juilliard Theatre
*The Inner Journey*, Repertory Theatre of Lincoln Center (Forum Theatre), NYC
*Julius Caesar*, Guthrie Theater, Minneapolis, MN
*The Homecoming*, Guthrie Theater
*Twelfth Night*, New York Shakespeare Festival (Delacorte Theater)
*The Time of Your Life*, Repertory Theatre of Lincoln Center (Vivian Beaumont Theater)

**1970**

*Paris Is Out!*, Brooks Atkinson Theatre, NYC
*The Disintegration of James Cherry*, Repertory Theatre of Lincoln Center (Forum Theater)
*Operation Sidewinder*, Repertory Theatre of Lincoln Center (Beaumont Theater)
*Mod Donna*, New York Shakespeare Festival (Public Theater)
*The Good Woman of Setzuan*, Repertory Theatre of Lincoln Center (Beaumont Theater)

**1971**

*The Playboy of the Western World* (S & C), Repertory Theatre of Lincoln Center (Beaumont Theater)
*An Enemy of the People*, Repertory Theatre of Lincoln Center (Beaumont Theater)
*The Losers*, Juilliard Opera Theatre
*Pictures in the Hallway* (S & C), Repertory Theatre of Lincoln Center (Forum Theater)
*Antigone*, Repertory Theatre of Lincoln Center (Beaumont Theater)
*Huckleberry Finn*, Juilliard Opera Theatre

*Der Jasager and Chocorua*, Tanglewood West Barn
*L'Incoronazione di Poppea*, Tanglewood West Barn
*The School for Scandal*, The Good Shepherd Faith Church, NYC
*The Hostage*, The Good Shepherd Faith Church
*Antigone*, Playhouse New York (National Educational Television)
*Women Beware Women*, The Good Shepherd Faith Church
*The Lower Depths*, The Good Shepherd Faith Church
*Enemies*, Repertory Theatre of Lincoln Center (Beaumont Theater)
*Happy Days* and *Act Without Words*, Repertory Theatre of Lincoln Center (Forum Theater)
*Play Strindberg*, Repertory Theatre of Lincoln Center (Forum Theater)
*The Merry Wives of Windsor*, American Shakespeare Festival, Stratford, CT
*Croquefer* and *Mahagonny*, Tanglewood West Barn, Lenox, MA
*Down By the Greenwood Side, Socrates* and *Aventures et Nouvelles Aventures*, Tanglewood West Barn
*Mary Stuart*, Repertory Theatre of Lincoln Center (Beaumont Theater)
*The Country Girl*, Eisenhower Theatre, Washington, DC
*People Are Living There*, Repertory Theatre of Lincoln Center (Forum Theater)
*The Wedding of Iphegenia*, New York Shakespeare Festival (Public Theater)

**1972**

*Narrow Road to the Deep North*, Repertory Theatre of Lincoln Center (Beaumont Theater)
*The Love Suicide at Schofield Barracks*, ANTA Theatre, NYC
*Grease*, Eden Theatre, NYC
*Twelfth Night*, Repertory Theatre of Lincoln Center (Beaumont Theater)
*The Country Girl*, Billy Rose Theatre, NYC
*Suggs*, Repertory Theatre of Lincoln Center (Forum Theater)
*And Miss Reardon Drinks a Little*, Berkshire Theatre Festival, Stockbridge, MA

*Krapp's Last Tape* and *Not I*, Repertory Theatre of Lincoln Center (Forum Theater)
*Mahagonny*, Kennedy Center Opera House, Washington, DC

**1973**

*The Plough and the Stars*, Repertory Theatre of Lincoln Center (Beaumont Theater)
*Aventures et Nouvelles Aventures* and *Satyricon*, Circustheater, Scheveningen, The Netherlands
*A Streetcar Named Desire*, Repertory Theatre of Lincoln Center (Beaumont Theater)
*Macbeth*, American Shakespeare Festival
*Measure for Measure*, Saratoga Spa Theatre, NY
*The Three Sisters*, Saratoga Spa Theatre
*A Breeze from the Gulf*, Eastside Playhouse, NYC
*Veronica's Room*, Music Box Theatre, NYC

**1974**

*Il Ritorno d'Ulisse in Patria*, Kennedy Center Opera House
*Enemies*, Playhouse New York (National Educational Television)
*An American Millionaire*, Circle in the Square, NYC
*Over Here!*, Shubert Theatre, NYC
*Love's Labour's Lost*, Saratoga Spa Theatre
*Play* and *Orchestra*, Saratoga Spa Theatre
*Edward II*, Saratoga Spa Theatre
*The Taming of the Shrew*, Art Park, Buffalo, NY
*The Time of Your Life*, Mendelsohn Theatre, Ann Arbor, MI
*Fame*, Golden Theatre, NYC
*Who's Who in Hell*, Lunt-Fontanne Theatre, NYC

**1975**

*Our Late Night*, New York Shakespeare Festival (Public Theater)
*Salome*, New York City Opera
*Kid Champion*, New York Shakespeare Festival (Public Theater)
*The Robber Bridegroom*, Saratoga Spa Theatre
*Truckload*, Lyceum Theatre, NYC
*Angel Street*, Lyceum Theatre

**1976**

*The Way of the World*, Power Center, Ann Arbor, MI

*Il Ritorno d'Ulisse in Patria*, New York City Opera (revival of Kennedy Center production)

*The Time of Your Life*, Theatre in America (National Educational Television)

*The Threepenny Opera*, New York Shakespeare Festival (Vivian Beaumont Theater)

*The Robber Bridegroom*, Mark Taper Forum, Los Angeles and Biltmore Theatre, NYC

*The Kitchen*, The Acting Company, Saratoga Spa Theatre

*The Miracle Worker*, Empire State Youth Theatre Institute, Albany, NY

*Angle of Repose*, San Francisco Opera

*Herzl*, Palace Theatre, NYC

**1977**

*Camino Real*, The Acting Company, Ruth Taylor Theatre, Trinity College, San Antonio, TX

*The Crazy Locomotive*, Theatre 4, NYC

*Rigoletto*, Opera Company of Boston

*Agamemnon*, New York Shakespeare Festival (Beaumont Theater)

Cabaret Theatre (Designer), New York Shakespeare Festival (Public Theater)

*The Dodge Boys*, Hudson Guild Theatre, NYC

**1978**

*Runaways*, New York Shakespeare Festival (Public Theater)

*Runaways*, Plymouth Theatre, NYC

*Stages*, Belasco Theatre, NYC

*Alice*, Forrest Theatre, Philadelphia

*Sunset*, Studio Arena Theatre, Buffalo, NY

*They're Playing Our Song*, Ahmanson Theatre, Los Angeles

**1979**

*They're Playing Our Song*, Imperial Theatre, NYC

*Peter Allen: Up in One* (S & C), Biltmore Theatre

*The Most Happy Fella*, Majestic Theatre, NYC

*Romantic Comedy*, Ethel Barrymore Theatre, NYC

**1980**

*Hillbilly Women*, Actors Studio, NYC

*The Most Happy Fella*, Great Performances (WNET Television)

*Sidewalkin'*, Manhattan Theatre Club, NYC

*The American Clock*, Harold Clurman Theatre, NYC

*Milliken Breakfast Show*, Waldorf Astoria Hotel, NYC

*To Bury a Cousin*, Cherry Lane Theatre, NYC

*Samson et Dalila*, San Francisco Opera

*Really Rosie* (Design Supervisor), Chelsea Theatre Center, NYC

**1981**

*Frankenstein*, Palace Theatre

*Boys in Autumn*, Marines Memorial Theatre, San Francisco

*Chekhov in Yalta*, Mark Taper Forum

*Twelfth Night*, Mark Taper Forum

*Aida*, San Francisco Opera

*Samson et Dalila*, Great Performances (WNET Television)

**1982**

*Another Part of the Forest*, Ahmanson Theatre

*The Tempest*, Old Globe Theatre, San Diego, CA

*The Death of von Richtofen as Witnessed from Earth*, New York Shakespeare Festival (Public Theater)

**1983**

*The Skin of Our Teeth*, Old Globe Theatre (also broadcast live on PBS American Playhouse)

*Porgy and Bess*, Arie Crown Theatre, Chicago and Radio City Music Hall, NYC

*Wings*, American Playhouse (PBS Television)

*Twelfth Night*, Old Globe Theatre

*Chaplin*, Dorothy Chandler Pavilion, Los Angeles

**1984**

*Detective Story*, Ahmanson Theatre

*The Genius*, Mark Taper Forum

*The Public Eye* and *Black Comedy*, Ahmanson Theatre

*Mozart Piano Concerto #21*, San Francisco Ballet

*Scapino!*, Old Globe Theatre

*The Loves of Don Perlimplin*, Pepsico Summerfare, State University of New York, Purchase, NY

## ROBIN WAGNER

**1953**

*Don Pasquale*, Golden Gate Opera Workshop, San Francisco

*Amahl and the Night Visitors*, Golden Gate Opera Workshop

*Zanetto*, Golden Gate Opera Workshop

Contemporary Dancers Company, Theatre Arts Colony, San Francisco

**1954**

*Tea and Sympathy*, Theatre Arts Colony

*Mr. Roberts*, Theatre Arts Colony

**1955**

*The Immoralist*, Encore Theatre, San Francisco

*Dark of the Moon*, Theatre Arts Colony

**1957**

*Waiting for Godot*, Actors Workshop, San Francisco

10 musicals, Sacramento Music Circus, CA

**1958**

*The Miser*, Actors Workshop

*The Ticklish Acrobat*, Actors Workshop

*Waiting for Godot*, York Theatre, NYC and World's Fair, Brussels, Belgium (revival of Actors Workshop production)

*Filling Station* (S & C), San Francisco Ballet

*The Guardsman* (S & L), Civic Theatre, Sacramento

**1959**

*Waiting for Godot* (revival of Actors Workshop production), San Francisco

*And the Wind Blows*, St. Mark's Playhouse, NYC

10 musicals, Sacramento Music Circus

*The Plaster Bambino*, Actors Workshop

**1960**

*The Prodigal* (S & L), Downtown Theatre, NYC

*Between Two Thieves*, Downtown Theatre

10 productions, Meadowbrook Dinner Theatre, Wayne, NJ

*Borak* (S & L), Martinique, NYC

**1961**

*A Worm in Horseradish* (S & L), Maidman Theatre, NYC

10 musicals, Carousel Theatre, Framingham, MA; Oakdale Theatre; Wallingford, CT; Warwick Theatre. Warwick, RI (stock tour)

**1962**

*Entertain a Ghost* (S & L), Actors' Playhouse, NYC

*The Days and Nights of Beebee Fenstermaker*, Sheridan Square Playhouse, NYC

*The Playboy of the Western World* (S, L & C), Irish Players (tour)

*Come Blow Your Horn*, Totowa Theatre, NJ

*West Side Story*, Totowa Theatre

**1963**

*Major Barbara*, Fred Miller Theatre, Milwaukee, WI

*Cages*, York Playhouse

*In White America* (S & L), Sheridan Square Playhouse

*The Burning*, York Playhouse

**1964**

*The White Rose and the Red*, Stage 73, NYC

*Dark of the Moon*, Arena Stage, Washington, DC

*Galileo*, Arena Stage

**1965**

*A View from the Bridge*, Sheridan Square Playhouse

*An Evening's Frost*, University of Michigan, Ann Arbor, MI

*He Who Gets Slapped*, Arena Stage

*Lonesome Train* and *Hard Travelin'*, Arena Stage

*An Evening's Frost*, Theatre de Lys, NYC

*Saint Joan*, Arena Stage

*The Skin of Our Teeth*, Arena Stage

**1966**

*Project Immortality*, Arena Stage

*The Condemned of Altona*, Repertory Theatre of Lincoln Center (Vivian Beaumont Theatre), NYC

*Serjeant Musgrave's Dance*, Arena Stage

*Oh, What a Lovely War!*, Arena Stage
*Macbeth*, Arena Stage
*The Magistrate*, Arena Stage

**1967**
*The Inspector General*, Arena Stage
*Galileo*, Repertory Theatre of Lincoln
  Center
*Phaedra* (S & L), Theatre of the Living
  Arts, Philadelphia
*The Andersonville Trial*, Arena Stage
*Oh, What a Lovely War!*, Alley Theatre,
  Houston
*Major Barbara*, Arena Stage
*Poor Bitos*, Arena Stage
*The Trial of Lee Harvey Oswald*, ANTA
  Theatre, NYC
*A Certain Young Man*, Stage 73

**1968**
*Hair*, Biltmore Theatre, NYC
*In Three Zones*, Repertory Theatre of
  Lincoln Center
*The Cuban Thing*, Henry Miller's The-
  atre, NYC
*The Great White Hope*, Alvin Theatre,
  NYC
*Love Match*, Palace West, Phoenix, AZ
  (pre-Broadway, closed in Los Ange-
  les)
*Lovers and Other Strangers*, Brooks At-
  kinson Theatre, NYC
*Promises, Promises*, Shubert Theatre,
  NYC

**1969**
*The Watering Place*, Music Box Theatre,
  NYC
*My Daughter, Your Son*, Booth Theatre,
  NYC
*Edith Stein*, Arena Stage
*Promises, Promises*, Prince of Wales The-
  atre, London
*Hair*, London

**1970**
*Gantry*, George Abbott Theatre, NYC
*Mahagonny*, Anderson Theatre, NYC
*The Engagement Baby*, Helen Hayes
  Theatre, NYC

**1971**
*Lenny*, Brooks Atkinson Theatre
*Jesus Christ Superstar*, Mark Hellinger
  Theatre, NYC
*Inner City*, Ethel Barrymore Theatre,
  NYC

**1972**
*Sugar*, Majestic Theatre, NYC
*Julius Caesar*, American Shakespeare
  Festival, Stratford, CT
*Antony and Cleopatra*, American Shake-
  speare Festival
*Jesus Christ Superstar*, Universal Amphi-
  theatre, Los Angeles, CA
*Lulu*, National Opera Company tour
*Lysistrata*, Brooks Atkinson Theatre
*Mary C. Brown and the Hollywood Sign*,
  Shubert Theatre, Los Angeles, CA
*The Old Man's Place*, Cinerama (film)

**1973**
*Seesaw*, Uris Theatre, NYC
*Full Circle*, ANTA Theatre, NYC
*Rachael Lily Rosenbloom and Don't You
  Forget It*, Broadhurst Theatre, NYC
Bette Midler Concert, tour
*Orpheus* (Director), Theatre in Space,
  NYC

**1974**
*Mack and Mabel*, Majestic Theatre
*Sgt. Pepper's Lonely Hearts Club Band
  On the Road*, Beacon Theatre, NYC

**1975**
*A Chorus Line*, New York Shakespeare
  Festival (Public Theater)
*The Red Devil Battery Sign*, Shubert
  Theatre, Boston, MA
*A Chorus Line*, Shubert Theatre, NYC
*The Rolling Stones Tour of the Americas*,
  Madison Square Garden, NYC

**1976**
*Hamlet Connotations*, American Ballet
  Theatre, NYC
*The Trojans*, Vienna State Opera, Vienna,
  Austria

**1977**
*A Chorus Line*, London
*Hair*, Biltmore Theatre
*West Side Story*, Hamburg State Opera,
  Hamburg Germany

**1978**
*On the Twentieth Century*, St. James
  Theatre, NYC
*Last Rite for Snow White* (Playwright),
  Ensemble Studio Theatre, NYC
*Ballroom*, Majestic Theatre

1979
*George and Rosemary* (Playwright), En-
  semble Studio Theatre
*Comin' Uptown*, Winter Garden, NYC

**1980**
*Swing*, Playhouse, Wilmington, DE
*42nd Street*, Winter Garden
*One Night Stand*, Nederlander Theatre,
  NYC

**1981**
*Semmelweiss*, Hartman Theatre, Stam-
  ford, CT
*Dreamgirls*, Imperial Theatre, NYC

**1982**
*The Barber of Seville*, Metropolitan Op-
  era, NYC
*Mahalia*, Hartman Theatre
Rolling Stones Concert, Madison Square
  Garden

**1983**
*Merlin*, Mark Hellinger Theatre
*Three Dances*, Eliot Feld Ballet, NYC
*Jewels*, New York City Ballet